# BIBLIOGRAPHIC INSTRUCTION

# Bibliographic Instruction
## The Second Generation

Edited by
Constance A. Mellon
Department of Library & Information Studies
East Carolina University
Greenville, North Carolina

1987
LIBRARIES UNLIMITED, INC.
Littleton, Colorado

LIBRARIES UNLIMITED, INC.
P.O. Box 263
Littleton, Colorado 80160-0263

**Library of Congress Cataloging-in-Publication Data**

Bibliographic instruction.

    Includes bibliographies and index.
    1.  Library orientation.    2.  College students--
Library orientation.    3.  Bibliography--Methodology--
Study and teaching.    4.  Libraries and education.
I.  Mellon, Constance A.
Z711.2.B53   1987       025.5'677       87-4049
ISBN 0-87287-563-6

Libraries Unlimited books are bound with Type II nonwoven material that meets and exceeds National Association of State Textbook Administrators' Type II nonwoven material specifications Class A through E.

To BRUCE SAJDAK,
the guiding force behind this publication,
my mentor and friend
in the chaotic days of early editorship, and

to EDITH and MARTIN MELLON,
the guiding force behind this editor,
my parents, who always believed I could do anything,

this book is gratefully dedicated.

# Contents

## Part II
## THE SECOND GENERATION
### Establishing an Identity

## SECTION A
### Understanding the Milieu of Bibliographic Instruction

## SECTION B
### Understanding the People We Serve

## SECTION C
### Bibliographic Instruction Librarianship

**Part III
THE NEXT GENERATION
Reflections on the Future**

# Introduction

*Bibliographic Instruction: The Second Generation* brings together the writings of many individuals whose ideas were instrumental in transforming user instruction from a grassroots movement to an established part of academic librarianship. Among the authors who were selected to represent the "First Generation" of instruction librarians, one finds the current and many past chairs of the Bibliographic Instruction Section of the Association of College and Research Libraries, the former director of LOEX, the National Library Instruction Clearinghouse, and writers and presenters whose names are a familiar part of the literature of library user instruction. Our book is intended as a forum for this First Generation of bibliographic instruction librarians to discuss the issues and ideas underlying the field today. We assume our audience to be those currently working in the area of user instruction who are thus conversant with the basic ideas and methods of the field; therefore, our purpose is to stimulate rather than to educate. We are the First Generation speaking to the Second Generation, our intellectual children.

The book uses as a framework key issues identified by the "Think Tank on Bibliographic Instruction," a preconference activity held in conjunction with the 1981 Conference of the Association of College and Research Libraries, and discusses, in its fifteen chapters, the current state of bibliographic instruction, its philosophies and theories, and its probable future. Organized into three parts, the book begins with "The First Generation: Beginnings of Bibliographic Instruction," a historical overview of the original Think Tank and its impact on the development of bibliographic instruction in academic libraries. Part 2, "The Second Generation: Establishing an Identity," which examines the characteristics of bibliographic instruction as it has developed over the past fifteen years, is the body of our work. The four sections which comprise part 2 organize the concepts and concerns of this new library specialization into areas for exploration.

Bibliographic instruction, which often seems to be a stepchild of the university curriculum, is not exactly teaching in the "coursework" sense of the word nor can it be considered simply a library service. "Where do our programs (and we) belong?" has long been the cry of the academic instruction librarian. In section A, "Understanding the Milieu of Bibliographic Instruction," we focus on the place of library instruction in the complex and changing world of academe. Possible academic library structures of the future which might evolve as the field reacts to developing technology and changing perceptions of information are described and alternate placement of library instruction, within the academic library or within the academic department, are the major issues discussed in this first section.

Bibliographic instruction is often a nearsighted specialization which focuses on "teaching" at the expense of "learning." The literature of the field is rampant with descriptions of what information, concepts, and strategies should be included in instruction programs or sessions and how these things can best be taught; yet all too frequently the audience for this teaching, the learner, is ignored. In section B, "Understanding the People We Serve," learners are examined as real people with needs and feelings that influence the effectiveness of bibliographic instruction. The two activities most likely to elicit anxiety in those using academic libraries, beginning experiences with library research and using automated retrieval devices, are discussed in this section from the perspective of the user.

In tracing the development of a discipline, a shift in perception from "topic of interest" to "area of study" can be observed. This shift in perception is currently occurring in the area of user instruction as organizations, journals, and monographs come into being which focus on what the Think Tank participants called the "underlying pedagogy of bibliographic instruction." Two conceptual areas, science of knowledge and learning theory, are universally acknowledged as basic to this pedagogy and a discussion of these areas as they relate to user instruction constitutes a major part of section C, "Bibliographic Instruction Librarianship." In addition, training for bibliographic instruction librarianship is discussed. Such training has, for the First Generation, been primarily informal, through mentoring, reading, and workshops; however, as the demand increases for librarians with at least the rudiments of training, the question arises as to the role of professional library education in preparing instruction librarians. This question is considered in depth in section C.

As bibliographic instruction has evolved over the years from an area of interest to an area of study, so has it evolved from a simple to a complex activity. Satisfied in the beginning with tours and orientation sessions, instruction librarians are beginning to delve into the complexities of search strategies, the differing information needs of "novices" and "experts," and the organization of knowledge within disciplines. In section D, "Increasing Specialization in Bibliographic Instruction," attention is directed toward instruction for special needs. Three chapters written by librarians with expertise in instruction for specific disciplines examine the structure of the literature and the needs of users in the sciences, the social sciences, and the humanities. In addition, in order to maintain and extend expertise in specific disciplines, librarians need to communicate with non-library professionals in these disciplines. The final chapter in section D suggests ways in which such communication might be accomplished.

Part 3, "The Next Generation: Reflections on the Future," is the concluding segment of our work. In this final part of our book, the author reflects upon bibliographic instruction, past and current, and raises some important questions to be addressed as the Second Generation moves into the future.

*Bibliographic Instruction: The Second Generation* is unique among most of the existing works on user instruction in two ways: its intent is thoughtful and philosophic rather than expository and it has grown from an organizing structure not usual in edited collections. First, as our readers, the new generation of instruction librarians, probably are aware, the literature of bibliographic instruction is largely expository. Reports of individual programs abound and where theory is the focus of a work, the work is often basic and descriptive. (Works of these two types are often referred to informally as "how-to" and "how-I-did-it-good." ) I myself have authored both of these types of materials and, while I do not question their value, I feel there is now a place for more sophisticated writing in the area of bibliographic instruction. Authors no longer need to assume that their readers must have the rudiments of each concept explained in detail. There exists a Second Generation of bibliographic instruction librarians familiar with basic methods and theory and with actual instructional experience "under their belts." It is to these, our colleagues, that we address this book.

Second, although this book is an edited collection of essays by twenty-two authors or coauthors, it differs from the usual edited collections in its underlying structure. To explain this difference, let me begin with my appointment in 1984 as editor of what was then called "the Think Tank publication." The editorship included assuming the chair of an ad hoc committee of the Association of College and Research Libraries, Bibliographic Instruction Section. The committee responsible for my selection as editor was led by Bruce Sajdak and included Donald Kenney, Maureen Pastine, Shelley Phipps, Mary Reichel, and Carla Stoffle. After my appointment, the committee served as an editorial board, meeting twice a year at the American Library Association conferences where it reacted to developments and provided suggestions and recommendations as the book slowly took form. In addition, two of the committee members, Maureen Pastine and Donald Kenney, kindly stepped in when identified authors backed out, to provide the full complement of chapters which had been planned.

One difference between this book and other edited collections is the planning which preceded the identification of authors. The book was to be based upon the recommendations of the 1981 Bibliographic Instruction Think Tank (described in chapter 1) but as my mentor Bruce Sajdak often assured me in my early phone calls for guidance, the form which it would take was my responsibility. Prior to the first meeting of the Think Tank Editorial Board, I spent hours pouring over the fat envelope of materials Bruce had forwarded to me, organizing and reorganizing concepts in the best Melvil Dewey tradition. The outline of this book is the fourth draft; it represents a broad view of the current state of bibliographic instruction, initially defined by the 1981 Think Tank and painstakingly filtered through the cataloger-trained mind of the editor.

With the outline for the book in place, the editorial board turned its attention to identifying authors. For each chapter, a list was developed of those whose work is known in connection with the topic and wherever possible, these are the authors of the chapters included in this book. Many of the names will be familiar; comprehensive lists of their achievements would fill a volume alone. All are previously published, many quite widely so. As editor, I spoke with each of the authors individually before they began to write. Authors were charged with developing chapters that were theoretical and/or philosophic, rather than expository, and were told to consider their audience as basically knowledgeable in bibliographic instruction. Authors stayed in close touch with the editor, the editorial board, and each other as their chapters grew and evolved. Nearly all chapters are second or third drafts, responding to my editorial comments which were designed to give a unity and coherence to the work as a whole. It is with deep gratitude that I acknowledge the cooperation and hard work of these authors, all of whom added this process to schedules already overloaded.

Several other acknowledgments are appropriate to the completion of this book: Bruce Sadjak and Mary Reichel, in many ways the father and mother of this work, and my friends and confidantes during the process of its editing; the Lyndhurst Foundation and Emily Boyce, who each, in their turn, provided me with the time, opportunity, and encouragement to fully develop all aspects of my expanding academic persona; and Gillian Greco, my daughter, who spent several years listening to the outpourings of joy and grief attendant upon the birth of any book. This volume is the collective effort of many people over a long period of time. I can only hope that our readers will be as stimulated by this work as its editor has been.

# List of Contributors

Rao Aluri
    Assistant Professor
    Division of Library & Informa-
        tion Management
    Emory University
    Atlanta, Georgia

Betsy Baker
    Bibliographic Instruction
        Librarian
    Northwestern University Library
    Evanston, Illinois

Anne K. Beaubien
    Head, Cooperative Access
        Services
    University of Michigan Library
    Ann Arbor, Michigan

Cheryl A. Bernero
    Assistant Librarian, Graduate
        Library Reference
        Department
    University of Michigan Library
    Ann Arbor, Michigan

Joseph A. Boisse
    Univeristy Librarian
    University of California at Santa
        Barbara

Emily S. Boyce
    Professor and Chair
    Department of Library &
        Information Studies
    East Carolina University
    Greenville, North Carolina

Bobbie L. Collins
    Assistant Head,
        Reference Department
        and Bibliographic
        Instruction
        Librarian
    Joyner Library
    East Carolina University
    Greenville, North Carolina

June Lester Engle
    Associate Professor
    Division of Library & Infor-
        mation Management
    Emory University
    Atlanta, Georgia

Joanne R. Euster
    University Librarian
    Rutgers University
    New Brunswick, New Jersey

Ruth M. Katz
    Director of Academic
        Library Services
    Joyner Library
    East Carolina University
    Greenville, North Carolina

Donald J. Kenney
    Head, Reference Department
    University Libraries
    Virginia Polytechnical
        Institute and State
        University
    Blacksburg, Virginia

David King
   Research Associate
   University of Illinois Library
      Research Center
   Urbana-Champaign, Illinois

Thomas G. Kirk
   College Librarian
   Berea College
   Berea, Kentucky

Carolyn Kirkendall
   Librarian, Instructional
      Materials Center
   Eastern Michigan University
   Ypsilanti, Michigan

Constance A. Mellon
   Assistant Professor
   Department of Library &
      Information Studies
   East Carolina University
   Greenville, North Carolina

Brian Nielsen
   Head, Reference Department
      and Coordinator of
      Research
   Northwestern University Library
   Evanston, Illinois

Kathryn E. Pagles
   Reference and Adult Services
      Librarian
   Edgecombe County Memorial
      Librarian
   Tarboro, North Carolina

Maureen Pastine
   Director of Libraries
   Washington State University
   Pullman, Washington

Sharon J. Rogers
   Director
   Gelman Library
   George Washington University
   Washington, D.C.

Carla J. Stoffle
   Associate Director for Public
      Services
   University of Michigan Libraries
   Ann Arbor, Michigan

Duane Webster
   Deputy Director and Director,
      Office Management Studies
   Association of Research Libraries
   Washington, D.C.

Sally B. Young
   Assistant Professor
   Department of English
   University of Tennessee at
      Chattanooga

# PART I

## THE FIRST GENERATION
### Beginnings of
### Bibliographic Instruction

In the beginning, there was Chaos. And the students moved aimlessly upon the face of the library. And the reference librarians said, "Let there be instruction." And there was instruction. The reference librarians brought forth the workbook, and the fifty-minute lecture; and the students no longer moved aimlessly about, but searched purposefully through the card catalog and the journal indexes and the serials catalog. And the reference librarians looked upon what they had wrought and they found it good.

The first generation of bibliographic instruction librarians were the founders, the innovators, the forgers of paths through the wilderness. As Donald Kenney reminds us in the final chapter of this book, the idea of instructing library users is not a new one; the mid-1960s, however, gave birth to a grassroots movement that has expanded the concept of librarianship. Early bibliographic instruction librarians soon moved beyond the workbook and the fifty-minute lecture to explore the contributions of learning theory and instructional design. Discussions of tool use gave way to outlines of search strategy as librarians explored the parameters of their own knowledge in an attempt to share it with the patrons they served. And most of all, questions were raised — about ways in which instruction might be most effective, about how programs might gain acceptance, and about whether the value of instructing library users might be measured.

The bibliographic instruction movement was a little over a decade old when the Association of College and Research Libraries, Bibliographic Instruction Section, sponsored a "Think Tank" to consider the future of this activity in academic libraries. The discussion, recommendations, and reports proceeding from the Think Tank had far-reaching consequences. It caused both controversy and advancement in this emerging specialization and the ripples that began with six librarians in a small room in San Francisco continue to be felt today.

Part I focuses upon the history of the Think Tank meetings out of whose deliberations this book was born. In chapter 1, Carla Stoffle and Cheryl Bernero provide a framework for the issues explored by the current generation of bibliographic instruction librarians. They begin with a historical overview of the original Think Tank meetings, then examine recent developments in bibliographic instruction in relation to the recommendations of the Think Tank. Finally, they offer a challenge from the past to the future generation, the "second generation," of bibliographic instruction librarians.

Chapter 2 presents a paper by Brian Nielsen which was seminal to the deliberations of the Think Tank. The only previously published essay in this otherwise original work, it is included because of its importance to the Think Tank and to the controversy surrounding some of its recommendations. In a commentary preceding this paper, Brian Nielsen explains the part it played in the original Think Tank meetings and its role in the resulting controversy.

# 1 Bibliographic Instruction Think Tank I: Looking Back and the Challenge for Think Tank II

*Carla J. Stoffle and Cheryl A. Bernero*

In June 1981, the Bibliographic Instruction Section of the Association of College and Research Libraries, as part of the 1981 ACRL/BIS San Francisco Preconference on Library Instruction, sponsored a Bibliographic Instruction "Think Tank." The general purpose of the Think Tank was to bring together a select group of practitioners with diverse backgrounds to discuss the present state and future directions of bibliographic instruction. Specifically, the group was charged with identifying the key issues shaping the future of bibliographic instruction as a whole; recommending a program of research and action to enable the profession to overcome obstacles and seize opportunities; and most important, stimulating widespread professional discussions which would raise the consciousness of librarians about these issues.

The Think Tank participants were selected by the BIS Preconference Planning Committee from nominations solicited through advertisements in the professional literature. The criteria for selection included demonstrated achievement in one or more of the following areas:

1. Significant and influential research on bibliographic instruction or issues germane to bibliographic instruction.

2. Planning and implementing a bibliographic instruction program of such exemplary quality that it has served as a model for others.

3. Publication and/or presentation of scholarly and/or theoretical material contributing to the development of bibliographic instruction.[1]

The six librarians who were finally selected were Frances Hopkins, Head of Reference, Temple University; Donald Kenney, Head of General Reference, Virginia Polytechnic Institute; Brian Nielsen, Head of Reference, Northwestern University; Anne Roberts, Coordinator of Library Instruction, SUNY-Albany; Carla Stoffle, Assistant Chancellor for Educational Services, University of Wisconsin-Parkside; and Paula Walker, Library Instruction Coordinator, University of Washington. Joanne Euster, Director of the Library, San Francisco State University, was selected to facilitate the group's discussions.

The members of the Think Tank met for two days. Their discussions focused almost exclusively on intellectual and social issues as opposed to modes and methods of instruction, developing materials, the characteristics of model programs, and the like, which were the frequent subjects of myriad instruction workshops, seminars, and conferences held during the 1970s. The recurring themes in the Think Tank deliberations were (1) "building bridges," to the rest of the profession, to the larger academic community, and to the library schools, and (2) consolidating the discipline by fostering research, publication, critical analysis, and development of an underlying pedagogy of bibliographic instruction.[2]

The final report was organized into six sections:

1.  Integration of bibliographic instruction and the library profession.

2.  Integration of bibliographic instruction and the whole of academic librarianship into higher education.

3.  Integrating library use skills, bibliographic concepts, and available technology.

4.  Relationships with schools of library science.

5.  Importance of research.

6.  Importance of publication.

Each section contained an introduction, recommendations, and a few statements or concepts which the participants agreed should be accepted as fact and no longer debated. An example of the latter was the statement, "Bibliographic instruction needs no more justification than instruction in composition or any of the liberal arts and evaluation studies aimed at justifying its existence are unnecessary." [3]

The report of the Think Tank was initially presented in draft form at the final preconference session and was received with "interest, enthusiasm, and even a little controversy." [4] Attention and discussion at the presentation focused mainly on two assertions. The first was that bibliographic instruction is not a secondary activity of the reference department but the core function. The second was that information on demand at a service desk (often defined as *reference*) is the "mop-up" activity for instruction — a minor but emotion-laden issue raised during the report.

A final report of the Think Tank deliberations was published in *College and Research Libraries News*.[5] This report stimulated a *Journal of Academic Librarianship* symposium called "Reactions to the Think Tank Recommendations." [6] The articles in this symposium both challenged and further explored the recommendations and their rationale in a more deliberate fashion. They called the attention of the profession to broader instructional issues which was, of course, the purpose of the whole exercise.

# IMPACT ON THE PRACTICE
# OF BIBLIOGRAPHIC INSTRUCTION

Regardless of how the ideas in the final document were received, the Think Tank report continues to stimulate discussion. The report also has created a general awareness of issues broader than the day-to-day creation and operation of instruction programs and provided direction for the activities of several ACRL presidents, BIS committees, and instruction librarians in general. A number of the recommendations of the group actually have been implemented, which may or may not be directly or solely attributable to their identification by the Think Tank. However, the documentation of some of these accomplishments within the framework of the Think Tank report is a worthwhile effort even if it only serves to remind us of some of the considerable advancements that have taken place in user education in five short years.

## Integration into the Profession

A major focus of the Think Tank discussion was the concern for the fuller integration of user instruction into the fabric of the profession. Many of the specific recommendations of the group were intended to counteract the existing tendency of those concerned with user education to talk only to each other and to focus their professional efforts exclusively in the units concerned with library instruction within ALA and other professional library associations. Since that time two former chairs of the ACRL Bibliographic Instruction Section have been elected president of ACRL. One former member of the BIS Executive Board and a Think Tank participant has been elected president of ACRL as well as to membership on the ALA Council and Executive Board. Countless other BIS members have assumed positions on "non-instruction" committees in ACRL and ALA including the ALA Council. Finally, a considerable number of instruction librarians have moved into middle level and senior level library management positions since 1981 and have begun to impact practice and policy in a number of academic libraries.[7]

## Integration into Higher Education

In the area of relations with other professional associations and with the higher education community in general, there has been an increase in presentations made by librarians at the meetings of other academic professional associations.[8] In addition numerous articles on user education and the role of the library have been published both in the higher education journals and journals of the academic disciplines.[9] Many of these recent activities were the result of efforts by Carolyn Kirkendall, who served from 1982 to 1984 as the ACRL Bibliographic Instruction Liaison. While the BI liaison position was created prior to the Think Tank deliberations, Kirkendall's efforts were guided by the recommendations of the group and the principles articulated by the group in its section on higher education.[10]

To continue and expand the work of Kirkendall, the ACRL Board under the leadership of ACRL President Sharon Rogers, who incidentally as Chair of the Bibliographic Instruction Section in 1981 initiated the idea of having a Think Tank, approved the creation of the ACRL Professional Liaison Committee. The purpose of the committee is to promote cooperative efforts with other higher education associations.[11] The committee will, among other things, help librarians participate in the programs of non-library professional associations by supplying some funds for travel and registration fees. In addition, Rogers and JoAn Segal, Executive Director of ACRL, during the 1984/85 year, visited the offices and met with the staff at the American Association of Higher Education, the Association of American Colleges, the *Chronicle of Higher Education*, and the American Council on Education.[12] These activities, designed to integrate libraries into the mainstream of academia, appear to be receiving a warm reception from the higher education community.

Another example of an integrating effort is the creation in 1984 of the Library Deans and Directors Roundtable within the American Association of Higher Education. This roundtable is the brainchild of Joanne Euster, recently appointed University Librarian at Rutgers. The roundtable was created to increase the interaction of librarians with academic administrators on the professional "turf" of the administrators. The roundtable met during the 1984 Annual Meeting under the leadership of Euster and at the 1985 meeting under the leadership of Beverly Lynch, University Librarian, University of Illinois at Chicago. These meetings are providing high visibility and legitimization for librarians as important administrators in colleges and universities.[13]

## Integrating Concepts and Technology

The concern for learning theory, conceptual frameworks, critical thinking skills, and the integration into user education programs of new technologies in the form of microcomputers and online catalogs, was only beginning to filter into the literature in 1981.[14] Members of the Think Tank picked up on these ideas and urged that, as a guiding principle for the future, all instruction be conceptually based; technology should be adopted to enhance instruction and new library technologies should not be viewed as reducing the need for instruction. Since that time, a number of librarians have explored the potential and applications of various learning theories; discussed the application of critical thinking development models to bibliographic instruction; described the bibliographic structure and research patterns in the sciences, humanities, and some social sciences; and provided enlightenment as well as guideposts for the development of more meaningful instruction programs.[15] In addition, instruction librarians in many libraries are now taking the lead through program development, presentations, and publications in exploring the potential impact of new technologies on the library, the user, and the role of the librarian.[16] Programs for instructing users in the use of online catalogs and commercial online databases are becoming increasingly prevalent.[17] A set of model goals and objectives for such instructional programs has been drafted recently.[18] Some libraries, including those at the University of Wisconsin-Parkside, Cornell, the Texas Medical Center at the Houston Academy of Medicine, and the University of Michigan, are providing instruction on the use of microcomputer software application programs such as those for word processing, spreadsheets, graphics, database management and manipulating personal bibliographic files. Finally, within ACRL, a Microcomputer Discussion Group and a Bibliographic Instruction Section Computer Concerns Committee have been created. The purpose of the discussion group is to provide a forum for information exchange on topics of mutual interest to academic librarians using or planning to use microcomputers. In the first year, some activities have included collecting policies and procedures for use of the micros, the development of a membership directory, and a survey of group members on the types of micros and software available, which was reported on by the chairperson, Linda Piele, at the 1985 ALA Midwinter.[19] The BIS Computer Concerns Committee, which began as an ad hoc committee, is now a permanent committee of the section. The charge of the committee is:

> To facilitate and promote the use of computers in bibliographic instruction; to act as a resource and information sharing vehicle for those involved in bibliographic instruction which either utilizes computers as teaching tools or teaches the use of computer-based information systems. Principal areas of interest include: online catalogs, online database searching, computer-assisted-instruction (CAI), end-user searching of online information resources.[20]

If this charge is implemented, the committee will provide an important forum for the future integration of information technology into libraries and instruction programs.

### Relationship with Schools of Library Science

Major advances in building relationships between instruction librarians and library education/educators along the lines suggested by the Think Tank also have resulted during the last five years. In 1983 and 1984, instruction librarians were involved in programs at the Annual Conference of the Association for Library and Information Science Education (ALISE). The actualization of the workshops came from the activities of Betsy Baker, Chair of the BIS Education for Bibliographic Instruction Committee, and Charles McClure, a noted library educator and member of the ALISE Board. Using the recommendations of the Think Tank as a guide, Baker contacted McClure about how they might work together. McClure responded enthusiastically, persuading the ALISE Board to sponsor a presentation by Baker. In January 1983, about 50 library educators attended the Baker session, which dealt with the activities of both the Bibliographic Instruction Section and the Education for Bibliographic Instruction Committee.[21] In her presentation, Baker stressed that library school faculty need to integrate user education concepts generally throughout the library school curriculum and that separate courses in bibliographic instruction are not the only means for introducing library school students to user education theories, philosophies, activities, and the like. Her talk opened the possibility for library educators and practitioners to discuss alternative methods for meeting the needs and demands of instruction librarians. The second program held during the 1984

ALISE meetings dealt more fully with "Education for Bibliographic Instruction." It consisted of three papers, an overview of the state of user education, a discussion of the daily activities and professional life of a library instruction librarian, and the view of a library administrator (about the kind of professional librarian to provide instruction he/she was looking for), followed by a discussion led by Baker on how library educators could accommodate the curriculum to meet the needs expressed in the papers.[22] Both these workshops are significant because, although academic instruction librarians had invited library educators to speak at their conferences, workshops, and so on, instruction librarians had not dealt with library educators on the educators' "turf." By talking with library educators at their own meetings, instruction librarians became resource persons, reached a larger audience, and legitimized their attempts to influence library school faculty—activities recommended by the Think Tank. Also, as a result of the workshops, these library educators have been appointed to, and currently two are serving on, the ACRL/BIS Education for Bibliographic Instruction Committee—an implementation of the recommendation to encourage faculty to be involved in ACRL activities.

In addition to their direct work with library educators, in 1984, the ACRL/BIS Education for Bibliographic Instruction Committee members applied for and received membership on the Library Education Assembly of ALA's Standing Committee on Library Education (SCOLE).[23] This action is important because it not only provides user education practitioners with the formal opportunity to exchange information, share ideas, and express concerns pertaining to library education with a broad range of library professionals, but it also provides a direct link to the membership of SCOLE—the ALA committee charged with developing and recommending ALA policies related to the training and education of library personnel.

## Research

While the Think Tank devoted substantial time and a fair amount of ink to the importance of research, comparatively limited advances have been made. The ACRL/BIS Research Committee has taken on the responsibility of identifying and disseminating information about relevant research on a selected topic yearly.[24] However, the most notable research activities took place in 1984/85 under the ACRL presidency of Sharon Rogers. Rogers initiated in *C&RL News* the "Research Forum" column to help stimulate research and research skills among librarians.[25] She also has created an ACRL Research Development Committee "to stimulate superior research among academic librarians" and established for potential researchers the first "Research Clinic," held in Chicago on July 8, 1985. The purpose of the clinic is to demonstrate the diagnosis and treatment of a researchable problem; stimulate a positive attitude toward research; and suggest ways to team up with academic colleagues.[26] The potential of these activities for increasing the research skills of instruction librarians, and thereby the quality of instruction programs, is enormous.

## Publication

The creation of a high-quality journal was stressed by the Think Tank report. Within eighteen months of the Think Tank meeting, the first issue of *Research Strategies: A Journal of Library Concepts and Instruction* was published by Mountainside Publishing, Ann Arbor, Michigan. The stated purpose of *Research Strategies* was to become the "primary medium of communication about [library] instructional content and techniques; [about] controversies in user education; [and about] problems of BI organization, administration, [and] evaluation."[27] The creation of *Research Strategies* was obviously a major achievement, signaling the recognition of user education as a legitimate and powerful component of academic librarianship. Articles in this publication provide a means to advance theory and practice in user education. Two articles by Donald Kenney, "Publishing BI Articles in Discipline Journals: Humanities" and "Publishing BI Articles in Discipline Journals: Social Sciences," have actually accomplished a separate recommendation made by the Think Tank.[28]

In addition to the creation of *Research Strategies*, at least six major books on bibliographic instruction and a substantial number of textbooks for use with students have been published since the Think Tank recommendations.[29] These materials have in the past and will continue to provide valuable resources for the advancement of instruction. They allow the transmittal of the accumulated knowledge of the field, providing materials for use so that every new instruction librarian need not start from scratch or have to "reinvent the wheel."

Another result of the Think Tank is this volume, *Bibliographic Instruction: The Second Generation*. Many librarians, especially Bruce Sajdak of Smith College, were stimulated by the ideas of Think Tank I but felt that it was important to immediately project beyond what had been done in two short days. Thus, Sajdak gathered an editorial committee and proposed a book-length publication that would:

1. Clarify in retrospect the ideas which resulted in the Think Tank recommendations.

2. Expand upon these ideas in essay format allowing for analyses (and second thoughts) not possible in a series of guidelines.

3. Encourage responses to and debate about each recommendation from those present as well as other interested librarians.

4. Provide perspectives on the ideas generated from the recommendations of non-librarians.

5. Articulate an agenda for action on bibliographic instruction in the 1980s.[30]

After much work, considerable discussion, and extensive review, an editorial committee, potential articles, authors, and an editor were identified. The resulting articles have been prepared in the hope that by looking beyond the day-to-day routines, instruction librarians will be stimulated and challenged. It is hoped that the information presented will aid them in actualizing the educational role of the library.

Before turning the forum over to the "Second Generation," the authors of the following chapters, these authors would like to briefly explore some of the developments which led to the original Think Tank. Then we would like to frame some issues which, in our view, still need to be addressed; issue, so to speak, a challenge to the "Second Generation."

# BACKGROUND

The history of library instruction as a user service is long and well documented.[31] However, it is widely recognized that the last 25 years, and especially the last 15, have been the most productive in terms of the development of programs, practitioner interest, and theoretical conceptualization and exploration.[32] The renaissance of the 1970s had its antecedents in the 1960s in the work of pioneers like Patricia Knapp, Vera Melum, and Millicent Palmer.[33]

The instruction renaissance of the 1970s was facilitated by:

> 1) the changing nature of higher education, along with a rapid growth of library collections and the construction of newer library buildings that gave emphasis to a book-centered educational philosophy; 2) technological developments and their effects on libraries, especially in the area of computer applications; 3) changes in the nature of reference service; 4) grants from governmental agencies and foundations; 5) the proliferation of published articles and books on the topic of bibliographic instruction; 6) the support and activities of professional library associations; 7) numerous conferences, workshops, and similar meetings dealing with the topic; 8) the establishment of clearinghouses, along with their bibliographic instruction-related newsletters and directories; and 9) standards established by various professional groups and accrediting agencies.[34]

The dominant influences of the 1970s were the instruction programs at Earlham College, the University of Wisconsin-Parkside, Sangamon State University, the University of Michigan, SUNY College of Environmental Science and Forestry, the University of Texas-Austin, and UCLA; the recommendations, publications, and programs of the ACRL Bibliographic Instruction Task Force; the conferences and publications of LOEX (the Library Orientation-Instruction Exchange) at Eastern Michigan University; and the writings and presentations of Tom Kirk, Hannelore Rader, Evan Farber, John Lubans, Miriam Dudley, Patricia Breivik, Jacquelyn Morris, Sharon Hogan, Anne Roberts, Nancy Fjallbrant, Carla Stoffle, and Richard Werking.[35] For the most part, instruction librarians in the 1970s were concerned with the mechanics of developing local instructional programs and materials and all the issues attendant with that, including how to gain faculty interest and support, organize and administer programs, market or sell programs, and plan and evaluate activities. Other major concerns centered on developing definitions and trying to appropriately label the activity;[36] justifying the need for programs and "proving" that the instruction was effective, that is, demonstrating that instruction improves the academic performance of students;[37] creating an underlying philosophy or foundation;[38] developing idealized models, such as the Model Statement of Objectives;[39] creating a history or sense of tradition for those engaged in instructional activities;[40] and gaining recognition and acceptance for instruction as a basic library service.[41] One indicator of the success of this latter activity was the increasing number of job advertisements for reference librarians which included instruction duties appearing during this time period. This is a continuing phenomenon; instruction is basically an integral part of the job description for most reference librarians today. A major failure during the period was the inability of instruction librarians to get user education integrated in an ongoing way in library school curricula and the inability to focus attention of library educators on the need to develop instructional skills among librarians.[42]

As with any major movement, the instruction movement in the 1970s experienced considerable growth pains. In addition to the problems of developing faculty interest and acceptance, administrative support, and maintaining the pace of growing demand, instruction librarians encountered problems with other library staff and with each other. Professional jealousy, both within institutions between non-instructional staff and instruction librarians and among instruction librarians from institutions across the country, for a time posed a serious threat to the continued development of local instruction programs. This competitiveness even threatened the creation of a permanent professional "home" for academic librarians engaged in instruction and the integration of instruction into professionally accepted standards and guidelines. Some professional splintering took place because of the insensitivity and lack of organizational sophistication of instruction librarians. (This was, after all, a "grassroots" movement.) Caught up in the local and sometimes national recognition gained for activities, their own enthusiasm, and imbued with having "learned to do it good," many instruction librarians did not recognize the need for the entire staff to share their commitment, vision, *and* recognition. Also instruction librarians did not know how to engage in constructive dialogue with colleagues at other institutions about differing viewpoints or approaches.[43]

By 1980, after a decade of ferment and development, instruction became an accepted basic public service activity in most libraries; it overcame most of the problems of splintering; and it gained recognition from the profession at large as evidenced by its inclusion in the various guidelines and standards issued by ALA units and by the adoption of the "Policy Statement: Instruction in the Use of Libraries" by the ALA Council.[44] Attention now shifted to issues such as the "personality" or personal characteristics of successful instruction librarians;[45] the high burnout rate among instruction librarians; how to develop tests to measure skills;[46] and the lack of sustained growth of most instruction programs, which was partly attributed to the growing realization that programs were being based on the talent of individuals rather than on educational principles.[47] Also about this same time, a number of instruction librarians began to feel that the movement had reached a plateau and was in danger of becoming stagnant. To identify new directions, challenge what had now become dogma, stimulate discussion and perhaps a little controversy, raise consciousness, and in general, create a "new" agenda and focus for the 1980s, a Think Tank was proposed and then held.[48]

The recommendations of Think Tank I reflected the state of development of instruction by the 1980s and achieved some of the previously mentioned goals. The question that remains is what should be the focus for Think Tank II or the Second Generation? What issues still need to be addressed? What areas explored? What new directions taken? What opportunities further exploited and recent advances built upon?

# CHALLENGE TO THE
# SECOND GENERATION

In the opinion of these authors, the Second Generation must again address the issue of definitions and labels for the instruction activity. Are the terms "library instruction," "bibliographic instruction (BI)," and "user education" too narrow? How do we gain acceptance for the premise that the educational role of the library includes teaching information management and use, and that this identity involves the development of critical thinking and problem-solving skills along with the traditionally accepted bibliographic identification skills and the ability to exploit the collection of a specific library? Also, how do we indicate that librarians should be responsible for teaching clients how to identify and exploit all types of information sources using a variety of tools including computers? Does the term "education for information management" as described by Matheson and Cooper, McClure, and Brassil better reflect the current stage of evolution of the educational role of the library and librarian?[49] Are there other more descriptive or meaningful terms?

Another problem of definition is the inability of instruction librarians to clearly label and articulate the characteristics of the successful product of instruction programs. More time and effort must be devoted to identifying characteristics of the "independent" or "self-reliant" user as described by Tuckett and Stoffle.[50] The concept of self-reliance needs to be further explored, expanded where necessary, and adopted if appropriate. The defensiveness of instruction librarians about the terms "independent" and "self-reliant" in regard to users must be overcome. The scenario of the users who, with a little bit of library instruction, assume they know it all and will not seek help is a myth that needs to be dispelled once and for all. Indeed, research shows that already large numbers of our users do *not* ask questions even when they have them because they do not know what librarians do, or do not want to appear to be unintelligent rather than because they think they know everything.[51] Instead, instruction creates more reference work, users more likely to seek out the instruction librarian for help with reference questions, and more demanding and critical users.[52]

Describing the characteristics of the successful products of instruction programs is only one area where instruction librarians need to focus attention. Performance standards for instruction librarians themselves along the lines of those first developed by Bruce Sajdak must be created, certified, and disseminated.[53] At the same time, criteria for assessing the suitability of librarians for the instruction role need to be identified. Some libraries ask candidates for positions involving instruction to prepare a presentation to be given during the interview and others ask for examples of instructional materials developed by the individual. A more expansive and systematic approach to measuring the potential of librarians to be good instructors must be undertaken.

In addition to reconsidering the labels and definitions for our activities, user education librarians should take the lead in initiating a more thorough review of the role and philosophical base of the academic library, both on their own campuses and within the profession at large. Rapid changes in technology have led to the creation of "information czars" at high levels of university administration. While most of these administrators do not as yet have responsibility for the library, the role of coordinating information technology will lead to involvement with the library. How will the library be viewed? Where will the library report? In addition, how will the organizational structure within the library be affected by technology? Who will teach faculty, staff, and students how to manipulate the new technology for information management? Guskin, Stoffle, and Baruth suggest that the library is ideally suited for this role but librarians must seize the initiative, prepare for this role, and then make clear their ability and willingness.[54] The future role and importance of the academic library in scholarship and teaching on most campuses could/will depend upon the clear articulation of values and a philosophical base that views the library as an educational, services-oriented operation. Who better than librarians to lead the university through the changes that will occur because of technology?

As libraries are automated and become more technologically sophisticated and diverse, it is not enough that instruction libraries teach users how to use the technology. Instruction librarians must apply what they have learned about users and how they learn, the structure of the literature in the various disciplines, and research patterns to the development of online catalogs and software for accessing the various bibliographic, numeric, and full-text databases. In addition to ideas about front-end packages and screen design, other examples of potential contributions instruction librarians might make to software design include notes referring users to the librarian for further information or providing messages about other sources of information available to the user, and skillful reminders of the weaknesses of online catalogs (what they do and do not contain and when they should be used). Instruction librarians must also ensure that they take part in the debate between "easy-to-use" versus "easy-to-learn." The need to develop sound information-seeking and research skills among clients still will be necessary to insure that the college-educated public of the future does not become dependent on the information provided by easy-to-use sources only. Recent studies of online catalogs with both menu-driven (easy-to-use) and command-driven (powerful, but often hard-to-learn) modules have discovered that many users do not move beyond using the menu-driven search, settling for less information or even no information rather than learning the command-driven search techniques.[55] Who will take the lead in demanding easy-to-learn but powerful research tools? Who will raise the appropriate issues? Who will determine what can and must be done? These must immediately become important questions for instruction librarians.

Think Tank I placed a heavy emphasis on the need to integrate instruction into the higher education community. Some advances, as described earlier, have been made in this area. However, since 1982 at least seven major national reports on educational issues were produced.[56] None of these contained explicit mention or even acknowledgement of a role for the library in helping to bring about educational change or in helping to provide students with a better education. Efforts to relate to the higher education community undertaken to date should be continued and expanded upon to correct this oversight. At the same time, mechanisms for providing a response to future studies need to be created — preferably before the studies are completed and issued. Perhaps ACRL or BIS within ACRL could establish committees to maintain files of pertinent information for such studies. These groups might be charged with preparing position papers in response to announcements of major studies. Also, instruction librarians need to establish networks of contacts to ensure that members of study groups or commissions hear from librarians that they know, or at least from individuals they know and respect, about the educational role of the library. Certainly additional creative approaches need to be explored.

In addition to responding to the higher education community in general, instruction librarians need to develop a better understanding of the higher education context and environment, especially the differences among the milieus of the various types of campuses and how change is successfully introduced. How do faculty operate and think? What constraints do they work under? What are the problems of middle-level academic administrators like department chairs? How does the governance structure operate generally and in specific situations? What powers do deans, provosts, and presidents have? What are their problems? How do they form their opinion of the library and how does one influence such individuals? How is an institution affected by national trends (changing demographics, increased state intervention, reduced federal funding, changing enrollment patterns by discipline, calls for increased industry/university cooperation, curricular change movements, and the like) and in what ways are the various kinds of institutions responding? These are only some of the areas where librarians need understanding, analytical skills, and frequent updates. Courses in higher education administration taught in education schools, continuing education courses provided through library schools or ACRL, and columns devoted to analyzing trends in higher education and their potential impact for libraries could be useful. Also, instruction librarians need to focus on identifying and understanding developmental change theories that will have applicability to the educational environment.

Work with library educators perhaps has been the area of the single greatest gain for instruction librarians. Initiative must not be lost. In addition to what has already been done, instruction librarians should consider working with library educators to create internships and/or residencies in user education on the model of the University of Michigan's Research Library Residency Program.[57] Also, instruction librarians should take advantage of the Council on Library Resources Cooperative Research Grant Program to institute research projects with library school faculty.[58] Finally, systematic training for instruction must be provided on a regular basis. Library educators and instruction librarians need to address the question of how this education can be provided and break through the impasse that has developed over the efficacy of credit courses devoted solely to library instruction.

Research is still an area in need of attention from instruction librarians. Developing research skills to facilitate program evaluation and identify more effective learning environments for users should be of prime importance over the next few years. Research problems need to be systematically identified and priorities designated. Perhaps funding agencies could be encouraged to consider funding proposals for projects dealing with problems identified in this manner. Another possible activity might be the development of materials on how to do low-cost, high-quality research and/or materials sharing insights on where to go for funding for research.

While the foregoing items do not provide an exhaustive list of issues or areas needing attention from instruction libraries, they do represent what these authors see as most important for the immediate future. However, before turning over this forum, an additional point must be made. Instruction librarians of the "Second Generation" need to focus on broad philosophical goals and values both in their daily work and in their professional activities. Instruction librarians must not allow themselves to become too attached to a particular method or methods or to specific configurations of activities that are then viewed as "traditional," "basic," or "core." If we as a group fall into this trap, the result will be an increase in "burnout." Additional tasks will overburden us to the point where no new activities will be undertaken. Also, the ability to change to meet new challenges or to take advantage of new ideas or technologies will be severely reduced. Instruction librarians must not let activities become "ends" in themselves, but must remain committed to broad goals and objectives based on the environmental context, user needs, and available resources, if the educational role of the library is to be successfully implemented.

## NOTES

1.   1981 Preconference Planning Committee, "Bibliographic Instruction 'Think Tank' Call for Nominations" (Bibliographic Instruction Section of the Association of College and Research Libraries, Chicago, n.d., Mimeographed).

2.   "Think Tank Recommendations for Bibliographic Instruction," *College & Research Libraries News* 42 (December 1981): 394.

3.   Ibid., p. 397.

4.   Judy Reynolds, letter to author, October 5, 1981.

5.   Think Tank Recommendations, pp. 394-98.

6.   Joanne Euster, ed., "Reactions to the Think Tank Recommendations: A Symposium," *The Journal of Academic Librarianship* 9 (March 1983): 4-14.

7.   Johnnie E. Givens, "User Instruction: Assessing Needs for the Future," in *Reference Services and Library Education: Essays in Honor of Frances Neel Cheney*, ed. Edwin S. Gleaves and John Mark Tucker (Lexington, Mass.: Lexington Books, 1983), pp. 95-108.

8.   Carolyn Kirkendall, "BI Liaison Project Update," *College & Research Libraries News* 45 (October 1984): 482.

9.   Ibid., p. 481.

10.   Carolyn Kirkendall, conversation with author, April 5, 1985.

11.   "Now There's Help," *College & Research Libraries News* 46 (May 1985): 229.

12.   JoAn S. Segal and Sharon Rogers, "ACRL and Higher Education," *College & Research Libraries* 46 (April 1985): 168-70.

13.   Joanne Euster, conversation with author, June 18, 1985.

14.   Paul G. Cappuzello and Sharon J. Rogers, *Information Gathering Skills for Pre-Service Teachers* (Toledo, Ohio: University of Toledo Libraries, 1979); Michael Keresztesi, "Bibliographic Instruction in the 1980s and Beyond," in *Directions for the Decade: Library Instruction in the 1980s*, ed. Carolyn A. Kirkendall (Ann Arbor, Mich.: Pierian Press, 1981), pp. 41-49; Pamela Kobelski and Mary Reichel, "Conceptual Frameworks for Bibliographic Instruction," *Journal of Academic Librarianship* 7 (May 1981): 73-77; Constance A. Mellon and Edmund Sass, "Perry and Piaget: Theoretical Framework for Effective College Course Development," *Educational Technology* 21 (May 1981): 29-33; Cerise Oberman-Soroka, *Petals Around a Rose: Abstract Reasoning and Bibliographic Instruction* (Chicago: Association of College and Research Libraries, 1980); Sharon Rogers, "Class-Related Bibliographic Instruction: A Philosophical Defense," *Proceedings from the Second Southeastern Conference on Approaches to Bibliographic Instruction*, ed. Cerise Oberman-Soroka (Charleston, S.C.: College of Charleston Library Associates, 1980), pp. 25-32; Sharon Rogers, "Research Strategies: Bibliographic Instruction for Undergraduates," *Library Trends* 29 (Summer 1980): 69-81.

15.   The following citations are a representative sample but not an exhaustive list of relevant publications.
      Rao Aluri, "Application of Learning Theories to Library-Use Instruction," *Libri* 31 (August 1981): 140-52; Rao Aluri and Mary Reichel, "Evaluation of Student Learning in Library-Use Instructional Programs Based on Cognitive Learning Theory" (Paper presented at the Second International Conference on Library Use Education, Oxford, England, July 1981); Patricia A. Berge and Judith Pryor, "Applying Educational Theory to Workbook Instruction," in *Theories of Bibliographic Education: Designs for Teaching*, ed. Cerise Oberman and Katina Strauch (New York: R. R. Bowker, 1982), pp. 91-110; Anne K. Beaubien, Sharon A. Hogan, and Mary W. George, *Learning the Library: Concepts and Methods for Effective Bibliographic Instruction* (New York: R. R. Bowker, 1982); Jon Lindgren, "The Idea of Evidence in Bibliographic Inquiry," in *Theories of Bibliographic Education*, pp. 27-46; Constance A. Mellon, "Information Problem-Solving: A Developmental Approach to Library Instruction," in *Theories of Bibliographic Education*, pp. 75-89; Constance A. Mellon, "Library Anxiety: A Grounded Theory and Its Development," *College & Research Libraries* 47 (March 1986): 160-65; Constance A. Mellon, "Process Not Product in Course-Integrated Instruction: A Generic Model of Library Research," *College*

& *Research Libraries* 45 (November 1984): 471-78; Mona McCormick, "Critical Thinking and Library Instruction," *RQ* 22 (Summer 1983): 339-41; Stephen H. Plum, "Library Use and the Development of Critical Thought," *New Directions for Teaching and Learning* 18 (June 1984): 25-33; Anne F. Roberts, *Organizing and Managing a Library Instruction Program* (Chicago: American Library Association, 1979); Topsy N. Smalley and Stephen H. Plum, "Teaching Library Researching in the Humanities and the Sciences: A Contextual Approach," in *Theories of Bibliographic Education*, pp. 135-70; Harold W. Tuckett and Carla J. Stoffle, "Learning Theory and the Self-Reliant Library User," *RQ* 23 (Fall 1984): 58-66.

16.    Carol F. Ahmad, *Bibliographic Instruction in ARL Libraries* (Washington D.C.: Association of Research Libraries, 1986); Nancy Fjallbrant, ed., *User Education in the Online Age* (Gothenburg, Sweden: International Association of Technological University Libraries Proceedings, 1982); Alan E. Guskin, Carla J. Stoffle, and Barbara E. Baruth, "Library Future Shock: The Microcomputer Revolution and the New Role of the Library," *College & Research Libraries* 45 (May 1984): 177-83; Constance R. Miller, "Scientific Literature as Hierarchy: Library Instruction and Robert M. Gagne," *College & Research Libraries* 43 (September 1982): 385-90; Brian Nielsen, "Teacher or Intermediary: Alternative Professional Models in the Information Age," *College & Research Libraries* 43 (May 1982): 183-91; Cerise Oberman, "Management of Online Computer Services in the Academic Reference Department," *Reference Librarian* 5/6 (Fall-Winter 1982): 139-42; Hannelore B. Rader, "The Teaching Library Enters the Electronic Age," *College & Research Libraries News* 47 (June 1986): 402-4.

17.    The following citations are a representative sample but not an exhaustive list of relevant publications.

Betsy Baker, "A Conceptual Framework for Teaching Online Catalog Use," *Journal of Academic Librarianship* 12 (May 1986): 90-96; Betsy Baker and Brian Nielsen, "Educating the Online Catalog User: Experiences and Plans at Northwestern University Library," *Research Strategies* 1 (Fall 1983): 155-66; Betsy Baker, "A New Direction for Online Catalog Instruction," *Information Technology and Libraries* 5 (March 1986): 35-41; Texas A & M University, Sterling C. Evans Library, *A Final Report from the Public Service Research Projects: A Comparison of Two End User Operated Search Systems* (Washington, D.C.: Association of Research Libraries, 1985); Pamela Engelbrech, "Instruction-Related Poster Sessions at ALA-Chicago," *Library Instruction Round Table News* 8 (September 1985): 10-11; Deborah Fink and Eddy Hogan, "Integrating Computer-Related Concepts into a Library Research Course," *Library Instruction Round Table News* 6 (March 1984): 1-3; Linda Friend, "Identifying and Informing the Potential End-user: Online Information Seminars," *Online* 10.1 (1986): 47-56; Linda Friend, "Independence at the Terminal: Training Student End Users to Do Online Literature Searching," *Journal of Academic Librarianship* 11 (1985): 136-41; Joan Lippincott, "Teaching End-Users to Search Online Bibliographic Databases," *Agricultural Libraries Information Notes* 9 (October 1983): 1-2; Deborah Masters, "Library Users and the Online Catalog: Suggested Objectives for Library Instruction" (Paper presented at the ACRL New England Chapter Spring Conference, Wellesley, Mass., March 19, 1982);

David R. McDonald and Susan Searing, "Bibliographic Instruction and the Development of Online Catalogs," *College & Research Libraries* 44 (January 1983): 5-11; Brian Nielsen, "What They Say They Do and What They Do: Assessing Online Catalog Use Instruction Through Transaction Monitoring," *Information Technology and Libraries* 5 (March 1986): 28-34; Sandra K. Ready, "Putting the Online Catalog in Its Place," *Research Strategies* 2 (Summer 1984): 119-27; Rader, "The Teaching Library Enters the Electronic Age," pp. 402-4; Carol M. Tobin, "Online Computer Bibliographic Searching as an Instructional Tool," *Reference Services Review* 12 (Winter 1984): 71-73; Linda Wilson, "User Education for Online Catalogs," *LIFline News Sheet* 24 (January 1984): 3-4.

18.   Baker, "A Conceptual Framework for Teaching Online Catalog Use," pp. 90-96.

19.   Linda Piele, conversation with author, June 3, 1985.

20.   *American Library Association Handbook of Organization 1985/86 and Membership Directory* (Chicago: American Library Association, 1985), pp. 59-60.

21.   Betsy Baker, telephone conversation with author, April 11, 1985.

22.   Sharon Hogan, "What Are the Skills and Academic Preparation Library Administrators Look For in Beginning Library Instruction Librarians?" (Paper delivered at the ALISE Teaching Methods Group and ACRL BIS Education for Bibliographic Instruction Joint Meeting, Washington, D.C., January 5, 1984); Anne J. Matthews, "How Can Library Schools Insure Their Graduates Acquire Bibliographic Instruction Skills Before Joining the Work Force?" (Paper delivered at the ALISE Teaching Methods Group and ACRL/BIS Education for Bibliographic Instruction Joint Meeting, Washington, D.C., January 5, 1984); Betsy Wilson, "A Day in the Life of a Bibliographic Instruction Librarian" (Paper delivered at the ALISE Teaching Methods Group and ACRL/BIS Education for Bibliographic Instruction Joint Meeting, Washington, D.C., January 5, 1984).

23.   Peggy O'Donnell, letter to Betsy Baker, February 13, 1984.

24.   John Collins, "ACRL BIS Research Committee Agenda, Midwinter 1985" (n.d., Mimeographed); Virginia Tiefel, conversation with author, April 10, 1985; Sandra Yee, conversation with author, April 7, 1985.

25.   Sharon Rogers, "Research Forum: A New C&RL News Column," *College & Research Libraries News* 45 (July/August 1984): 350-52.

26.   Dorothy J. Anderson, "Stimulating Quality Research: Starting with the Basics," *College & Research Libraries News* 46 (April 1985): 180-83.

27.   Sharon A. Hogan and Mary W. George, "Start-up Thoughts," *Research Strategies* 1 (Winter 1983): 2-3.

28.  Donald J. Kenney, "Publishing BI Articles in Discipline Journals: Humanities," *Research Strategies* 1 (Spring 1983): 64-76; Donald J. Kenney, "Publishing BI Articles in Discipline Journals: Social Sciences," *Research Strategies* 2 (Summer 1984): 128-35.

29.  Mignon S. Adams and Jacqueline M. Morris, *Teaching Library Skills for Academic Credit* (Phoenix: Oryx Press, 1985); Beaubien, Hogan, and George, *Learning the Library*; Patricia S. Brevik, *Planning the Library Instruction Program* (Chicago: American Library Association, 1982); Nancy Fjallbrant and Ian Malley, *User Education in Libraries* (London: Bingley, 1984); Cerise Oberman and Katina Strauch, eds., *Theories of Bibliographic Education: Designs for Teaching* (New York: R. R. Bowker, 1982); Anne F. Roberts, *Library Instruction for Librarians* (Littleton, Colo.: Libraries Unlimited, 1982).

30.  Bruce T. Sajdak, "Bibliographic Instruction, the Second Generation: A Prospectus," (June 29, 1982, Mimeographed).

31.  Carolyn A. Kirkendall and Carla J. Stoffle, "Instruction," in *The Service Imperative for Libraries* ed. Gail A. Schlacter (Littleton, Colo.: Libraries Unlimited, 1982), p. 69.

32.  Kirkendall and Stoffle, "Instruction," pp. 42-93; Givens, "User Instruction," pp. 95-108.

33.  While the work of Louis Shores in regard to the "Library College" concept has some followers and was highlighted by the journal *Learning Today*, this work did not substantially influence academic library instruction or instructors of this period.

34.  James E. Ward, "Trends in the Growth of Bibliographic Instruction in Twentieth-Century American Academic Libraries," in *Reference Services and Library Education*, p. 75.

35.  Kirkendall and Stoffle, "Instruction," pp. 42-93.

36.  Jacqueline M. Morris, *Bibliographic Instruction in Academic Libraries: A Review of the Literature and Selected Bibliography* (Syracuse, N.Y.: ERIC Clearinghouse on Information Resources, Syracuse University, 1979).

37.  For a list of some appropriate studies, see Kirkendall and Stoffle, "Instruction," p. 72.

38.  For a review of relevant literature, see Kirkendall and Stoffle, "Instruction," pp. 71-72.

39.  Thomas J. Kirk, "ACRL Bibliographic Task Force Report 1971-1976" (Chicago: Association of College and Research Libraries, November 1976, Mimeographed).

40.   For a review of histories of instruction written during this period, see Kirkendall and Stoffle, "Instruction," pp. 69-70.

41.   Ward, "Trends in the Growth of Bibliographic Instruction," pp. 75-94; Givens, "User Instruction," pp. 95-108.

42.   Sharon Anne Hogan, "Educating Librarians for User Education in the United States or Who Is Teaching Us to Teach?" in *Library User Education: Are New Approaches Needed?* ed. Peter K. Fox (London: British Library, 1980), pp. 18-27; Sue Galloway, "Nobody Is Teaching the Teachers," *Booklegger* 3 (January 1976): 29-31.

43.   The following provide some insight into this issue.
Frances Hopkins, "User Instruction in the College Library," in *College Librarianship*, ed. William Miller (Metuchen, N.J.: Scarecrow Press, 1981), pp. 199-200; Carolyn Kirkendall, "Cooperation, Coordination and Communication: The LOEX Clearinghouse Experience," in *Library User Education*, pp. 39-42; Jacqueline Morris, "The Effect of an Active Bibliographic Instruction Program on Interpersonal Relations Within a Library" (Paper presented at Second Annual Conference on Integrating the Library into the Educational Mainstream, Kenosha, Wisconsin, June 23, 1978); Cerise Oberman-Soroka, "Personality to Education: A Necessary Change," in *Directions for the Decade*, pp. 34-39; Anne Roberts, "The Politics of Library Instruction: Internal and External," in *Proceedings from the Second Southeastern Conference*, pp. 1-9.

44.   American Library Association, "Policy Statement: Instruction in the Use of Libraries," Council Document no. 45 (Document approved at the annual meeting of the American Library Association, New York, 1980).

45.   Judy Avery, "The Challenge of the 80's," in *Directions for the Decade*, pp. 25-27; Roger W. Fromm, "Tuesday Morning Live—Personality and Bibliographic Instruction," in *Directions for the Decade*, pp. 28-30; Bonnie J. King, "A Librarian for All Seasons," in *Directions for the Decade*, pp. 31-33; Oberman-Soroka, "Personality to Education," pp. 34-39; Virginia Tiefel, "Why Are Most Instruction Librarians Young?" in *Directions for the Decade*, pp. 36-40.

46.   Eileen Dubin, "The Library Skills Test: Helping to Set Benchmarks," in *Teaching Library Use Competence: Bridging the Gap from High School to College*, ed. Carolyn A. Kirkendall (Ann Arbor, Mich.: Pierian Press, 1982), pp. 69-78; Ann Hyland, "The Ohio School Library Media Test," in *Teaching Library Use Competence*, pp. 35-68; Anne Roberts, "Library Skill Tests: A Defense and Critique," in *Teaching Library Use Competence*, pp. 79-86.

47.   Oberman-Soroka, "Personality to Education," p. 35.

48.   Sharon Rogers, conversation with the author, April 21, 1985.

49.   Ellen C. Brassil, "Information Management Education: Policies and Procedures for a Reference Department Manual," *Medical Reference Services Quarterly* 2 (Winter 1983): 49-59; Nina W. Matheson and John A. D. Cooper, "Academic Information in the Academic Health Sciences Center: Roles for the Library in Information Management," *Journal of Medical Education* 57 (October 1982): 1-89; Charles McClure, "Library User Education Services: Issues and Strategies" (Paper presented at the American Library Association Annual Meeting, Dallas, June 26, 1984).

50.   Tuckett and Stoffle, "Learning Theory and the Self-Reliant Library User," pp. 58-66.

51.   Kathleen Coleman, "Library Instruction and the Advancement of Reference Service," *The Reference Librarian* 10 (Spring/Summer 1984): 241-52; Mary Jane Swope and Jeffery Katzer, "Why Don't They Ask Questions?" *RQ* 12 (Winter 1972): 161-66.

52.   Coleman, "Library Instruction and the Advancement of Reference Service," pp. 241-52; Joan C. Durrance, "The Influence of Reference Practices on the Client-Librarian Relationship," *College & Research Libraries* 47 (January 1986): 57-67; Janice Z. Koyama, "Bibliographic Instruction and the Role of the Academic Librarian," *Journal of Academic Librarianship* 9 (March 1983): 12; David W. Lewis and C. Paul Vincent, "An Initial Response," *Journal of Academic Librarianship* 9 (March 1983): 4-6; Constance McCarthy, "Library Instruction: Observations from the Reference Desk," *RQ* 22 (Fall 1982): 37; Billy R. Wilkinson, *Reference Services for Undergraduate Students: Four Case Studies* (Metuchen, N.J.: Scarecrow Press, 1972).

53.   Bruce T. Sajdak, "Draft Performance Standards for Library Instruction," (1979, Mimeographed).

54.   Guskin, Stoffle, and Baruth, "Library Future Shock," pp. 177-83.

55.   Stephen P. Harter, "Online Searching Styles: An Exploratory Study," *College & Research Libraries* 45 (July 1984): 249-58.

56.   Gordon K. Davies and Kathleen F. Slevin, "Babel or Opportunity: Recent Reports on Education," *The College Board Review* 130 (Winter 1983-84): 18-21, 37.

57.   Richard M. Dougherty and Wendy P. Lougee, "Research Library Residencies: A New Model for Professional Development," *Library Journal* 108 (July 1983): 1322-24.

58.   Council on Library Resources, *Research Grants* (n.d., Pamphlet). For more information, contact the council at 1785 Massachusetts Ave., N.W., Washington, D.C. 20036.

# 2 Alternative Professional Models in the Information Age

*Brian Nielsen*

## A COMMENT: UNDERCURRENTS IN THE VALUE PREMISES OF THE "FIRST GENERATION"

The paper that follows, published originally in *College & Research Libraries* (May 1982), appears in this collection among what are otherwise new essays because of its special relationship to the first Bibliographic Instruction Think Tank held in San Francisco in June 1981. Revealing the nature of that special relationship through its republication here, and commenting briefly on the paper's content will help people in the field understand the roots of a controversy sparked by the original Think Tank.

"Teacher or Intermediary" was written to be delivered at the 1981 ALA San Francisco conference during the regular Bibliographic Instruction Section program meeting titled "Will Bibliographic Instruction Survive the Online Age?" I had prepared a reading version (virtually identical to its published form except in its opening paragraph and the many footnotes, which were added later to form what is practically a second text) in advance of my arrival in San Francisco for the Think Tank Preconference. Early on in the Think Tank deliberations, I shared the paper with the other six participants. Its content served to stimulate thinking in a number of directions, particularly in considering the relationship between BI and what goes on at the reference desk. Though the paper did not argue the primacy of user education over one-on-one reference service per se, it did suggest a line of reasoning that placed the two forms of service in opposition to each other. It thus provided a perspective on reference service which was, and perhaps still is, somewhat radical for its time.

Rather than continuing to view BI as an "add-on" to traditional reference, "Teacher or Intermediary" argued that BI was fundamental to the development of service objectives oriented to the academic community as a whole; and, in that special sense, it was different from reference service, which provides help for a relatively small group of library users who ask reference questions. A less radical, but in some ways similar, position was taken by Fran Hopkins, another Think Tank participant, in a paper she read at the beginning of the preconference (also published in *College & Research Libraries*).[1] These affirmations of BI as a "core activity" were echoed in the Think Tank document and were not controversial when presented for wide discussion near the end of the preconference.

What *did* generate some heat was the characterization of one-on-one reference service as a "mop-up activity." This phrase, which emerged out of the cloistered Think Tank discussions of the "Teacher or Intermediary" paper, was used in a report to the audience at the preconference's conclusion, but without the benefit of the context the paper provided; ALA conferees did not hear the paper until three days later. The paper critiqued "traditional reference" for the way in which it limited service distribution; the point was to challenge the idealized model of service, based on such classic reference texts as those of James Wyer, Margaret Hutchins, and Bill Katz, that the "First Generation" was taught in library school. Though the paper critiqued a *model* of service, the preconference audience heard only what appeared to be a critique of the service as it was provided, and thus by extension, the servers. It was unfortunate that some of the heat generated by this misunderstanding found its way into a *Journal of Academic Librarianship* symposium on the Think Tank, without benefit of the light which might have been shed by reading "Teacher or Intermediary."

"Teacher or Intermediary" does touch on some deeper issues which gave the First Generation of BI workers its special character. The First Generation was rebelling against the reference model taught throughout the 1950s and 1960s (and probably still taught in some schools). There were strong undercurrents of a deprofessionalization movement in the early 1970s in BI, not unlike movements in other occupations that advocated greater client control in matters otherwise thought to be within the professional's exclusive domain.[2] This sentiment to empower library users by giving them more sophisticated knowledge of bibliographic matters created a paradox when it combined with the professionalization drive as expressed through the faculty status movement; such a paradox was bound to engender conflict.

As a final note, let me point out that this reprinting restores the essay's opening paragraph to its original form as read in San Francisco. The panel for which the paper was written bore a title that put BI practitioners very much on the defensive in relation to the then-glamorous online search practitioners. My intent was to raise a strong counteroffensive, and thus I sought to address fundamental premises. In the five years since the paper was written, academic librarianship at large has come to recognize what the paper argued: that bibliographic instruction can play an important role in advancing technological change for the benefit of users.

# NOTES

1. Frances L. Hopkins, "A Century of Bibliographic Instruction: The Historical Claim to Professional and Academic Legitimacy," *College & Research Libraries* 43, no. 3 (May 1982): 192-98.

2. For an interesting parallel in another field, see Robert J. S. Ross, "The Impact of Social Movements on a Profession in Process: Advocacy in Urban Planning," *Sociology of Work and Occupations* 3, no. 4 (November 1976): 429-54.

\* \* \*

# "TEACHER OR INTERMEDIARY: ALTERNATIVE PROFESSIONAL MODELS IN THE INFORMATION AGE" *

The question posed as the title for this series of papers, "Will Bibliographic Instruction Survive the Online Age?", has an urgent, almost ominous, ring to it. Unlike the general conference theme "Libraries and the Pursuit of Happiness," we here in the Bibliographic Instruction Section program meeting are looking to the future with some sense of trepidation. Will we bibliographic instruction specialists who have invested considerable amounts of our creative talents and time in what we saw as an up-and-coming career path be displaced? Is the future of reference to be in online database searching and the realization of that dream in which librarians cease to teach and instead provide directly all the information users need? Facing a new technological environment, we who define ourselves as user education specialists seem not to be thinking about how we are to further develop and modify our specialty in the Online Age; our panel title suggests we are worrying about our own survival.

Rather than consider the future, this paper will look into the past—the past of bibliographic instruction, of reference service, and of some larger issues about the status of librarianship. The past treated here is not the consideration of specific historical events, but an examination of certain ideas that have shaped the development of librarians and their current ways of thinking about bibliographic instruction and reference service. Though many do not find such "philosophizing" particularly useful in day-to-day problem solving, a historical and sociological perspective can help librarians to better understand their present circumstance. Working toward a deeper understanding of the path to their current dilemmas may in the end allow librarians to see new options for the future that they didn't know existed.

A brief outline of the train of thought this paper will pursue may be helpful. The conceptual foundation underlying the argument presented here is the well-established relationship between instrumental value change and technological advance that has influenced many spheres of modern life, but especially environmental policy.[1] The first objective is to consider the professionalization issue within librarianship and to show how reference work has played a very special role in the occupation's long struggle for higher professional status. This paper will argue that reference work has the qualities of what sociology has called a "core task" for the occupation as a whole. The second section will comprise a fresh look at the old "information versus instruction" debate, which has occupied reference theorists for at least twenty years. It will argue that the information versus instruction debate hides deeper issues and values that are related to librarianship's status and the "core task" nature of reference. These issues and values are

*Reprinted by permission of the American Library Association, "Teacher or Intermediary: Alternative Professional Models in the Information Age," Brian Nielsen, from *College & Research Libraries*, May 1982; copyright © 1982 ALA.

not often discussed at meetings and in the literature, but deserve attention because of their effect on decision making. Following discussion of how these values may shape the future, this paper will touch briefly on some of the technological and economic factors that will also be important in the years ahead. It will conclude with a call to set aside the "information versus instruction" debate and replace it with a new model for a reference role that better reflects the fundamental values shared by librarians.

Regardless of whether the specific programmatic conclusions presented here are accepted by a sizable number of librarians in the field, it is hoped that this paper will open debate on value issues that have received scant attention in the literature up to now. Like other occupational groups (and especially those concerned with professionalization), librarianship has an unfortunate tendency to assume value consensus among its membership and is reluctant to open value debate because such debate threatens group solidarity.[2] The value issues implicit in any technological advance, however, result in the concrete expression of values that may not be held in common by all group members, and so while solidarity may appear to be maintained on the surface, underlying contradictions may grow. This condition is exacerbated by the still-prevalent argument that technological (and professional) decision making can somehow be "value free."[3] By exploring the value choices that accompany technological decision making in librarianship, librarians may in the long run clarify considerably their grounds for decision making.

With these preliminaries out of the way, attention is called to a social fact of librarianship that, over the years, has had an enormous influence in how librarians act, talk about themselves, and relate to the larger social world around them. That social fact is the tenuousness of their collective claim to professional status. Social status for librarianship has for most of the past hundred years been bound up with the fortunes of women in our society. The demeaning but widespread stereotypes, the low salaries, the organizational arrangements that so frequently make males the administrators and females the underlings, all attest to the status problems with which librarianship continues to struggle. As a "feminized profession" librarianship has encountered a variety of problems related to self-concept, problems that have at their root the same issues now being confronted quite effectively by elements of the contemporary women's movement.[4]

A common response in dealing with problems of self-concept is to diagnose the difficulty as an "image problem," which is what much of librarianship has done. When trapped into thinking of its status condition as the result of "image problem," it retaliates by creating counter-images, like the image of the high-technology "new librarian," the occupation's equivalent of a Virginia Slims commercial.

A key rhetorical device librarianship has used to legitimate itself and raise its status has been to seek in the occupation parallels with other higher-status fields.[5] An important means librarians use to draw those parallels involves reference work and what sociologists Rue Bucher and Anselm Strauss have called "core professional tasks."[6]

"Core professional tasks" are those tasks that are shared by large numbers of a particular occupation's membership and that serve to make the members distinctive as a group to the lay public. For lawyers, the core task is arguing in a courtroom, for doctors it is interacting on an intimate basis with clients—the so-called doctor-patient relationship. Never mind that most lawyers seldom come close to a courtroom, never mind that doctors' interactions with patients may often be perfunctory or through an EKG chart rather than face-to-face; the symbolic power of the "core task" in the public mind provides a ready identification for the profession as a whole that conveys status, the performance of special and esoteric skills, and a sense of the critical role that the professional members play.

The performance of reference work is a "core professional task" for librarianship as a whole, and as such, all of librarianship (and particularly its professional leadership) has a stake in defining reference work to suit rhetorical purposes. Though reference is only one of many specialties, it is a unique specialty that resonates in so many ways with that other "core task" of a most high profession, the doctor-patient relationship. This paper attempts to show how librarianship as a whole benefits from the image that that particular specialty can convey.

There are a number of features of reference work that reveal the sense in which this task mirrors tasks of higher-status occupations. First of all, reference is a librarian role that involves a "professional-client" relationship, unlike other task areas such as cataloging, book selection, and administration, where the contact with library users is not often direct. Because there is user contact, reference is the "public face" of the occupation. It is the most visible occupational model, if one discounts the person who checks books out at the circulation desk, who is more often not a librarian, anyway. Reference work is also a specialty area in which the "application of special and esoteric knowledge," that criterion so important to achieving professional status, is patent: the public perception of the all-knowing reference librarian (which coexists with other, less flattering images) is testimony to this special characteristic of reference. Still other qualities of reference work that give weight to its "core task" nature are that the work is not reducible to rules, it is difficult to measure, and its practice relies on intuition, hunches, and bits and pieces of information that only long experience and a retentive mind—not a textbook—can develop. Finally, there is a "private practice" character of reference work that is not shared with other library specialties. The reference librarian, though a member of the library staff like the cataloger or the circulation librarian, performs work on the behalf of specific, identifiable users rather than directly on behalf of the organization as a whole. Such a position enables the reference librarian to bend the rules, take shortcuts, and in other ways demonstrate autonomy in relation to the bureaucratic red tape with which the public sees the library organization encumbered.

All of these characteristics of reference combine to provide librarianship as a whole with a set of images that serve to enhance the occupation's status. Librarians know that reference work is not any more important or necessary than cataloging, circulation, administration, or any other area of librarianship. One can't provide good library service without all of the different specialties working together. Yet in all this, it is reference that provides a number of paradigmatic work roles which give considerable ammunition in the occupation's fight for higher social status.

The problem of the status of librarianship and this special role that reference plays in the striving for professional recognition has had a subtle but important influence on an old debate in the reference field. I refer to the "information versus instruction" debate.[7]

For those unacquainted with this debate, the basic positions may be stated very simply. The information side argues that it is the role of the reference librarian to concentrate practice on the delivery of information extracted from the source in which the information is found in as complete and digested a manner as possible—in short, "question-answering." Teaching users how to retrieve information themselves, it is felt, falls short of the ideal professional goal of maximum service delivery.[8] The instruction side argues that an appropriate and desirable reference activity, though not the sole activity, is to help users by teaching them how to find answers for themselves. A key element of the instruction side of the debate is the advocacy of self-reliance.[9]

In their extreme forms, the two sides of the debate define two alternative role models for the reference librarian: the information intermediary on the information side, and the teacher on the instruction side. It is difficult at this point to see whether one role model will win out in acceptance over the other as more relevant to our time. It is possible that the two will come to coexist, resulting in two specializations competing between each other for resources, and the likely decline of general reference service as we have known it. Through describing some of the technological, organizational, and social factors involved in the "information versus instruction" debate, the present situation will be made a bit clearer, and in the end, a resolution that fashions a new role (which is neither teacher nor intermediary, but which combines some of the features of each) will be proposed.

The growth of online bibliographic searching, in which librarians play out to the fullest the intermediary role, has been an important causal factor in reopening the "information versus instruction" debate. Reference librarians are now having to decide which area—online searching or bibliographic instruction—will better further their individual careers, and reference administrators are being forced to decide how best to allocate scarce resources between these two expensive functions.[10] Making decisions requires some projection into the future, and any projection is based on assumptions and values presently held just as much as on assessments of technological and economic trends. Because the trends in technology are for the most part outside the domain of librarianship, we can have some notion of their nature but little control over their direction. Although assumptions and values too often go unexamined, it is time we look at and articulate them more carefully, for through such examination librarians can not only better predict the future, but also perhaps take part in shaping it.

The intermediary role has always had the edge as a role model among those who have a strong interest in the status aspirations of librarianship. The reason for that advantage is plain: the intermediary role expresses the "core task" nature of librarianship. The intermediary role, if fully implemented, would provide considerably more status value to librarianship than the instruction role, just as the doctor has higher status than the teacher. Advocates of the intermediary role, such as Samual Rothstein, Bill Katz, and Tom Galvin, seem often preoccupied with image; they speak of the role in glowing terms that have limited correspondence to practice, for in practice, answering questions often seems closer to Band-Aid dispensing than to brain surgery. Bibliographic instruction is frequently attacked on grounds of the poor user evaluation it receives, but these critics totally ignore the few careful evaluations of question-answering in libraries, evaluations which are so distressing that we all often pretend they never appeared in print.[11]

A significant boost to the intermediary role was provided with the innovation of the online searching in the early 1970s, because the technology was sufficiently complex and the economics were such as to make intermediaries attractive to both librarians and end users. It was great for those who were concerned about high status for the field because of the status value provided by the visible and public association with computer technology.[12] Early experiments by some researchers to provide users with direct access met in failure, a very common result in the eyes of many librarians who enjoyed the newfound status. User dependency on librarians seemed assured by the new technology.

But what about the consequences of the intermediary role for service? What other values does the choice express? The most basic organizational issue in reference service, like any social service, is how it is to be distributed. Although this has long seemed to be a nonissue in reference—those who receive the service are those who ask for it—it is a genuine and serious issue that is unfortunately hidden under the debate over appropriate modes of reference practice.

As a service that has seen little, if any, design changes since its origin in the late nineteenth century, librarians tend not to think of the value choices implicit in that design that they have also inherited.[13] They all accept as a basic postulate that reference service is useful to anyone, at least potentially. Almost every user walking in a library door has one or more questions to which a librarian could provide answers.[14] Yet it is known that many if not most library users do not ask questions of librarians, and are actually only vaguely aware of the range of services a reference librarian may perform. Those few questions that are asked relative to the much larger number which users choose to keep to themselves are thus typically of a lower level than the questions for which answers are sought; and most questions go unasked of a reference librarian.[15] Serious questioners are a small minority of users. This leads to the realization that reference service as it is classically performed in an intermediary role is a service for the few. The intermediary role model, of necessity, advocates providing information only to those who ask, and promises maximum service to that minority. The maximum service that the intermediary promises can be delivered only if there is a substantial limitation on demand, that is, if most questions don't get asked of a librarian. That limitation on demand is provided quite conveniently by the learned behavior of users to not ask questions.[16]

With online searching as it is presently practiced (the logical extension of the intermediary role), other means of limiting demand have been found, such as charging fees, providing minimal publicity for online, and creating the impression that the service is only appropriate for advanced and sophisticated researchers.

In contrast to the value choice of service to the few, which is implicit in the information-giving mode of service, those who advocate instructing users make the opposite value of distributing reference service in as egalitarian a manner as possible. Helping users to help themselves provides for a wide distribution of service, though of course not all of the service is provided by librarians. Those who have had experience in mounting effective instruction programs know, too, that such programs do not reduce the number of questions reference librarians must answer across the desk; the programs increase the number, and, as well, typically make the questions more interesting. By allowing users to become their own question-answerers, instruction advocates to some degree blur the distinction between librarian and layperson, a blurring that has caused problems for those anxious about the occupation's status. The instruction side of the debate values self-reliance and devalues the dependence on experts which results in service disequilibrium and general service scarcity.[17]

Technological advances such as online tend to clarify the implications of value choices that were made long ago without full awareness of their ultimate consequences. These advances require librarians to look harder at their values and perhaps seek change in them. The choice between service to the few and service to many implicit in the "intermediary versus teacher" decision provides just one more example of this general phenomenon. Medicine, of course, provides the best-known example. The notion of the doctor as the all-responsible healer led to the development of high-technology medicine, and now we are realizing the huge economic and social costs of the dependency relationship fostered by that kind of medicine.[18] The economics of information retrieval technology, however, which librarianship has only very limited control over,[19] will result in a lessening necessity for information intermediaries.

With computer costs still dropping and the information producers seeing a need to increase the size of their markets, the development of more user-friendly systems seems highly likely. The information industry has used librarians as effective and cheap retailers up to now, but only through direct appeal to end users can the industry achieve the size market it needs. New systems are being developed for the growing home computer market, and terminals are becoming about as common as the family encyclopedia. New pricing structures may be implemented to ensure that maximum market saturation is achieved. Although current pricing methods for online now favor the utilization of intermediaries, changes may be in the offing. Proposals have been made to charge a flat upfront admission fee to a database plus a "viewing" charge for partial output, which would virtually eliminate the economic advantage that highly skilled intermediaries now have over novice end users.[20] Many other technical innovations in online searching combined with new economic conditions make end-user access more and more likely.[21]

The president of Dialog Information Services, Inc., has recently mounted a new counter-argument to the economic argument for end-user access.[22] Since Dialog's experience has been that providing telephone assistance to naive end users is very expensive, it is argued that end-user access is not viable. What such an argument neglects, of course, is the factor of alternative system design criteria. Systems such as Dialog have made considerable development investment in a market of trained librarian searchers; the retooling of these systems to accommodate a new market of nonintermediary users may require more capital than is now available to Dialog. Thus, while the older established commercial search systems may not move into the end-user market, other newer systems are likely to do so.[23]

In academic libraries the development of online catalogs may also lead to the intermediary role becoming an anachronism. Catalogs *must* be user friendly, or at least have the appearance of friendliness; if they were not, the amount of time required for staff assistance would be staggering. At Northwestern, for example, there is now an online author-title catalog reflecting virtually all of the library's monographic holdings processed since 1970, and all of its serial holdings, including the latest issue checked in, can easily be displayed on public terminals. Subject access to the online file is now available in a test mode. With members of the Reference Department and other public service staff members working closely with system developers to design online instructions into the catalog itself, the teaching functions of reference again come to the fore. As the library staff members gain more experience with such systems and machine costs continue to drop, it may be from there but a simple step to acquire tapes from other database producers, load them onto their systems, and let their users search them as they do the library's catalog.[24]

The present competition between those who advocate the intermediary role and those who advocate the teaching role is unfortunate and unnecessary. It divides the ranks of reference librarians at a time when unity of purpose on behalf of user needs has never been more important. Those who favor exclusive practice of an intermediary role lock themselves into the practice of a specialty that is rapidly approaching obsolescence due to continuing economic and technological change. The intermediary role also cannot hope to satisfy the information needs of more than a small minority of library users, and thus cannot meet a critical social need for greater equity in the distribution of knowledge. Attempts to foster a dependency relationship between librarian and user may promise short-term gain for librarianship, but they are, in the long run, counter to the interests of both librarians and users.[25]

Though the critique presented here has focused principally on the intermediary role, it must be said that the teaching role as it has been implemented is also in need of much critical examination.

Much of what is being taught in bibliographic instruction programs is mind-deadening. Teaching about the problem of information retrieval can be intellectually challenging, as the problem touches on some of the most difficult questions in philosophy, linguistics, psychology, and sociology. The bibliographic instruction curriculum should be broadened to treat more thoroughly and creatively basic principles, including such things as set theory for online searching. At the same time, it should take the teaching of technique out of the classroom and into self-instructional learning packages, hands-on experience, and other less expensive mediated methods. Above all, advocates of the teaching role should not make a cult out of teaching. Librarians provide many helpful and necessary services besides teaching, and the totality of that contribution deserves recognition in its own right. Attempts to emulate academic faculty roles can be just as dysfunctional as attempts to mold reference into a doctor-patient model. The teaching cult also tends to divide instruction librarians from all other librarians, which is harmful to all librarianship. For all of these reasons, librarians must work toward defining a new role for reference service.

Forging a new role model for reference librarianship requires first the disabusing of the idea that reference must be a "core task" of a status-seeking profession. The intermediary role is the embodiment of the "core task" idea, and as such serves the status interests of librarianship at the expense of the information needs of library users. If librarians truly wish to work toward the best interests of their users, it is absurd to continue to advocate the old classic professionalism, which places users in a dependency relationship with librarians. Such a relationship does a disservice to users and ultimately retards the development of library services, of librarians, and of much library technology.

The intermediary role still has a powerful appeal to many in librarianship, especially to many library school faculty members, because of the professionalization interests that the role serves. Librarians cannot work to discard it without offering an alternative that is also powerful and intellectually sound. Pauline Wilson is essentially correct in her critique of the teaching role as being inadequate, and even harmful in some respects, for our field,[26] so further search for a new role is in order.

Though no alternative model adequate to librarianship has yet been fully developed, there are movements afoot in other human service fields that bear close watching for the examples they may provide. These movements all have in common a characteristic that lies at the heart of the ideals of librarianship: they value the sharing of information. The movements are also radically humanistic and show a healthy skepticism toward technological fixes, though they are not antitechnology. The holistic health movement is perhaps the best known of these, but other occupational areas besides physical health are involved in forging a new role model, among them psychotherapy, social work, media and computer activism, and economics. Some useful texts [that] may help librarianship explore new models for reference service include the book *Helping Ourselves: Families and the Human Network* by Mary Howell, Theodore Schultz' new book *Investing in People: The Economics of Population Quality*, a very interesting article by Paul Hawken in the spring 1981 *CoEvolution Quarterly* called "Disintermediation," the work of Ival Illich, and that of Gregory Bateson.[27-31] Their message calls upon experts of all kinds to rethink their relationships to nonexperts, and to work toward the sharing of knowledge rather than its opposite, the monopolization of knowledge implicit in the classic professional model.

Undertaking the project of redefining appropriate helping roles for librarians will require the work of many individual librarians, experimentation and research in libraries, and much communication with users. Such redefinition cannot be merely a paper exercise practiced by authors in library journals.[32] But the undertaking appears valuable and librarians, in the end, might not only provide better service for our users but also be the happier for it.

### References

1.  Emmanuel G. Mesthene, *Technological Change: Its Impact on Man and Society* (Cambridge: Harvard University Press, 1970); Jon Wagner, "Defining Technology: Political Implications of Hardware, Software, Power, and Information," *Human Relations* 32:719-36 (1979); Victor Ferkiss, *Technological Man: The Myth and the Reality* (New York: Braziller, 1969).

2.  An interesting illustration of this avoidance of value debate is provided by Carolyn F. Etheridge, "Lawyers versus Indigents: Conflict of Interest in Professional-Client Relations in the Legal Profession," in Eliot Friedson, ed., *The Professions and Their Prospects* (Beverly Hills, Calif.: Sage, 1973), pp. 245-65.

3.  For some discussion of this point, see Manfred Stanley, *The Technological Conscience: Survival and Dignity in an Age of Expertise* (New York: Free Press, 1978), pp. 23-24. Also very useful is Hazel Henderson, "Systems, Economics, and 'Female'," *CoEvolution Quarterly* 7:61-63 (Fall 1975).

4. A useful historical explanation of the current condition is provided by Dee Garrison, *Apostles of Culture: The Public Librarian and American Society, 1876-1920* (New York: Macmillan, 1979). Some interesting prescriptions for change are presented in Pauline Wilson, "Librarians and Their Stereotypes" (Paper read at the Library Research Round Table, American Library Association Annual Conference, Dallas, 1979). Kathleen Weibel, "Toward A Feminist Profession," *Library Journal* 101:263-67 (Jan. 1, 1976) has articulated some linkages between librarianship and the women's movement.

5. Acknowledgement is made here to Donald W. Ball, "An Abortion Clinic Ethnography," *Social Problems* 14:293-301 (Winter 1967), from which the author has borrowed a way of looking and the idea of a "rhetoric."

6. Rue Bucher and Anselm Strauss, "Professions in Process," *American Journal of Sociology* 66:328-30 (1961).

7. Robert Wagers, "American Reference Theory and the Information Dogma," *Journal of Library History* 13:265-81 (Summer 1978), provides excellent complementary historical perspective on this point.

8. A large number of papers supporting this position have appeared over the years, among them, Samuel Rothstein, "Reference Service—The New Dimension in Librarianship," *College & Research Libraries* 22:11-18 (Jan. 1961); William Katz, *Introduction to Reference Work, Volume II: Reference Services and Reference Processes*, 2d ed., (New York: McGraw-Hill, 1974; Thomas Galvin, "Education of the New Reference Librarian," *Library Journal* 100:727-30 (April 15, 1975); and Anita Schiller, "Reference Service: Instruction or Information," *Library Quarterly* 35:52-60 (Jan. 1965), which is the best reasoned. Other papers support the position in passing, such as Mary Lee Bundy and Paul Wasserman, "Professionalism Reconsidered," *College & Research Libraries* 29:5-26 (Jan. 1968), and Herbert S. White, "Growing User Information Dependence and Its Impact on the Library Field," *Aslib Proceedings* 31:74-87 (Feb. 1979).

9. Useful texts in support of this position are provided by Harvie Branscomb, *Teaching with Books: A Study of College Libraries* (Chicago: Association of American Colleges and American Library Asociation, 1940); Patricia Knapp, *The Monteith College Library Experiment* (New York: Scarecrow, 1966); and Evan Farber, "Library Instruction throughout the Curriculum: Earlham College Program," in John Lubans, ed., *Educating the Library User* (New York: Bowker, 1974), pp. 145-62.

10. Trudy A. Gardner, "Effect of On-line Data Bases on Reference Policy," *RQ* 19:70-74 (Fall 1979), highlights the competition, though the paper fails to address the value premises that might form the basis for deciding appropriate relative emphases on online and instruction.

11. F. Wilfrid Lancaster, *The Measurement and Evaluation of Library Service* (Washington, D.C.: Information Resources Press, 1977), pp. 91-109.

12. James M. Kusak, "Integration of On-line Reference Service," *RQ* 19:64-69 (Fall 1979), provides a good illustration of the status and image issues advanced.

13. Writing on the history of reference service has suffered from an ahistorical approach that is biased toward a high degree of professionalization. Frances L. Hopkins, "A Century of Bibliographic Instruction: The Historical Claim to Professional and Academic Legitimacy," *College & Research Libraries* 43:192-98 (May 1982), has fortunately broken new ground to provide a more objective viewpoint. See also Burton Bledstein, *The Culture of Professionalism: The Middle Class and the Development of Higher Education in America* (New York: Norton, 1976).

14. Patrick Wilson, *Public Knowledge, Private Ignorance: Toward a Library and Information Policy* (Westport, Conn.: Greenwood, 1977), has persuasively argued the error in that postulate. His prescription for remedy merits discussion in the field; it may be that through such discussion, values different from Wilson's alone will be seen to bear on the issues presented.

15. Mary Jane Swope and Jeffrey Katzer, "The Silent Majority: Why They Don't Ask Questions," *RQ* 12:161-66 (Winter 1972), provides some empirical verification that a small percentage of user questions are posed to reference librarians.

16. Gregory Bateson, "The Logical Categories of Learning and Communication," in his *Steps to an Ecology of Mind* (New York: Ballantine, 1972), pp. 279-308, explains the sense in which such behavior is learned. Erving Goffman, *Behavior in Public Places: Notes on the Social Organization of Gatherings* (New York: Free Press, 1963), p. 106, proposes an alternative explanation, that of an "implicit contract" between questioner and answerer. Both theories have merit.

17. John McKnight, "The Professional Service Business," *Social Policy* 8:110-16 (Nov.-Dec. 1977), provides a good summary of the general argument.

18. Everett Mendelsohn, Judith P. Swazey, and Irene Traviss, eds., *Human Aspects of Biomedical Innovation* (Cambridge: Harvard University Press, 1971), especially the essay by Victor Sidel, "New Technologies and the Practice of Medicine," pp. 131-55.

19. Anita Schiller, "Shifting Boundaries in Information," *Library Journal* 106:705-9 (April 1, 1981). A contrasting but in some ways similar viewpoint can be found in Arthur D. Little, Inc. (Vincent Giuliano, project director), *Into the Information Age: A Perspective for Federal Action on Information* (Chicago: American Library Association, 1978), and Isaac L. Auerbach, "The Information Industry: An Invisible Industry," in *Information Demand and Supply for the 1980's* (Proceedings of a seminar organized by the International Council of Scientific Unions, Abstracting Board at the U.S. National Academy of Sciences, Washington, D.C., June 23-24, 1976) (Paris: ICSU AB, 1978), pp. 91-97.

20.   P. L. Holmes and C. B. Wooten, "An Alternative Approach to the Pricing of Online Services," *2nd International Online Information Meeting Proceedings*, London, Dec. 5-7, 1978 (Oxford: Learned Information, 1979), pp. 115-21; T. P. Barwise, *Online Searching: The Impact on User Charges of the Extended Use of Online Information Services* (Paris: International Council of Scientific Unions, Abstracting Board, 1979).

21.   Brian Nielsen, "Online Bibliographic Searching and the Deprofessionaliza-tion of Librarianship," *Online Review* 4:215-24 (Sept. 1980).

22.   Roger Summit, "Popular Illusions Relating to the Costs of Online Services" (Address delivered at the ALA RASD MARS Program, "Cooperation: Facilitating Access to Online Information Services," New York, June 29, 1980). The argument is also touched on in Roger Summit, "The Dynamics of Costs and Finances on Online Computer Searching," *RQ* 20:60-63 (Fall 1980).

23.   A. K. Kent, "Dial Up and Die: Can Information Systems Survive the Online Age?" *Information Scientist* 12:3-7 (March 1978) argues for a governmental policy that would encourage alternative system designs to those that presently exist and dominate the market.

24.   The soon-to-be-available GPO *Monthly Catalog* on RLIN may be cited as an example.

25.   For a more general perspective on the future of service delivery, see Milan Zeleny, "The Self-Service Society: A New Scenario of the Future," *Planning Review* 7:3-7, 37-38 (May 1979), and Jonathan Gershuny, *After Industrial Society? The Emerging Self-Service Economy* (London: Macmillan, 1978).

26.   Pauline Wilson, "Librarians as Teachers: The Study of an Organizational Fiction," *Library Quarterly* 49:146-62 (April 1979).

27.   Mary Howell, *Helping Ourselves: Families and the Human Network* (Boston: Beacon Press, 1975).

28.   Theodore Schultz, *Investing in People: The Economics of Population Quality* (Berkeley: University of California Press, 1981).

29.   Paul Hawken, "Disintermediation," *CoEvolution Quarterly* 29:6-13 (Spring 1981).

30.   Ivan Illich, *Toward a History of Needs* (New York: Pantheon, 1978).

31.   Gregory Bateson, *Steps to an Ecology of Mind* (New York: Ballantine, 1972), especially the essays "Effects of Conscious Purpose on Human Adapta-tion" and "The Roots of Ecological Crisis."

32. For insight into this point, see Paolo Freire, "Extension or Communication," in his *Education for Critical Consciousness* (New York: Seabury, 1973). This is not to say that critical writing is not helpful. For a useful discussion paper, see Ray Lester, "Why Educate the Library User?" *Aslib Proceedings* 31:366-80 (Aug. 1979). Lester, unfortunately, makes a curious separation between culture and work.

# PART II

## THE SECOND GENERATION
### Establishing an Identity

Twenty years have passed since the grassroots movement began which was to establish bibliographic instruction as a recognized part of librarianship. Bibliographic instruction, following closely the stages of a developing profession, has moved from an area of interest with informal meetings and internally circulated papers to a recognized area of study with its own organizations, literature, and bibliographies. Nonetheless, it is still an area in its infancy, striving for identity and arguing among its adherents as to what it should be and where it should go.

Part II is the body of our work, designed to explore those areas considered part of the current identity of bibliographic instruction. The four sections comprising Part II provide an organizing framework within which to examine issues arising from the original Think Tank. This framework developed over a period of a year as the editor, with the close involvement of the editorial board, studied the findings of the original Think Tank and worked to discover an organizing structure for the findings in light of current bibliographic instruction needs and practices. The chapters comprising the sections emerged both from the original Think Tank issues and from current needs identified out of the developing specialization of bibliographic instruction.

In section A, "Understanding the Milieu of Bibliographic Instruction," the changing nature of academic librarianship due to developing technology and organizational restructuring in higher education is discussed. The impact of these changes on bibliographic instruction and its place in higher education is explored. Bibliographic instruction is depicted as a complex activity, consisting of both basic and specialized levels that may require separate places within the academic curriculum. Section B, "Understanding the People We Serve," is designed to remind librarians that the focus of bibliographic instruction is real people with real needs and feelings. To consider instruction without considering those to be instructed is a futile activity destined to fail. In section C, "Bibliographic Instruction Librarianship," the issues of library education for bibliographic instruction and the conceptual areas that have been identified as the base for bibliographic instruction theory are explored. The fourth and final section, D, "Increasing Specialization in Bibliographic Instruction," carries on the themes of differing needs of academic researchers and differing levels of instruction as well as non-library liaisons required to meet those needs.

The authors of the twelve chapters comprising Part II were charged with producing essays that are theoretical or philosophic in intent rather than providing "helpful hints" or descriptions of "model programs," with which the literature of bibliographic instruction is rife. They are writing for an audience assumed to have a basic understanding of bibliographic instruction and, if not a conviction of its legitimacy, at least an open mind. Part II, then, presents the Second Generation addressing the Second Generation.

41

# SECTION A

## Understanding the Milieu
## of Bibliographic Instruction

Bibliographic instruction is, by its very nature, an activity greatly influenced by the setting in which it takes place. User instruction occurs regularly in four types of library settings (school, public, academic, and community college) and, regardless of setting, focuses upon the basic function of information retrieval; however, depth, content, and approach vary for each type of library. Moreover, wide differences are found among libraries of the same type as programs are developed and adapted to individual library settings.

Bibliographic instruction in academic libraries, the focus of this book, is likely to be the most responsive to setting among the four types of libraries which support this activity. There are four reasons for this. First, academic libraries encompass a broad range of institutions, varying from the small liberal arts college to the huge, multibranch university libraries. Second, the political climate of individual institutions, and the academic library's place within its politics, can dictate the library's freedom to develop such services as a library instruction program and the availability of funds to support these programs. Third, the academic freedom of faculty and the place, or lack thereof, of bibliographic instruction in the curriculum, affects whether or not librarians have access to students. Finally, the complexity and dominance of various academic programs influence the type and depth of library instruction needed on individual campuses.

The importance of setting in establishing an identity for bibliographic instruction is the theme of this first section. Library concepts and structures are shifting and changing as librarians react to developing technology: thus, the models that may emerge to provide information to the academic community are a matter of uncertainty and debate. Without first understanding the parameters that encompass this change, it is difficult to discuss intelligently the future of bibliographic instruction. The three chapters which form this section explore three broad aspects of the academic milieu in relation to their impact on the Second Generation of bibliographic instruction librarians.

In chapter 3, Joseph Boisse and Duane Webster present four scenarios which represent organizational extremes for academic libraries of the future. These scenarios are based on an ARL discussion of the future organizational structure of academic libraries. Each includes a projected institutional philosophy and context, an assessment of its impact upon library organization, and a discussion of the possible effects on bibliographic instruction.

The effect of emerging technology on academic library operation is the focus of chapter 4. In this chapter, Joanne Euster discusses how information technology has changed the way individuals perceive and use information resources and how this changed perception affects the role of the bibliographic instruction librarian.

Chapter 5 explores the place of bibliographic instruction in the academic curriculum. It begins by expanding and clarifying the ongoing debate on whether library instruction should be presented and controlled by the library or by an academic department. Emily Boyce, Chair of an academic department which offers a one-credit, required course in library skills, and Ruth Katz, Director of Library Services for the same campus, present the two sides of the debate. Constance Mellon, who is currently involved with the design of the credit course and who formerly developed and coordinated a major library instruction project as part of an academic library staff at another campus, discusses the pros and cons of each argument from an applied standpoint and suggests possible ways of integration. The second part of this chapter explores the levels of specialization within bibliographic instruction and how they differ from the basic library skills instruction appropriate for all college freshmen.

# 3 Looking Ahead: An Administrative View

*Joseph A. Boisse and Duane Webster*

The past quarter century has been an eventful one for American colleges and universities. During that time American higher education experienced the most rapid growth of its three-and-one-half-century history; it struggled through the upheavals of the 1960s; it experienced the impact of technology as computers were introduced in many of its ongoing operations; it slid from a period of unprecedented affluence to one of great financial stringency; it witnessed a rapid incursion of the courts into all aspects of its existence; its doors were suddenly flung open to large segments of the population not hitherto exposed to postsecondary education.

During the same period, academic libraries have experienced an equal amount of turmoil. Every change in the general landscape of higher education has produced a ripple effect in the academic library. The rapid growth of student populations on campuses across the country resulted in a period of extensive construction of library facilities. The introduction of countless new academic programs brought about the rapid, and in some cases almost geometric, growth of library collections. The demonstrations and violence of the 1960s forced libraries to develop and implement security measures. Government subsidies brought new controls as well as more money to libraries. The swing from affluence to straitened circumstances inevitably resulted in reduced funds for academic libraries, with an accompanying cancellation of subscriptions and purchase of fewer books. The introduction of computers necessitated fundamental changes in the way staffs of academic libraries performed their day-to-day tasks.

Of these many changes, technology has had the most profound impact on both the institutions and their libraries. Automation has affected virtually every facet of higher education. Its influence has been so pervasive that it has brought about changes in the very organizational structure of academic institutions. New senior administrative posts have been created in some institutions specifically to deal with technology and automation. New power struggles have been generated over the control of technology and vast sums of money have been diverted from other functions to support it. The impact of technology has just begun; future automation will entail more radical, more pervasive, and more profound change.

What that change will be and how it will alter activities that we are all familiar with in academic libraries are questions with which library administrators must grapple on a daily basis. The library administrator is expected to have a vision of what the future will be for his/her library; the library administrator is expected to identify the forces which are affecting the library from all sides; and finally, the library administrator is responsible for developing a strategy which will enable his/her library to reach the envisioned future both in spite of, and with assistance from, those forces.

Any attempt to look into the future is filled with danger. When one considers the forces, previously described, at play on the higher education scene, the attempt is almost foolhardy. Nevertheless, this chapter will attempt to look at the future of bibliographic instruction in academic libraries from the point of view of an administrator.

## LIBRARY ADMINISTRATION AND THE HISTORY OF BI

Before the future, however, there is the past. The history of the instruction movement, especially from the mid-1960s to the present, is well documented. Although there is no need to recount that history, three comments bear repeating at this time.

The bibliographic instruction movement, as we know it today, was a grassroots movement. There were few administrators to be found at the meetings which were held on the subject in the late 1960s and early 1970s. It did not come on the scene as a glamour issue in the same way that automation and preservation did. Those issues provided academic library administrators with topics that were relatively easy to explain to institutional administrators and which to some extent, could be more easily used to justify additional resources. The impact of seeing the pages of a book crumble when they are turned is formidable. The demonstration in California of a computer searching the library catalog of a university in New York is awe-inspiring. Not so the sight of a librarian conducting a research skills seminar for graduate students in English literature. A request for funds to develop a comprehensive bibliographic instruction program is likely to be met with comments such as, "That's the role of the faculty," "Librarians aren't paid to teach," or "That's a waste of time and money."

Grassroots movements invariably go through a phase in their development in which they operate in a sort of guerilla fashion. Such was the case with bibliographic instruction. In many libraries, it was practiced by reference librarians without the knowledge of the library administration. Such a low profile is especially possible in large complex academic libraries, where a great many activities are carried on that the administration knows little or nothing about. In a sense, bibliographic instruction had to fight its way to the threshold of administrative interest and concern.

Unfortunately, even today, user education all too frequently receives more lip service than actual support. In too many colleges and universities it remains a stepchild both in terms of its place within the organizational structure and in terms of the level of financial support it receives. As we dream of the future role of libraries, we discuss scholars' workstations and access to information from every campus office. Little time or effort, however, is devoted to the careful examination of the educational role of the library and the future role of librarians themselves.

# ORGANIZATIONAL OPTIONS FOR ACADEMIC LIBRARIES AND THEIR IMPACT ON BI

At the Fall 1984 meeting of the Association of Research Libraries, the directors of the nation's largest research libraries discussed the future staffing needs of their libraries. Staffing needs, in the context of the discussion, referred not only to number of individuals but also to the kind of preparation those individuals would be expected to have in order to be able to contribute meaningfully to the work of the library in the future.

The discussion was structured around four organizational options which were identified as likely to categorize higher education as it moves toward the year 2000. Each option flows from a different institutional philosophy. While ARL directors were obviously concerned only with academic research libraries in the university context, the institutional philosophies and the options which flow from them apply to all of higher education in varying degrees.

Without a doubt, a distinct, and in many cases very unique future, lies ahead for each of the three thousand institutions of higher education in this country. Attempting to categorize them all rigidly into four groups would be presumptuous. The comments that follow are simply a discussion of four philosophies which may guide the development of the institutional context within which libraries must exist. These philosophies of higher education range from the very traditional to the highly experimental or, as some past discussants have noted, from the warehouse approach to the "startrek" approach.

The remainder of this chapter, then, will examine each of the four options starting with an explanation of the institutional philosophy which underlies it, the organizational context which flows from it, and its likely impact on the library. Only then can we attempt to assess the impact of each of the options on bibliographic instruction in terms of both its place within the organization and how it will be provided to the library clientele.

## The Conservative University

The first option is guided by an institutional philosophy of conservatism. Caution is the byword of the administration which sees itself in a passive role of coordination rather than in an active leadership role. There exists a hesitancy, bordering on paralysis, to introduce change, especially technological change. Different units of the institution go their separate ways with little chance for or interest in cross-fertilization. The administration does nothing to foster the bridging of historical barriers between disciplines.

All of the campus agencies dealing with information have their separate agendas; they are in active competition for the limited resources available. The library is not recognized as the intellectual hub of this educational enterprise. It is seen by the institutional administrators as just another cost center and its success is frequently measured by how well its expenditures are controlled. It is the administrators of these institutions who are most frequently heard to refer to the library as a "bottomless pit." It is as though they consider the library a necessary evil which they would rather do without but which tradition does not allow them to eliminate. The institutional administration has never made the transition from the concept of books to that of information. Another measure of the library's success is the size and scope of its book collections with little or no concern for how well, or poorly, the information contained therein is transmitted to the users. The "information society" will pass this institution by.

Taking its cue from higher up, the library administration is likely to be conservative in its approach. Since "boat-rockers" are not encouraged in the institution, the library administration will not be noted for its risk-taking. The desire to be a catalyst for change in the institution does not characterize the library; the librarians tend to melt into the institutional woodwork. New approaches to library service are rarely, if ever, tried. The organizational structure is the same as it always has been. Outreach to the campus community is actively discouraged. Bibliographic instruction, if it exists, does so with virtually no support from the library administration. The best administrative attitude an instruction librarian can hope for is benign neglect.

Clearly, the institution of higher education which chooses to follow this path for the future will be a rarity. It will have to resist every trend currently discernible on the higher education landscape. What is important to note is the philosophy which underlies the option. This philosophy still exists and, where it does, one cannot hope to establish new bridges to the educational community. The vision of the role and function of the library does not allow for the kind of partnership with other campus information units and with teaching faculty that will insure adequate, effective access to information. The next generation instruction librarian cannot hope to find much job satisfaction in such an institution. Even the most committed and energetic instruction librarian will face certain discouragement in this situation. More challenging and satisfying positions will undoubtedly exist elsewhere.

## The Innovative University

The second option along the continuum describes institutions in which campus administrators perceive their role to be one of leadership. They promote change and encourage technological innovation. The institution is engaged in some kind of strategic planning. To a considerable extent, the effort is propelled by a desire to control and, if possible, reduce overall institutional costs in an attempt to position the institution for a viable future.

Following in the path mapped by the institutional administration, the library administration is no less involved in change and automation. Because the library administration recognizes the new and changing demands placed on it by the evolving college or university, it will be considering and experimenting with organizational changes within the library itself. The traditional dichotomization between technical and public services will become blurred although not entirely obliterated; organization of the library along strict functional lines will begin to weaken and the assignment of professionals will cut across functions significantly. Librarians, expected to possess a solid base in traditional skills, additionally will be required to demonstrate an ease in dealing with and using technology.

These new skills will be required because, as a result of the institutional context, the library will have made significant strides in computerization. Various technical services functions are automated and circulation is controlled by computer. Retrospective conversion is substantially complete and the online catalog is the primary means of access to the in-house collection. The library administration recognizes that access to information must be provided in new ways. While the library's success continues to be gauged primarily on the basis of size and scope of collections, there is an awakening awareness that other means of satisfying user needs already exist. There is a commitment to outreach and an ongoing search for new services which can be provided to the academic community.

Because there will be less specialization by function, it follows that more librarians will be involved with bibliographic instruction. These librarians necessarily will be versatile and comfortable with change. Individual librarians will be more responsible for satisfying the information needs of users. The need for user education is recognized not only by the library administration; even the institutional administrators are beginning to understand the concept and the need for its development and implementation.

In this option, with the parent institution moving from the comfort of decades of tradition to the unease of pervasive technological advancements, librarians can play a very important role; they can serve as the bridge between the old and the new. Even in academic institutions that encourage the use of technology, all disciplines cannot be expected to adopt such use at the same rate. Faculty in the sciences and engineering usually have been in the forefront in the use of computers; the social scientists and humanists have come along at a slower pace. Librarians will be working with people whose technological sophistication covers a very broad spectrum.

Instruction librarians can play a key role in the shift from manual to computer-based information systems. If they approach their task with enthusiasm and confidence, they can serve as a catalyst to introduce information technology to an ever-widening group of scholars. The instruction librarian in this second option can be a leader in shaping the attitudes with which institutional users approach this information technology. The opportunity exists for librarians to pass from a reactive to a very proactive stance.

Option two, in summary, is characterized by an institutional philosophy which promotes experimentation and change. Risk-takers are encouraged to try out new solutions to old problems. This open attitude carries over into the library where new approaches to information service are encouraged and where the pervasion of technology in information services is welcomed. User education not only receives support from administrative leaders, but it is seen as an opportunity to move the library to a proactive stance. Because of the movement away from narrow functional assignments, many more librarians will be involved in bibliographic instruction and, inevitably, a closer affiliation will develop between librarians and scholars.

## The Specialized University

The third option, recognizing certain trends toward specialization which already exist in higher education, projects them to the extent that they become the driving force behind the restructuring of the institution. The option is based on a philosophy which recognizes the sovereignty of disciplines or disciplinary groups in the institution. This trend results in an organizational fragmentation of the college or university. Larger research institutions will focus on extensive research in very specialized areas; smaller institutions will follow in this direction on the assumption that bringing faculty with similar interests together will result in better instruction and will increase personal satisfaction.

In this option, the entire institution takes on quite a different image. The central administration assumes a coordinating role or function while greater control over budget, program, and curriculum devolves to the smaller units. In this context, the library as we know it is likely to become an anachronism. As the discipline-oriented groupings assume more power over budget and programs, they are likely to demand more control over information services as well. This option will hasten the creation of branch information centers. These extensively automated centers will emphasize the use of technology in meeting institutional information needs. It is likely that tension will develop between these information centers and the central library. In recruiting librarians, an increasing emphasis will be placed on subject expertise. Pressure will develop to bring the librarians in the information centers directly under the control of the faculty in the discipline or groups of disciplines served by the individual centers. Provision of library services will become bifurcated with basic information services provided centrally and specialized services provided by the discipline-oriented centers. This option will be most disruptive and unsettling for the entire library organization. The library will be caught in a major power struggle and could come out of the situation in a very weak position indeed.

In this most decentralized of the options, bibliographic instruction necessarily will be decentralized and, to some extent, fragmented. It will become increasingly difficult to provide any kind of standardized instruction; more so if the central or main library loses administrative control over the control centers. The development and maintenance of a well-planned, carefully designed, comprehensive user education program will present an almost insurmountable challenge. What may well result is an instruction program in the central facility which deals with traditional information resources and others in the information centers focusing on the information technology of the discipline or disciplines served by the various centers. If an understanding of, and a commitment to, both levels of bibliographic instruction is developed, there may be a possibility that a rational program can exist. The tensions created by the decentralization of institutional processes and information-related services are more likely, however, to tax personal energies and delay the development of a rational program.

The librarians involved in bibliographic instruction in the information centers undoubtedly will develop close working relationships with faculty. This will result in part from a common disciplinary interest and in part from the dynamics usually characteristic of a small working group. On the other hand, those librarians relegated to the main library facility and involved only in teaching the use of traditional sources probably will be alienated from the intellectual mainstream of the institution. Such a two-track library system is not likely to improve the overall support between instruction librarians and the higher education community.

**The Technological University**

The last option for the future assumes a dominant role for technology in all disciplines and in all facets of academic life. The library is replaced by something called the Academic Information Center which administratively brings together the following traditional functions: the library, the computer center, telecommunications, publishing, and media services. Everyone in the institution will have ready access to a terminal which will become the major, and in many instances the sole, method of access to information.

Of the four options, this is the most highly centralized. It brings about major institutional reorganization. The most important and powerful position in the institution becomes that of vice-president or vice-chancellor for information services.

The impact on the library will be radical. In many disciplines, the acquisition of books and journals as we know it today will become of secondary interest. As electronic publishing proliferates, it will provide the primary means of access to much of the scientific information of interest to scholars. The acquisition function will consist of establishing relationships with databases maintained nationally by either the public or private sector. For scholars and researchers whose needs are met in this manner, a visit to the library might become as rare as an excursion to Antarctica.

Even in the case of individuals who will continue to use printed books and journals, the role of the library will be significantly altered. Through the use of computer terminals, faculty and students will, of course, have access to the library's card catalog. For these materials, it is inevitable that they will expect a delivery service. For reference materials which ordinarily do not circulate from our libraries today, these scholars will rely on databases.

In a world so radically different from what we are familiar with and accustomed to, what are the implications for librarians generally and for bibliographic instruction librarians in particular? Subject skills will probably no longer be required; indeed traditional library skills will be virtually unknown. The Academic Information Center will be managed and operated by management specialists and technicians. The user-friendliness of the databases will so reduce the need for personal interplay between librarian and user that librarianship as we know it will cease to exist. Indeed, users will not have to rely on learning how to use the terminal keyboard since the means of oral communication between the user and the computer will have been perfected and will be widespread.

With this option, bibliographic instruction will be obsolete just as the library as we know it will. Because the use of computers will be universally taught in primary and secondary schools, there will not even be a need to teach students how to use their computers to access and manipulate the databases.

# LOOKING AHEAD:
# UNCERTAINTY AND CHANGE

Where, in these options, will a particular institution find its home for the future? That is impossible to say. Indeed, no one can foresee what kinds of new developments, unheard of at the present time, may suddenly appear on the horizon and push institutions in directions as yet unimagined. It is, however, reasonable to expect American colleges and universities to be characterized by one of these options ten years from now. Even the fourth option, which to some may seem too radical to give any credence to, has its adherents. A number of institutions have appointed "information czars" whose responsibility combines, as a start, the library and the computer center. Several other institutions, both colleges and universities, have committed themselves to creating a technological environment for scholars and students very much in line with what has been presented as the fourth option. Brown University, in Providence, Rhode Island, has launched a program that, in ten years, will make available to every faculty member and student a workstation which, among other things, will give the user access to the card catalog and to a whole range of databases currently available only in the library.

Where does the role of the bibliographic instruction librarian lie in such a future? We can only be certain that it will be radically different from what it is now because our libraries will be totally changed. Many of the premises on which our instruction efforts are based will no longer be valid. Not so many years ago a long-distance telephone call could not be completed without the intervention of a telephone operator. Today, new telephones make it possible to call anywhere in the country, and many places abroad, without any human intervention whatever. Telephone calls to specific numbers can even be placed by passengers from airliners traveling at altitudes of thirty thousand feet, again without human intervention.

The future is full of uncertainty. But it also presents a challenge. Success for bibliographic instruction librarians will depend on whether they can remain flexible enough not only to cope with the enormous changes already underway, but also to influence that change and help guide it. If the Second Generation is as energetic and determined as the First, success will be assured.

# 4 Technology and Instruction

*Joanne R. Euster*

Emerging technologies affect many aspects of library organization and services. Building plans must take into account not only existing technologies, with their enormous appetites for electrical and cable connections, but also must include flexibility to accommodate future developments. The possibility of remote access to informational databases introduces the issue of where informational activities should or will take place. The impending availability of full-text online brings into focus the already critical issues of ownership of materials versus access to information.

Technological capabilities inevitably outrun the development of social conventions for managing the results of technology. In anticipating the future it is possible to predict the general nature and direction of effects of change, but very difficult to predict the precise effects and how they will complement one another. A major challenge facing librarians and instruction librarians is to rethink the role of what has been called "bibliographic" instruction, and to focus on what will inevitably become "information" instruction. As the technologies of information continue to change, the nature of information instruction must change as well.

A decade ago, a chapter entitled "Technology and Instruction" would have been expected to cover the basics of utilizing audiovisual techniques for delivering bibliographic instruction to students. Now, however, while the use of appropriate teaching technology is as important as ever, technology is no longer merely a means for improving the quality of instruction. Rather, it has become the engine which drives the need to consider the structure and nature of information instruction. This chapter will focus on the impact of emergent technology on the ways individuals view and use information resources and how these changes affect library instruction.

## THE ACCESS RELATIONSHIP

Three principal shifts in the access relationship between the library user and information resources have occurred. First, geographic barriers to information have broken down to a large extent. Books can be borrowed from all over the country. Photocopying and telefacsimile have made it possible to acquire a copy of virtually any journal article in any language. Increasingly, online bibliographic databases, including the bibliographic utilities, allow the user to discover quickly what has been published or is owned on the topic of interest. The barriers to access are less a matter of *de facto* availability than of costs, time, and above all, interpretation.

Howden and Boyce have described establishment of electronic branch libraries (which may or may not include some print materials) in order to provide informational access to the central library's resources.[1] Brown also describes such a branch.[2] These branches include a mix of online access to the library's holdings files, telefacsimile transmission, and telephone assistance. It is a small leap of the imagination to anticipate the same access and services from the individual's home or dormitory workstation. Once the individual no longer has to go in person to the library (although the user may have other needs that take him/her to the library), it is a logical extension to enlarge the concept of "library" to include any library or database which can be reached electronically from the individual workstation.

Second, a change in users themselves has occurred. While personal computers are not yet widespread in home use, their availability to children and teenagers has been greater than to the population as a whole. Furthermore, those under fifteen years of age are more receptive to interaction with computers.[3] The first wave of students who are interested in and familiar with computers is only now reaching colleges in significant numbers. Those students' expectations of the formats, speed, and convenience of information resources are considerably different from the expectations of their predecessors. Their expectations, however, may be unrealistically inflated when compared to the present state-of-the-art of automated information storage and retrieval.

Third, technology is creating a new public consciousness of information as a consumer good. In this context, information, time, and money are beginning to be seen as interchangeable concepts. Evidence of this is found in willingness to pay for the use of computers, for computerized bibliographic and data searches, for interlibrary loans, and for paper copies of microforms, computer data, and library-owned books and journals. A recent full-page spread in the "Scene/Arts" section of the *San Francisco Examiner* focused on individual strategies for managing information flow: the use of video recorders for television time shifting, time management techniques, reading and scanning strategies, and computerized access to informational databases, such as The SOURCE and COMPUSERVE.[4] Libraries have lost any presumed monopoly on information sources, but in the process, the commercial value of information has been accepted. The result is that information now has value dimensions beyond simple content. The time to acquire it, both the consumer's time and waiting time, are factored into the information equation. The form in which information arrives also has economic value, and users are willing to pay to have personal copies to mark up or to use at leisure. Finally, the organization of information has economic value. A computer-generated bibliography is quicker and easier to use than laboriously hand-copied index cards, for example.

Whether the willingness to view information resources as consumer goods with prices attached is desirable is a matter for another debate. The fact remains that the purchase of information in premium forms has many analogs in other sectors: broadcast television is free; cable television has a whole spectrum of charges attached; local telephone calls are unlimited, while long-distance calls entail additional charges; the neighborhood "shopper" is free, but the daily newspaper continues to increase in price, and in some localities, online versions at even greater cost are available. The list of possible examples grows when one loosely defines what constitutes information.

# REFERENCE VERSUS INFORMATION INSTRUCTION

Technology is giving librarians and patrons the means to be semi-self-sufficient. However, the library is hampered by the double bind of too little time to teach information management skills which would render the user information independent and by the traditional reference orientation. The compromise is often to teach only enough to ensure user dependency.

John Naisbitt, in *Megatrends*, speaks eloquently of the trend which he sees from institutional help to self-help.[5] This shift takes many forms, from the upswelling of community action programs to the concern for total personal well-being instead of treatment of illness alone. Libraries, as "the people's university," have long emphasized self-help. The earliest conception of the reference librarian was of one who taught or was an advisor, rather than a purveyor of books and information.[6]

Control of one's own life is generally accepted as a human need. By helping students to become more information self-sufficient, librarians have the opportunity to empower them. Those who empower others are seen as powerful in their own right, a description which generally has not been applied to librarians, but one which is sought. The opportunity can scarcely be ignored.

The reference assistance orientation to library service is an honorable tradition and has many advocates. To many, it is the essence of librarianship as a service profession. When the first Think Tank recommendations were published, reactions included strong support for the view that " ...the best instruction in the use of the library remains the one-to-one interaction of the single library user with the reference librarian." [7] Yet others feel strongly that the purpose of reference and information services is to provide the user with the needed information as quickly and painlessly as possible, and that the emphasis on teaching information skills completely misses the purpose of reference services. Is the user in need of a particular fact to be put off until he or she has enrolled in a library skills course the following semester?

Beyond the desirability of emphasizing information education for self-sufficiency, there is an overriding managerial reason for shifting toward information independence training. As library users develop greater expectations of the library's ability to provide them with information resources quickly and in manageable form, there simply will not be enough information professionals to deliver individualized service at all levels. Unfortunately, too many libraries find that by teaching students to make better use of library resources, they have only increased the level of sophistication of demands, thus increasing the pressures for reference assistance and consultation. The solution to this dilemma is certainly debatable; nevertheless, it is not unrealistic to compare the current situation to the introduction of microforms in order to conserve space. Small-scale efforts result in reduced efficiency and redundancies; only through large-scale commitment does the program become effective. New priorities and reallocation of resources are required to make effective commitment to this, as any other, change.

What role would the instruction librarian play in empowering the information-savvy student? William Miller accurately describes the conflict in attempting to provide both traditional reference services and instructional services.[8] Given the explosion in technology, which has barely begun, and the growth in user expectations, libraries are being faced with the need not only to perform a teaching role, but also to rethink the entire function of user assistance and training.

One likely scenario is the evolution of the librarian as a combination mediator and teacher. The function of the teacher is to help the user develop information access and management skills, while in the mediator role the librarian interprets and assists in use of information resources. In the mediator role the librarian helps to retain the human interaction dimension, or in Naisbitt's terms, responds to the need to accompany high tech with "high touch." [9] As teacher, the role is more complex. Teaching the use of a specific library and the reference tools that it contains is useful, but more is needed. To be truly information independent, the user needs to understand:

- The processes through which information is generated, organized, and made available in reference sources, whether those are printed or computerized.

- How to differentiate among the levels of information available, in particular between unanalyzed data and critical interpretations.

- How to evaluate information critically and develop individual bases for granting cognitive authority to sources.[10]

- How to scale expectations of the entire universe of information available to fit the requirements of a particular information need.

- How to evaluate information sources for cost-effectiveness in relation to the individual's need, in terms of time, money, and inconvenience.

An instruction program based on these concepts is clearly aspiring to teach underlying principles and critical analysis, a far cry from most bibliographic instruction programs, but an honored paradigm in other academic disciplines.

## THE PARADIGM SHIFT

To some extent, the problem facing libraries is political and territorial. Is the library to maintain its legitimate place as the focus of information activity in the university? If it is to do so, it must find the time and resources first, to teach information skills and second, to teach the use of a specific library and the resources contained therein or accessible therefrom. This is scarcely a new idea, but one which is honored more often in the breach than in actuality. The problem is exacerbated by the fact that the technological imperative has only partly arrived, and the present, perceived need is to respond to immediate short-term student needs to learn how to negotiate the bibliographic maze of a particular library.

Although it can be argued that the full impact of technological change on library education has yet to be felt, the need for reorientation is already present. Indeed, it can be equally well argued that the "full impact" will never be realized, since by its very nature technology changes continuously. Bibliographic instruction has clearly reached a stage of maturity as a recognized essential element of most academic library programs. Yet the resources to expand teaching programs while maintaining all other services simply do not exist, nor are they likely to in the near future. Journals continue to carry articles deploring librarian burnout and overload at the circulation desk.[11]

In light of the perceived crisis in allocation of resources between "Instruction" and "Reference," the need for rethinking the relationship is not only present, but urgent. However, to deal with the present problem of emphasis and allocation is inadequate. Solutions to today's problems leave us little better prepared to deal with tomorrow's problems than before. A more desirable strategy is to set new instruction and reference priorities in light of expected future developments, and to design plans for moving in orderly steps from meeting today's needs to adjusting to those of tomorrow.

How can this be achieved? The first step is widespread discussion of the purpose of instruction programs. Before any future-oriented planning can take place, there must be agreement on a near-future information scenario and the greatest possible library involvement in it. Such agreement might include:

- A goal of information literacy instead of library literacy.

- An emphasis on lifelong information management skills (completion of a college course presumes that the student has acquired knowledge which will serve the rest of his/her life; should information education be anything less?).

- Acceptance of strategies for dealing with short-term information and reference needs in ways that require little librarian time.

The reordering of priorities following from such a consensus would then permit service techniques which would free professional staff time for teaching information concepts. A wide variety of service strategies has been proposed in many forums. Possible options include (but certainly are not limited to):

- Development of short point-of-need media devices for teaching use of specific indexes, catalogs, and reference tools.

- Allowing patrons to place their own interlibrary loan requests.

- Development of in-house online files of ready reference and informational queries for direct patron use.

- Use of peer advisors and tutors, similar to the use of student consultants in computer labs, to assist in use of standard reference tools and conduct orientation tours.

- Regular instruction in end-user searching of bibliographic databases and arrangements allowing students to conduct their own searches.

- Use of clerical and student staff to handle routine informational queries.

These strategies may or may not be feasible for a given library. Some entail risks. Yet failure to think creatively and to take some risks leaves us in danger of being locked into an unending dilemma of too much to do and too few librarians to do it well.

## THE ROLE OF THE "LIBINFOSCI" SPECIALIST

Regardless of the strategies employed, the overriding goal is to enable library patrons to make effective use of more technologically complex information resources. However, in achieving this goal, the role and status of the librarian is almost certain to be enhanced. Indeed, the relative status of academic librarians and classroom faculty may be reversed: " ...librarians will gain new powers and respect ..." while education in many aspects will become more remote and mechanized, and "teachers will understand at last what drove the Luddites and some of them will teach themselves to destroy cable-lines." [12]

Consider the university in the electronic age soon to be upon us. Many elements of classroom teaching will be replaced by self-paced, computer-assisted learning packages. Lectures will be taped for remote replay at the student's convenience. Even consultation and discussion between faculty member and student may take place partially through electronic conversations. Whatever level of personal interaction will be optimal — higher education, after all, is not just facts and concepts, but absorption of less tangible attitudes from faculty and other students as well — it is clear that the student will not travel to campus daily and possibly not even weekly.

In this setting, librarians cannot assume that they will maintain a personalized service which mediates between the user and information resources. Ways will have to be found to parallel geographic independence from the university with informational independence from the library and the librarian. Librarians will have no choice but to focus on teaching analytical abilities, comparable to the teaching of writing, while leaving instruction in use of bibliographic tools, like the teaching of typewriting, to others.

The function of the librarian as the teacher of what can only be classed as a survival skill is bound to elevate librarian status. At the same time, the intellectual content of what is taught must be both theoretical and practical; greater emphasis on thorough understanding of information dynamics and on research will place higher level responsibilities on librarians. Currency in the field will be not only a criterion for promotion, but an essential attribute for adequate teaching. Specialization, both in subject matter and in specific information management techniques, may well become essential as the discipline becomes increasingly complex.

This scenario is both encouraging and threatening. On the one hand, the professional future of what has been called "libinfosci" specialists is bright indeed. The library profession will need to move forward in development of a coherent body of thought regarding information education, trying out transitional curricula and teaching methods. Agreement on long-term and short-term future visions of higher education and information services must occur first, however. The original Think Tank was criticized for speaking of bibliographic instruction as a discipline.[13] Yet the mandates of technological developments in information clearly call for a discipline of information literacy, including a primary body of concepts, practical skills for applying those concepts, and a pedagogy for teaching both. As the scholars and theorists of this discipline, librarians will occupy the preeminent position.

# NOTES

1.   Norman Howden and Bert R. Boyce, "The DELTA Center Concept: A Modest Proposal for the Improvement of Research Library Infrastructure," *Information Technology and Libraries* 4 (September 1985):236-39.

2.   Doris R. Brown, "Three Terminals, a Telefax, and One Dictionary," *College & Research Libraries News* 46 (November 1985):536-38.

3.   David Godfrey and Douglas Parkhill, eds., *Gutenberg Two*, 3d ed. (Toronto: Press Porcepic, Ltd., 1982), p. 223.

4.   Jane Ferrell, "In the Know, How You Can Manage the Information Crunch," *San Francisco Examiner*, June 10, 1984, Scene/Arts section.

5.   John Naisbitt, "Institutional Help—Self Help," chap. 6 in *Megatrends: Ten New Directions Transforming Our Lives* (New York: Warner Books, 1982), pp. 131-57.

6.   Frances L. Hopkins, "A Century of Bibliographic Instruction: The Historical Claim to Professional and Academic Legitimacy," *College & Research Libraries* 43 (May 1982):192-98.

7.   David W. Lewis and C. Paul Vincent, "An Initial Response," *Journal of Academic Librarianship* 9 (March 1983):4-6. See also "The Shifty Shoals of Bibliographic Instruction" by Joseph Rosenblum in the same issue, page 8. Other points of view are included in the issue, under the title "Reactions to the Think Tank Recommendations: A Symposium," pp. 4-14.

8.   William Miller, "What's Wrong with Reference: Coping with Success and Failure at the Reference Desk," *American Libraries* 14 (May 1984):303-06, 321-22.

9.   Naisbitt, *Megatrends*, pp. 39-54.

10.   For an excellent discussion of the bases of cognitive authority, see Patrick Wilson, *Second-Hand Knowledge* (Westport, Conn.: Greenwood Press, 1983).

11.   Miller, "What's Wrong with Reference."

12.   Godfrey and Parkhill, *Gutenberg Two*, p. 2.

13.   Lewis and Vincent, "An Initial Response," p. 5.

# 5 The Place of Bibliographic Instruction in the University Curriculum

*Emily S. Boyce, Ruth M. Katz, and Constance A. Mellon*

While it seems to be generally acknowledged, if not universally accepted, that bibliographic instruction has a legitimate role to play in higher education, the way in which that role can be played best remains a matter of debate. This debate centers largely on the issue of control: should bibliographic instruction be considered strictly a library function and, as such, offered and controlled by the academic library or should it be offered as a regular part of the university curriculum and thus controlled by an academic department? Each viewpoint has its strengths and weaknesses and each is compounded by complexities which frequently are not mentioned (or perhaps not considered) by their proponents. In this chapter we will explore the place of bibliographic instruction in higher education, combining our various types of expertise as library director, chair of a graduate library education program, and bibliographic instruction librarian with experience both as coordinator of a program within an academic library and as instructor in a credit course offered by an academic department. Our discussion will begin by examining basic bibliographic instruction for entering freshman, usually the area around which the controversy over control is focused, and will then move on to consider some of the complexities of bibliographic instruction in higher education. Finally, we will offer a model for consideration which attempts to integrate the strengths and minimize the problems presented by each of the two traditional approaches.

## BIBLIOGRAPHIC INSTRUCTION AND THE ACADEMIC LIBRARY

Bibliographic instruction in higher education began as a grassroots movement arising out of the concern of academic reference librarians for the library research needs of students. Librarians were confronted with more and more students who had little or no understanding of library research and with declining staff resources to fill information needs on a one-to-one basis. Thus, the idea of teaching library skills to groups of students was a logical one. The rapid growth of bibliographic instruction from a movement to a recognized part of librarianship further demonstrates that the idea was sound. And while instruction librarians in academic libraries, whether program coordinators or members of reference staffs, advocated various teaching approaches and argued among themselves about how to define bibliographic instruction, how it should be done, and who should do it, very few suggested that it belonged outside the aegis of the academic library.

Much of the argument ranges around basic bibliographic instruction, for it is here that large numbers of students are involved. If we believe, as most advocates of bibliographic instruction do, that all students require some type of library instruction as they begin their college careers, we could be talking about teaching more than a thousand students per semester.

The strongest argument for bibliographic instruction as a function of the academic library is the expertise of the reference librarians who generally provide the teaching. Reference librarians argue, and rightly so, that no one can understand the resources and the needs of the users better than those who work with both daily. It is their job to know the resources that comprise their collections, to keep up-to-date on the new materials which are added and the old materials which have been superseded, and to understand the intricacies and problems encountered in using various finding tools. In their day-to-day work, reference librarians have developed shortcuts through the sometimes incomprehensible maze of bibliographic organization; they understand how to meet the information requirements implicit but inadequately explained in course assignments. They know many of the faculty and their attitudes toward "acceptable" sources: "Dr. Smith considers everything obtained through ERIC as worthless and Dr. Jones will accept only scholarly journals." Most important, they understand the library behavior of students: which ones you can give information to in a few short sentences, which ones you need to take by the hand and lead to the resources, and which ones are going to leave the reference desk and walk right out of the library unless you monitor them every step of the way.

The strength of this knowledge brought to bear on bibliographic instruction is threefold. First, academic librarians can select the best, or the simplest, tools to meet a particular information need. Second, they can identify search strategies that work within the constraints of their individual libraries. Third, they have immediate feedback on the problems presented by the instructional materials they design. A strong memory which supports this latter point involves one of us who sat at the reference desk, trying to field questions, as six hundred freshman scurried frantically around the library trying to complete an assignment she had designed. Unfortunately, cataloging reconversion activities had wiped out materials to be used in this carefully constructed educational experience and the result was mass confusion!

A second argument in favor of keeping program control in the hands of the academic library is ownership. In the situation described above, although the problems with the assignment created difficulty for the reference staff, the attitude was generally one of good humor. They were willing to pull together to create order out of chaos (in this instance to help revise the assignment and to disseminate it from the reference desk to confused or hostile students) because the mistake was made "by one of us." The reference staff was fond of the library instruction person and proud of the program being created; thus they could laugh about the incident rather than becoming irritated or angry.

These are strong arguments for bibliographic instruction as a function of the academic library; however, there are three major weaknesses in this model. The first weakness is that of power—the power of the grade. While librarians may think the intricacies of tool use and library search are fascinating, students do not. Moreover, students have plenty of work to do anyway, generally more than they can complete effectively. Add to this the fact that, until they are faced with their inability to locate library materials for a specific assignment (often due the next morning), many of them think they "know how to use" the library; there is a real problem with motivation. To get their attention, the power of the grade is irreplaceable. Should this seem doubtful, try a simple experiment. Proceed with a library instruction session in the usual way; for the second session, have the professor whose class is being instructed begin by telling students they will be tested on what they learn. The difference between the attentiveness of students who are and are not being tested is amazing!

Not only do academic librarians lack power, they also lack time. Bibliographic instruction is rarely a librarian's only responsibility; instruction librarians generally are part of a reference staff, participating in all the activities required of reference librarians. In addition, since many academic librarians hold faculty rank, they are expected to do research, to publish, and to be actively involved in professional organizations—those activities whose reward is tenure. Moreover, library administrators may not be aware of the time involved in preparing to teach (two hours of preparation for one hour of instruction is not uncommon) and may approve little or no released time for such work. In such instances, instruction librarians arrive early, work late, and quickly burn out. As a general rule, offering bibliographic instruction from the pool of personnel in the library's reference department places an enormous strain on a library staff that is already overextended. The logistics of managing both responsibilities may result in neither job being performed with maximum effectiveness.

One final problem with bibliographic instruction centered in the academic library stems from programs that are too successful; the demand soon exceeds the supply. It is unlikely that the academic library can add staff to meet increased demands and thus either the bibliographic instruction program or the regular work of the library must suffer.

## BIBLIOGRAPHIC INSTRUCTION AND THE ACADEMIC DEPARTMENT

Paradoxically, the weaknesses of centering the massive program of beginning bibliographic instruction in the library are the strengths of placing it in an academic department. Perhaps the greatest strength of placing the program within an academic department is its acceptance as a legitimate part of the university's curriculum. With this type of placement, it becomes a recognized course: it carries the power of a grade, instructors are provided whose sole responsibility is the teaching of the course, and as the course succeeds or is accepted as part of the general education requirements of the university, sections can be added as they are needed. Moreover, in order to become an accepted part of the curriculum, such a course has been subjected to the scrutiny of the university's various curriculum committees. These committees, composed of teaching faculty and administrators have, in essence, approved the library instruction course to assume its rightful place among other courses that comprise the curriculum.

The process by which a course is approved as part of the university's curriculum is a long and rigorous one, requiring careful, up-front design to include clearly stated objectives, methods by which students will be evaluated, and a content outline. Both the chair of the sponsoring department and the person who will be teaching or coordinating the course must agree upon and be thoroughly familiar with the design of the course, for they undoubtedly will be required to clarify and defend it to their teaching colleagues on the various committees who must approve it. There are certain prerequisites to offering a bibliographic instruction course for credit within an academic department. These include, though they may not be limited to, the following: a course syllabus on file; a course coordinator (for a large program) or a course instructor (for smaller programs) with bibliographic instructor expertise; a structured means of interaction with library reference staff; cooperative arrangements with other appropriate areas and individuals such as the Writing Center and the Director of Freshman Composition; and an organized process to evaluate both the course content and the instructors. While all of this does not necessarily assure that students are better instructed than they might be in sessions taught by instruction librarians, it does provide a documented means of quality control not available in the academic library.

One immediate advantage to the parent university of giving the library instruction course as part of the accepted curriculum is its generation of FTE (Full-Time Equivalency) Units. It is by this means that a university monitors the need for, and the success of, the courses it offers. Normally, academic libraries cannot generate FTEs. Thus, bibliographic instruction performed as part of the reference function "loses" students taught in this way from the reporting practices of the university. When library instruction becomes a course within an academic unit, these FTEs are regularly reported and documentation of need becomes a matter of university record.

While quality control was discussed above in relation to structured university courses, it is quality of instruction that is frequently questioned when library instruction courses are housed in academic departments. First, and without question, teaching faculty cannot have the same type of expertise that their reference colleagues, who work daily with the materials and the students, have. While this may not constitute a major problem when discussing basic bibliographic instruction, particularly for instructors who maintain a close working relationship with their colleagues in the reference department, it certainly can have an impact on more discipline-specific instruction. Then, too, instructors rarely accompany students to the library to supervise their use of the materials and their work on the assignments the instructor has prepared. Thus instructors may be unaware of the inadequacy of their materials or of the problems they create for both students and reference staff.

The large, required course in basic bibliographic instruction can experience problems in providing effective, or sometimes even adequate, learning situations for students. Such courses, like their general education counterparts throughout the university, usually are offered in multiple sections and are taught by a variety of different instructors, the majority of whom are graduate students. On our campus we are fortunate: the credit course in library instruction is coordinated by a member of the faculty whose content expertise is in bibliographic instruction and who works closely with the instructors in the program as well as with the reference staff of the academic library. Even so, her hours are long and her work is complicated by the day-to-day logistics of running such a large-scale program. In universities where similar programs are located in departments other than library science or coordinated by individuals who are not librarians, control may be less stringent. When thirty to forty sections are needed each semester, identifying and providing minimal orientation for enough instructors to cover these sections can be a herculean task. This may mean sections taught by instructors with little or no real understanding of, or interest in, the workings of the academic library. And no matter how effective the coordinator of a large, multisection general education course may be, the limits of time and energy put parameters on how carefully each section of the course can be monitored.

Many of the credit courses, and thus much of the controversy about the place of bibliographic instruction in the higher education curriculum, occur on campuses where a library and a library school coexist. In theory, a library school is just another academic unit with which librarians develop a working relationship; in practice, however, there often are problems. A library school or department is the obvious place in which to center a credit course in basic bibliographic instruction and, if the library school uses its own faculty and graduate students (preferably doctoral students with longer time on campus) to offer such a program, then this is of great assistance to the academic library. If the library school uses non-librarians, that is, graduate students in other fields, then the effectiveness of instruction may suffer.

## A MODEL FOR BIBLIOGRAPHIC INSTRUCTION THROUGH THE CREDIT COURSE

In describing the strengths and weaknesses of placing beginning library instruction programs either in the academic library or in an academic department, one interesting point emerges: the strengths of each are the weaknesses of the other. Clearly, then, the way to maximize the strengths and minimize the weaknesses of an academic program in basic bibliographic instruction is to have it coordinated by a full-time faculty member with a joint appointment in the library and in an appropriate academic department. The debate over ownership is a futile one, weakening the position that library instruction might attain in the university curriculum if the ownership were shared.

On a campus without a library school, the library will likely need to initiate such a structure—a structure, it might be added, that may take considerable time, energy, and investment to realize. An appropriate department must be identified to house the credit program and, while the English department is the logical choice, political constraints may make this impossible. Our experience includes work on a campus where the majority of English faculty, including the chairperson, refused to officially recognize that library research had a teachable content. The next step is the development and submission to appropriate university committees of the proposed library skills course. This step is a delicate one requiring much political expertise on the part of the administrative sponsors of the course: the library director and the chair of the involved academic department. In addition, it is helpful if the person who eventually might be proposed to fill the joint appointment is already part of the library staff and has strong credentials, including a doctorate and a publication record, to meet the requirements for teaching faculty. Needless to say, such a person should first and foremost be an experienced professional librarian.

The joint position should be tenurable, being at least at the assistant professor level. If the course begins as a general education requirement, it should carry with it only the requirement for coordinating/presenting the course and the related responsibilities expected of all teaching faculty. It should be mentioned that beginning efforts to have such a course accepted on an individual campus may not at first include the designation of "required general education course"; this, however, should be the goal. As the course provides its students with skills that other students find they need and that faculty would like to see in students entering their courses, the likelihood of a general education designation increases.

The joint appointment must not be in name only. It is vital that the course coordinator attend reference meetings; observe (though not necessarily participate) regularly at the reference desk; have an office or at least a desk in the library where office hours are conducted; and establish and maintain close working relationships with library administrators, librarians, and library staff. These same "rules of thumb" apply to the academic department of which the course coordinator is a part.

While the appointment should be "joint," it does not necessarily have to be equally funded. As the course begins to generate more and more FTEs, it may become reasonable for the department to fund up to three-fourths of the position with the library providing the remainder. For the library to maintain some control over the course and thus a true feeling of ownership, the position should continue to be partly funded by the library and not come to carry merely an "adjunct" designation.

In large institutions where multisection courses are likely, it is important that the course coordinator be given sufficient time to maintain quality control over the sections which she or he coordinates. Two methods for providing this control are the standardized syllabus and the required course for section instructors. In the standardized syllabus approach, the coordinator, in consultation with the reference staff, determines objectives for student learning, instructional methods by which students will be guided toward mastery of these objectives, and evaluation activities to determine if mastery has been achieved. In addition, exercises and supporting materials should be prepared. As new instructors are identified for course sections, they will be provided with these materials and with training and, from time to time, will be observed as they conduct class sessions.

Another approach, as yet untried, but with strong implications for the professionalization of bibliographic instruction in higher education, stems from a model frequently used for composition instructors. Freshman composition courses, like the proposed bibliographic instruction course, can be huge. As required general education courses to be completed during the first two years of college, they too are multisectioned and are often taught by graduate students rather than regular teaching faculty. Larger campuses generally appoint a Director of Freshman Composition, a special faculty position often within the English department. In order to teach freshman composition, instructors are required to take a graduate course in theories of composition, a course which generally includes the latest research on composition as well as surveying methods of instruction in this area. With the growing literature on bibliographic instruction, it seems reasonable to suggest that the coordinator of the library skills course could develop a graduate course on theories of bibliographic instruction. This graduate course, to be offered by the department housing the library skills course, would be required of all instructors in the program.

# AN ALTERNATIVE METHOD OF INSTRUCTION: MAINSTREAMING BI

One further model for basic bibliographic instruction that deserves mention might be called the "mainstreaming" approach. It is similar to the effort by that name to integrate appropriate perspectives into all courses where they should reasonably be included. Such an approach is receiving much attention in the literature on women's studies, where it is suggested that the feminist perspective be included within the existing framework of university courses rather than being offered as a separate area of study. In this model, the academic library would designate a lead person to coordinate the introductory program for entering freshman. This coordinator would work with faculty who teach in the university's general education program (or core curriculum) to integrate library use with course syllabi. While this approach is both simple and logical, two major problems stand in the way of its effectiveness. The first problem is similar to what is encountered with the credit course; many of those who are teaching general education courses are the same graduate students we cited earlier as the weak link in library instruction offered by academic departments!

The second problem is foreshadowed in the mainstreaming efforts for women's studies; that is, the difficulty in guaranteeing that the designated perspective, once integrated into specific courses, would continue to be effectively represented. The BI perspective, like the feminist perspective, would be incorporated into specific courses as the result of interaction between the course instructor and a BI librarian. The problem occurs in making certain that perspective continues to be integrated, and to be correctly represented, when the BI librarian is no longer involved or when the current faculty member leaves and a new faculty member assumes responsibility for the course. Since the turnover of instructors is usually greatest among those teaching general education courses, this could present a real difficulty, particularly on larger campuses.

# COMPLEXITIES OF BIBLIOGRAPHIC INSTRUCTION IN HIGHER EDUCATION

The problems and the recommended models discussed above are focused primarily on basic bibliographic instruction: a general understanding of academic libraries and their use appropriate to all beginning college students. But effective bibliographic instruction cannot be limited to basic instruction; it is an area of many levels and many specializations. The following discussion describes some of the complexities of bibliographic instruction beyond the basic level and explores ideas and issues related to them.

### Bibliographic Instruction and Subject Specialization

It seems clear, considering the arguments advanced for the knowledge and understanding of librarians whose daily business is reference work, that when subject specialization and advanced methods of use and retrieval are the focus of library instruction, reference expertise is vital. In addition, at this level of instruction, student motivation becomes less of a problem than it is in the large, general classes. Therefore, in discussing the more complex levels of bibliographic instruction, an agreement can be assumed that the academic library is the best place to develop and house these programs. Where advanced or specialized programs might most effectively be housed, however, does require an understanding of the individual campus, the size of its student body and its courses of study, and the resources, both physical and administrative, available to support needed BI programs.

At the undergraduate level, attention must be given to those freshman and sophomores who declare early for a professional area such as nursing, music, or business. Reference librarians with appropriate subject backgrounds are usually best for this type of bibliographic instruction, not only for their subject expertise, but because they are likely to work with these same students and the faculty who teach them for four years or more. The development of a comfortable and personal relationship with the librarian(s) who will continue to help students fill their information needs during the course of their studies can be more valuable than the initial information imparted. It is not unreasonable for the library director to ask professional school deans to designate faculty members to serve as liaison to the library. In some universities, these deans have provided faculty members or graduate students who spend time working in the library to help provide reference and information services to their own majors.

While subject area librarians may be the preferred instructors in professional area instruction, numbers of declared professional area majors and availability of appropriate reference librarians must be considered. Universities with large undergraduate professional schools may present bibliographic instruction problems in those subject specializations which are very similar to the problems discussed in relation to basic library instruction. Where subject specialization is an issue, however, it is vital to have the close involvement of a reference librarian with a background in the subject area, even if constraints dictate that the involvement be primarily supervisory.

Perhaps the most neglected persons in any university are the graduate students. They often are thought to be mature enough and motivated enough to find their own way around the campus. Even if this is so, many graduate students may come from an undergraduate campus that has a library quite different in size and organization from that on their new campus. Added to this change may be a department chairperson or an advisor who is too busy to spend much time with new students and who may expect a graduate student to know enough about libraries to do the advisor's library research. Where such students are too few in number or too varied in subject need to be the focus of organized classes, there are some simple ways in which an academic library can meet their needs.

Graduate students are very receptive to expressions of the library's interest in them. Packets explaining library collections, hours, and services can be prepared and offered to the graduate school office and to graduate coordinators in the professional schools for distribution to entering graduate students. These packets should include a list of subject bibliographers who can meet with them individually to discuss research needs or materials useful in classes that a student may be assigned to teach. At this level, the responsibility for bibliographic instruction is spread more evenly among subject specialists even though the overall BI program may be coordinated by a single individual.

## Bibliographic Instruction and the Library Director

While the library director involved in the writing of this chapter (and her fellow library directors who have authored other chapters in this book) are clearly advocates of bibliographic instruction, this is not necessarily a universal situation. Needless to say, the support of the library director is vital to the success of a bibliographic instruction program and to its ability to acquire needed resources for its expansion and development.

There are two basic "givens" that can be suggested to help an academic library director understand the responsibility for bibliographic instruction. First, regional accrediting associations for postsecondary institutions typically expect basic library services provided by an academic library to include programs that teach library users how to gain access to a full range of library services and materials and also that a variety of instructional methods be considered for delivering this instruction to users. Second, an acquaintance with the teaching/learning process suggests a role for libraries.

F. Coit Butler, in an excellent three-part article on the teaching/learning process, presents several points to inform a discussion of the responsibility of the academic library for bibliographic instruction:[1]

1. Demonstrating the practical application of new material heightens awareness; especially when the knowledge or skill clearly has value for students' personal lives or future occupations.[2]

2. The mere act of organizing information involves a certain degree of comprehension....[3]

3. Regardless of the instructional media or method, some means must be used to insure that students directly interact with the new information conveyed, as it is conveyed.[4]

4. The most important ... knowledge and skills are those that are generalizable.[5]

Raising the consciousness of the library director about the appropriate fit between the teaching/learning process and the mission of bibliographic instruction, in combination with highlighting the instructional expectations of accrediting associations, will help to increase the director's understanding of the relevance of instruction to effective library programming. The importance of an informed and supportive library director to the development and growth of a functional bibliographic instruction program cannot be overemphasized.

## Bibliographic Instruction and Faculty/Library Relations

The library's relationship with the teaching faculty is a vital link to the success of bibliographic instruction programs in higher education, a link that is sometimes difficult to forge. Librarians have two selling points in working with faculty. First, if Butler's model of the teaching/learning process is accepted, then it is clear that librarians are the experts in areas in which many faculty have weaknesses. Second, if teaching faculty want to have a major (if not a dominating) role in collection development, they can increase their understanding of the organization of the literature in their own fields by participating with librarians in bibliographic instruction programs.

Some libraries hold seminars for subject area faculty in order to work out a joint approach to library instruction and some work closely with a school or department only if an individual librarian has developed an unusually good working relationship with a colleague in that school or department. Both approaches are time-consuming initially and very dependent upon good people skills and good matches of library-department partners. Library directors must be painfully realistic (as necessary) in selecting staff members to work with schools and departments if teaching within those units is to be included in that librarian's recognized scope of responsibility. A related issue stems from the legendary lack of understanding of librarianship expressed by the world in general and by our university colleagues, specifically, the teaching faculty. It therefore seems likely that success of library programs such as bibliographic instruction is enhanced in settings where librarians have faculty status and/or are serving on university committees that provide an opportunity for them to demonstrate that their knowledge of and interest in higher education and its governance is equal to that of their teaching colleagues.

A further complexity, rarely discussed, which presents a potential obstacle to a good organizational plan for bibliographic instruction occurs on a campus with many department and professional school branch libraries. This arrangement may limit the library director's choice of librarian-instructors, may dampen the enthusiasm of even the most library-minded students, and may encourage teaching faculty to have a narrow view of library services and collections, depending upon service from library staff rather than on their own knowledge of the literature.

## Bibliographic Instruction and Academic/High School Library Relations

Colleges and universities in general are beginning to recognize the need to work with high schools much more closely than they do now. Some of the more obvious reasons for this collaboration are that universities can provide an outlet for gifted and talented students, special resources for learning disabled students and for others with special needs, and continuing education for teachers and administrators. Less obvious, perhaps, is the need for collaboration between high school and college librarians.

High school librarians (and district offices) are often unable to provide a full range of resource materials for teachers and administrators who have to deal with very complex and tightly scheduled programs of instruction, with legal matters, and with transportation, censorship, or other topics that have a way of springing up unexpectedly in the middle of a school year. Indeed, with the limits on staffing and budgets, high school librarians have all they can do to provide resource material and leisure reading for a wide range of student needs.

University libraries can develop programs to supplement the resource needs of high school libraries and thus can establish a colleagueship with advantages for both parties. When high school and university librarians work together, the benefits may include library-wise high school graduates, high school librarians who find pleasure in being involved with a larger number of professional colleagues than might otherwise be possible, and university librarians who learn, painlessly, something about teaching methods and teachers.

## AFTERWORD

The problems and ideas presented above are neither as complicated nor as simple as they may seem to many readers. Regardless of this, one thing is particularly clear: we should not be arguing about the division of responsibility but rather about the division of labor. Our responsibility is to students and for the teaching/learning process. Librarians in all aspects of bibliographic instruction should seize the opportunities to get on with the work at hand.

## NOTES

1.  F. Coit Butler, "The Teaching/Learning Process: A Unified, Interactive Model," Parts 1-3, *Educational Technology* 25, nos. 9-11 (September, October, November 1985): 9-17, 7-17, 7-17.

2.  Ibid., Part 1: 16.

3.  Ibid., Part 2: 7.

4.  Ibid., 11.

5.  Ibid., Part 3: 12.

# SECTION B

## Understanding the People
## We Serve

Librarianship is a service profession highly dependent upon interactions among people: those who need information and those who would supply it. Yet all too often the literature of the field ignores the fact that the real business of the library is "human" service. We delve into "search strategy" and "cognitive theory" and "automated processes," meanwhile reducing the people we serve to the operational definitions of such words as "patron" and "end-user." For any public service offered by a library to truly serve the public, it is important to remember that behind the terms we use to describe a participant's role in library activities — terms such as "student" and "instruction librarian" — are individuals, with individual needs, abilities, and emotions.

In the preceding section, the focus was upon the broad aspect of setting: the place in which bibliographic instruction does or should occur. In section B, the focus narrows to examine those toward whom instruction is directed and, since the two cannot be realistically separated, those who are doing the instructing. This section builds upon the first in that the participants in bibliographic instruction, student and teacher alike, are shown to be people acting within the settings described in chapters 3 through 5. In the chapters that comprise secton B, the interrelated nature of people and setting is clearly shown as is the central role played by the needs and feelings of individuals in relation to all aspects of the instructional situation.

Chapter 6 discusses the most naive of the audience for bibliographic instruction, the beginning researcher. Coauthored by two experienced bibliographic instruction librarians and a composition teacher who has taught for many years both in high school and in college, this chapter starts with a description of the assumptions made by teaching faculty and librarians about the library skills of college freshmen. It then presents the reality behind these assumptions. Data are provided to support the theory that unrealistic assumptions lead to "library anxiety" in students, an emotion which must be addressed as an integral part of any bibliographic instruction program. In addition to recommendations for reducing library anxiety in students, the authors consider beginning bibliographic instruction from the viewpoint of the other group of participants in this activity: the instruction librarians. Stress experienced by librarians with major instruction responsibilities is discussed within the framework of "burnout."

In chapter 7, two leading researchers in the area of automation and user education explore library technology from a human perspective. Pointing out that technology is all too often considered in isolation, apart from the human endeavors it is intended to facilitate, they reflect upon the misconceptions such a view can foster. They explain how technological developments based on librarians' perceptions of "user friendliness" might complicate rather than satisfy the actual information needs of individuals and how librarians' assumptions about the "correct way to search" might conflict with the information-seeking behavior which is part of the intellectual life-style of academic library users. New educational roles for librarians are suggested, based on the needs of both library users and the library profession itself.

# 6 The Needs and Feelings of Beginning Researchers

*Bobbie L. Collins, Constance A. Mellon, and Sally B. Young*

In our professional writing about bibliographic instruction, we all too often neglect the audience for our instruction: the students. We tend to consider them, if we consider them at all, as an absorbent mass, rather like a sponge, who will operate well in our library if only we can determine the correct things for them to soak up. Therefore, we concentrate on the content of our instruction sessions; students never seem to become to us individuals with knowledge, thoughts, and feelings about the library that must be understood, and perhaps overcome, before learning can begin. Yet without a deep understanding of those we address, designing effective library instruction programs is impossible.

It is the purpose of this chapter to develop the view of beginning researchers as individuals exposed for the first time to a complex cognitive task in an unfamiliar and confusing setting. To do this, we will call upon studies and informal surveys we have conducted in three different academic institutions and upon our combined experience in reference work, in teaching bibliographic instruction sessions, in teaching sections of a credit course in library use, and in teaching high school English and college composition.

## EXPECTED KNOWLEDGE AND ITS REALITY

Most university teachers were good students in college. They listened in class, took notes, and exercised resourcefulness when faced with new problems. If they were asked to write a term paper and didn't know what was expected of them, they probably found an appropriate section in their textbook and felt their way around the library until they were successful. And, if they were once reluctant to ask questions of their own professors or reference librarians, they can no longer remember the fact. For this reason, university teachers tend to think that the students they have now in class, exhibiting similar dedication and resourcefulness, should have no problems finding information in libraries.

University librarians expect far less actual library knowledge and resourcefulness from students. After all, they have been observing library behavior more closely and for a far longer time than have their teaching colleagues. Yet librarians often assume a sophistication of reasoning ability on the part of college students that is not accurate. Research on the cognitive development of college students has shown that abstract reasoning and reasoning by analogy is not common during the first two years of college and may not necessarily be attained by graduation.[1] Yet librarians expect that instruction on the use of a single tool can be translated into the ability to use all similar tools and that describing how knowledge is organized in a library can be translated into search strategy to fit any information need.

Students, for their part, tend to support rather than disprove these misconceptions on the part of their instructors and librarians. When we ask students if they already know something we are about to teach them, many feel they should politely nod their heads "yes," indicating they have already heard of the concept. Later, after we have lectured on something they supposedly know, they again nod politely that they understand even when they don't. Thus when we inquire about students' knowledge of the library and the research process, we cannot always trust the information they give us.

## Data from Composition Classes

A poll of students in freshman writing classes conducted at a small Southern university over several semesters reveals some surprising facts. Of the 66 students responding to the questionnaire, 61 said that they had written a term paper in high school. With this knowledge, most teachers would assume that students are somewhat familiar with the resources of a library as well as being aware of proper procedures for writing note cards and avoiding plagiarism. Further questioning of these people, however, showed that their high school research experience was either very superficial or easily forgotten!

The library feature most often identified correctly by students is the card catalog. Eighty-nine percent of the students showed some understanding of what this object is, recognizing it as the place to look up books by title, author, and subject. They do not, however, understand how to use the *Library of Congress List of Subject Headings* to help narrow their topic, nor can they use the information about publication date, number of pages, bibliography, and the tracings on the card to advantage. Their ignorance of the Library of Congress system (only 26 percent of them had any idea of what it was) prevents them from searching for books on the shelf by subject.

A surprising 71 percent of the students identified microfilm with some degree of accuracy, though their description was likely to be of the "small film with print" variety. Many students were not sure just what was stored on microfilm, and others who had some experience using it described it as "a pain." Some students believed that articles were condensed from the original magazine length before being placed on microfilm.

*The Readers' Guide to Periodical Literature* was correctly identified by 62 percent of those questioned; however, many students were confused about just what the index did. Some said it was a "list of titles and events," while others were sure it was a "list of magazines." Their uncertainty was not confined only to what they would find in the index; they also did not understand what to do once they had found an article with a promising title.

The reference librarian, whose title, we assume, indicates her function, was recognized by more than half of the students (58 percent). According to these students, her duties ranged from "helping people with the different types of research that can be done" to "helping people find library material." It might be hoped that students would ask her what call letters and numbers are for, because 49 percent of them did not understand that these were used for locating materials on the shelves.

Even a fairly common term, such as periodical, posed a problem for many students. Only 48 percent of those questioned identified this term accurately as meaning magazines and newspapers. Can you imagine their confusion when the teacher assigns them a paper in which more than half the sources must be from periodicals?

The fewest number of students, only 1 percent, could explain what an index was when they were told the term did not, in this case, refer to the pages in the back of a book. Even having been asked what the *Readers' Guide* is did not give them a hint.

## Data from Bibliographic Instruction Classes

Combined information collected informally from bibliographic instruction classes, both fifty-minute lectures as part of reference work and credit classes within an academic department, yielded similar results. Most students were familiar with the Dewey Decimal system as a means of locating books on shelves, but few had used (or even heard of) the Library of Congress system. In fact, many identified LC numbers as Dewey numbers, bypassing the letter designations and attempting to retrieve books using numbers alone. When the letters were called to their attention, they explained them away as acronyms (e.g., LB as "library building" and RM as "room"). Students also had a nodding acquaintance with the card catalog (although many thought it included journal articles by author and title as well as monographs) and with *Readers' Guide* ("Yeah, I think I've used it.").

The three things we can be sure entering college students know about the library are these: (1) academic libraries are larger and more complicated than any libraries they have ever seen; (2) collections in academic libraries are more scholarly, therefore duller and more intimidating; and (3) college freshmen are expected to know how to use the library. It is only the "dumb" freshman who goes on a tour of the library.

It is far easier to suggest the gaps that exist in entering students' knowledge of library use; however, from the standpoint of the librarian, that list could be endless. Some important intellectual concepts, beyond the obvious ones of organization and tool use, include how to select a topic for research, how to compile a bibliography, what a style manual is, how to use microfilm and microfiche (and often, how to find the courage to even touch microprint hardware!). Library language constitutes another big gap in students' knowledge.

Librarians who use the language of their field daily and who can't imagine there is anyone in college unfamiliar with such terms as "entry" and "journal" need to rethink the jargon with which they sprinkle their information. After all, less than half of the students in fifty-minute sessions held over a three-year period had any idea what the word "reference" meant! Which leads to a related problem — students' confusion with the functions of different library departments such as Circulation, Reserve, Reference, and Manuscripts. (Some think Special Collections are for librarians to read.)

One final area deserves mention: transferability of skills. Many students do not understand that all libraries organize material in similar ways and that the skills they are learning can be used at other times and in other libraries. They think of these skills as useful only for a specific course, such as composition, or for a specific setting, such as college, rather than as a lifelong competence.

**View from the Reference Desk**

Supplementing the data reported above are some informal observations from the reference desk. First, that selecting or defining a topic for research is a formidable task, which students just do not know how to start. All too often topics are loosely described by composition teachers as "anything you're interested in" or "something relating to your major." More than one scared freshman has begged the reference librarian to "tell me what I'm interested in."

Second, that the sign "Reference" indicates some obscure, but important, library function being performed by the individual who sits beneath it and that to interrupt this function is a vile and dastardly deed which must occur only at the point of desperation. Can we help but notice that nearly everyone who approaches the reference desk begins the request for help with "I'm sorry to interrupt you ..." or "I know this is a stupid question, but ..."?

Third, that if you use the library correctly, there are no dead ends in search. Many students feel that, as Harvard psychologist William Perry once stated, "All knowledge is known." This is especially true of freshmen and sophomores. It is therefore hard to explain why information may not be immediately and readily available on any and all topics students choose and why some topics are preferable to others for beginning researchers.

Finally, and this is a big one, that students think it is a mark of stupidity to ask their professors for clarifying information. Many students would rather do anything, including buying a term paper, rather than question a professor about an assignment.

# WHY THE KNOWLEDGE GAP EXISTS

There are several sides to the knowledge gap story. The bibliographic instruction librarian working on the college level cannot understand why her colleagues, the school librarians, send students on to her totally unprepared. What have they done with those twelve years they were allotted?

Inquiry brings surprising results. Bibliographic instruction in K-12 is often innovative and well-designed, proceeding from a list of competencies that would be the envy of any college reference librarian. The problem appears to be one of structure and understanding rather than one of competence.

First, and foremost, we must face once again the fact that people outside the field of librarianship have no idea what we do! If anything, the stereotype persists that we keep books in order, hide (or lose) everything anyone wants, and become hysterical at any sound above a whisper! How then, can school librarians convince teachers to give them either time or support in assuring that effective library instruction reaches all students? And how can they compete for funds and personnel to build adequate library resources to teach the rudiments of research?

It is on the middle school/high school level that the gap appears and widens. Elementary school librarians are usually allotted time within the curriculum to teach, but beyond grade six librarians live by tolerance alone. This is being compounded by the current accountability model that is stirring up public education. The "Time on Task" method of evaluating effective teaching, and tying that evaluation into salary increases, is sweeping the country leaving disaster in its wake. This method measures the effectiveness of the teacher by his or her ability to keep students working on specified learning tasks. If we think motivation is bad among students now, what will happen when teachers are afraid to let them glance up from their "tasks" for fear of an evaluator appearing in the doorway! Added to this are the standardized tests or competency tests that test both students and their teachers. Even the most competent and highly respected school librarian has trouble convincing the classroom teacher to give up one precious moment of instruction time under a system such as this.

High school teachers, from their side, often view the school library as a sanctuary reserved for use by only the most deserving students: students who are exemplary in study hall and can be trusted to be quiet so that the librarian can get on with the work of due dates and acquisitions; honor students who appear to have serious work to do; and students who have actually read a book and can be expected to check out another one. Further, high school libraries often appear to teachers to lack the resources, either in staff or materials, for library research. The faculty of such high schools, concerned with the limitations of library resources, may neglect term papers altogether or resort to the source book approach.

Even the fortunate student who, during the course of his/her high school career, has done a paper requiring the use of the library may be unprepared for college research. High school libraries are very different from college libraries. While high school libraries use the Dewey Decimal system, college libraries usually use the Library of Congress system. While high school libraries are generally housed in one large room, college libraries may be spread out over many floors or even housed in different buildings across campus. In addition, school libraries generally close right after school, so library research may have been conducted in the public rather than the high school library. The differing service orientation of the public library makes it likely that students had retrieval functions performed for them, including the loading of a microfilm reader, thus adding little to their knowledge of either search strategy or tool use. Even a student who has found information successfully in high school faces a challenge in college research.

## HOW THIS MAKES STUDENTS FEEL

Students are unnerved by the library; it is large and filled with many unfamiliar objects. Because of their personal fear of failure or of appearing stupid, many of them will avoid going to this imposing place, and thus risk failing a course, rather than attempt to use an unknown resource.

Students who seem otherwise intelligent balk at trying to thread the microfilm reader and will hike several blocks to the public library where the librarians load the machine for them, despite the fact that each machine bears a simple threading diagram. Even the reassurance that everyone has somehow wound it wrong at least once or rewound it so fast that it made a loud noise is insufficient to make students attempt its use unless there is no alternative.

Although it is impossible to know from a distance whether or not someone is having difficulty finding a particular page using microfiche, most students act as if the machine was projecting their fumbling first attempts on a giant screen on the wall. They will approach the machine furtively, as if they were about to steal it, before sliding their card into the reader. If someone approaches as they are searching, they act nonchalant, stop on whatever page the pointer had found, and appear to be absorbed in the text.

These students also approach the *Readers' Guide* with tenseness. Although it is obvious to an experienced user that not every issue will have articles on a given topic, the students who cannot find their topic the first time usually abandon the topic and try another, rather than checking other volumes or trying the same topic under a different heading. They see page turning and exchanging one volume for another as signs of defeat, rather than good research practices.

Even their so-called friend, the card catalog, is an obstacle for them. It is massive! The sheer number of cards in it makes it difficult to find a narrow subject. And because, for many subjects, there will be an incredible number of sources, which ones shall they choose to look up? The first five alphabetically? The ones with the cleanest cards? All of them?

And then there are the reference librarians. Students are convinced that they are spies for the English department (many of them do make marks on a calendar or chart when you ask them a question), ready to tattle whenever a student has trouble finding something the first time. Even students who don't think that reference librarians are informers for their professors are apprehensive about them because they can go immediately to the shelves and find lots of things. Perhaps they are all witches!

These observations are supported and extended by a study conducted at a small Southern university which explored students' feelings as they did research in an academic library for the first time.[2] With the cooperation of twenty composition instructors, diary-like writings were collected from beginning composition classes over a two-year period. Analyzing this data for recurrent themes, it was found that 75 to 85 percent of students in every class studied described their initial response to using the library for research in terms of fear or anxiety.

Most of the students who discussed their fear of the library talked about the feeling of being "lost." One student claimed she felt like "a lost child," while another declared that he was "lost in there and actually scared to death."

Feelings of being lost seemed to stem from four causes: the size of the library ("[it] seems like a huge monster that gulps you up after you enter it!"), and a lack of knowledge about where things are, how to begin, and what to do. One student summed up the feelings of many when she wrote: "When I first entered the library I was terrified. I didn't know where anything was located or even who to ask to get some help. It was like being in a foreign country and unable to speak the language."

Descriptions such as these led to the construction of a theory of library anxiety: that many students become so anxious when confronted with the need to gather information in the library for their first research paper that they are unable to approach the problem logically or effectively. Three concepts arising from the data help in understanding the basis of library anxiety: (1) that students' fears are due to a feeling that other students are competent at library use while they alone are incompetent; (2) that this lack of competence is somehow shameful and must be kept hidden; and (3) that asking questions will lead to a revelation of their inadequacy.

One student who signed his paper "Knucklehead" wrote, "I can't believe I don't know anything about this!" A second student summed up library anxiety with these lines: "I was scared to ask questions. I didn't want to bother anyone. I also didn't want them to think I was stupid."

These observations and the documenting of library anxiety suggest problems with previous models of bibliographic instruction that ignore the emotional attitudes which beginning researchers bring to the learning situation. Before the work of instruction can begin, attitudes must be changed, reassurances must be offered, and anxieties must be allayed.

## ALLAYING ANXIETY: COURSE-RELATED INSTRUCTION

Twenty years ago, an English instructor could assign a term paper at the beginning of the course and set a due date light years away near the end of the semester. Perhaps he asked to have note cards turned in with the final product, but generally he assumed that students would read the handbook and follow the guidelines to prepare the paper.

An instructor using this method today would likely discover at the end of the term that the students had no papers or that they had copied papers written by other people. Because most incoming freshmen lack library and writing experience, an unmonitored research paper assignment would be futile. Today, the English instructor needs to work hand in hand with the bibliographic instruction librarians in the university library in order to prepare students for a successful library research experience.

Both teachers and librarians must continually reassure students that they are not expected to know how to use the library already. Students entering a university library for the first time are like the six-year-old boy who joined a neighborhood swim team and did not know how to swim. He took his place in line to jump into the pool during a drill. He watched each child in front of him jump in, begin moving his arms and legs, and progress in some fashion toward the other end of the pool. When it was his turn, he jumped in, began moving his arms and legs, and almost immediately sank. As he planted his feet on the bottom of the shallow end, he looked up at the coach apologetically and said, "Gosh, I'm sorry; I just can't seem to get the hang of it!" Similarly, our students often behave as if they thought being able to use the library was an inborn trait rather than an acquired skill; they are afraid of attempting many library tasks because they fear looking stupid — or, even worse, looking like freshmen!

To overcome some of this reluctance to enter the library, the composition teacher can define in class certain terms librarians use. It might help to explain generally how the Library of Congress system of classification works, what indexes are, what periodicals are, what microfilm and microfiche are, some basic guidelines for using the card catalog (to refresh students' memories about the type of information available on the cards), and what the reference librarians does. This often requires that the instruction librarian spend tactful and extended sessions with composition teachers to agree on the definitions of terms and on the library tools and processes to be used.

Once the students have been given a brief introduction to some of the concepts and have physically toured the library with a knowledgeable guide, it is time for them to get hands-on experience. Here the instruction librarian plays a key role. With a simple and well-organized program explaining library search, he or she can assure students that using the library is not beyond their capabilities.

In selecting library resources to introduce at this initial session, a logical place to start is with journal indexes. These are probably the most valuable, and the least understood, resources for the beginning researcher. The session should begin by placing journal indexes in the perspective of search strategy, explaining how, why, and when they are appropriate to use. We feel strongly that such a session should include a component of hands-on practice, preferably with the *Readers' Guide to Periodical Literature.* By first introducing the *Readers' Guide,* an index whose name, at least, many students already know, students can be shown how mastery of this index opens up to them the use of other Wilson indexes in a broad spectrum of subject fields. Hands-on practice should include introduction to the serials holding tool used by the library. Two other components of an effective session should be included: short, simple, and accurate information sheets on the tools introduced and a follow-up assignment to be collected and graded by the composition teacher. Once again, the latter activity may require a tactful approach to the teacher and help in designing and grading the assignment.

Most students will take off confidently on their research after the introductory library session and assignment; however, there will be a few who are still confused. Abstracting a topic out of a general field is a more difficult task than is generally realized and even intelligent people have trouble doing it. As a good follow-up to the library instruction session, composition teachers should hold at least one class meeting in the library near the indexes being used. Students who are having no difficulty can work independently finding sources; those who are still unsure of what to do can work on an individual basis with the instructor.

Later in the term, once students have gained confidence in their ability to use an index, they might return for a second library session on how to use such resources as *Newsbank* and the *New York Times Index.* These types of tools are important since many of the papers students write in college deal with current issues not covered in books. Thus, the more resources students can use to find current information, the better off they are.

An assignment which can be helpful in allaying students' fears throughout their experience of learning to use the library is the search diary. The search diary can serve many purposes in the research-and-writing process, such as having students record their preliminary bibliography, commenting on sources, and proposing tentative outlines for their papers, but it can also be a document in which the student and the teacher interact. Students who would never ask a question in class or raise their hands when the class is asked, "Who didn't understand?" will often confess in the privacy of their search diary that they are confused or had trouble using some library tool. The teacher can answer the student's questions by writing in the search diary itself or suggest via the search diary that the student come to the library for some individualized help. These diaries, if turned in weekly, can keep less-confident students from getting too far behind and, eventually, either dropping out of the course or failing it.

Another important element which the teacher can encourage is a spirit of camaraderie among the members of the class—a "we're all in this together" attitude. Students who begin to feel comfortable with one element of library work are usually pleased to share their expertise with frightened classmates. Often the student who is helped first is able to assist his "teacher" with something else later in the term. This reciprocity has several benefits: teaching a concept to another student makes that concept more ingrained in the one doing the teaching; a spirit of cooperation among students leads to more profitable classroom discussion, as students will be more willing to share both their successes and frustrations; and the library becomes a friendlier place when students see their classmates there doing the same type of work and having the same difficulties they are experiencing.

## GENERIC SEARCH VERSUS DISCIPLINARY SEARCH: AN INSTRUCTIONAL APPROACH

It must be remembered that writing a research paper presents beginning researchers with two complex cognitive tasks that they must master and complete in a relatively short period of time: the library search process and the writing process. In addition, librarians soon come to realize that the lion's share of instruction time will be devoted to the writing process. Since this is so, we would like to suggest an approach to research developed out of experiences with library instruction classes and work with faculty in a broad range of disciplines. College research consists of two types: disciplinary research and what might be called "generic" research.

The first, disciplinary research, is what comes to mind when the term "research" is used: that is, a thorough search of the literature to learn as much as possible about a specific area of interest. But there is a second type of college research: "generic" research. This type of research, like the generic labels on grocery products, indicates something that is adequate for the general purpose intended. We feel this is an important distinction and that the generic research approach is a legitimate one for librarians to recognize and to teach. Generic research is the answer to constructed interest: Professor Smith tells his students, "For the next six weeks, you WILL be interested in this topic," — with the unspoken, but understood prepositional phrase being — "if you want to pass the course."

The information need created in the situation described above is best handled by generic research. Using a reference tool such as a journal index, the student can narrow the topic while, at the same time, being assured that information on the topic does exist. While the result may not reflect the finest or most thorough research ever conducted on the topic, it does help to eliminate some of the most frustrating dead ends that beginning researchers encounter by narrowing the field in the direction of available articles on a topic. It also provides a less frustrating, but adequate, introduction to the process of library research.

## LIBRARY INSTRUCTION FOR BEGINNERS: EFFECT ON THE INSTRUCTOR

While the purpose of this chapter has been to present a picture of beginning researchers and to suggest some problems and solutions in familiarizing them with library research, the picture would be incomplete without some mention of the effect of all this on the instruction librarian. Many of the leaders of the bibliographic instruction movement of ten years ago have moved on to other roles. While one reason for this is certainly upward mobility, a second is bibliographic instruction burnout.

Providing bibliographic instruction at a major university of 35,000 students, or even at a small college of less than 2,000 students, can prove to be a very challenging experience frequently producing an undesirable phenomenon — BI burnout. In recent years, burnout has become a topic of increasing public and professional concern. According to Christina Maslach:

> Burnout is a syndrome of emotional exhaustion, depersonalization, and reduced personal accomplishment that can occur among individuals who do "people work" of some kind. It is a response to the chronic emotional strain of dealing extensively with other human beings, particularly when they are troubled or having problems. Thus, it can be considered one type of job stress.[3]

In general, burnout seems to creep up on an individual. At first, the person is enthusiastic about the job and looks forward to getting up each morning, and going to work. The nature of the work is very satisfying and the person feels that he or she is making a significant contribution to the organization. After a while, however, certain job stress factors begin to emerge — things like lack of opportunity for advancement, conflicting job demands, too heavy a workload, lack of information on which to make informed decisions, and very little feedback on job performance. Eventually, this continuous stress takes its toll. The individual no longer has positive feelings about the job and is aware of an undefined sense of stress. Awakening in the morning, he or she still feels physically and emotionally drained. In addition to extreme fatigue, other burnout symptoms such as insomnia, depression, irritability, and headaches are experienced.

While the physical aspects of burnout are alarming, the resulting organization consequences, including job performance, absenteeism, and creativity, are also significant. If burnout is a serious and pervasive problem among individuals whose jobs keep them in constant contact with other people, it is important for beginning instruction librarians to learn as much as possible about the effects of burnout and about ways of coping with or reducing it.

As mentioned previously, too heavy a workload is a factor in producing stress. In some cases, the beginning instruction librarian may find himself or herself in a situation where the program becomes so successful that there is an increasing demand for this service. As more sessions are given, more are requested. For example, depending upon the size of the facility and the number of staff members, some libraries may schedule two or more instruction sessions at the same hour. Thus, during the peak time for instruction during a semester, some large libraries may book as many as 12 sessions a day, even providing sessions for evening classes.

In addition to conducting instruction sessions, some instruction librarians work at the reference desk, do computer searches, participate in collection development, and serve on library or university committees as well as state and national ones. Furthermore, academic librarians who have faculty status and are working toward tenure may have to show evidence of scholarly pursuit, a particularly stressful situation for junior faculty members. Because of such job pressures, some instruction librarians claim they have little time to prepare for classes and to develop handouts and other instructional materials. Since courses vary in organization as well as in subject matter, the beginning instruction librarian must decide what information to present as well as how to present it. Often, this requires rethinking and new preparations in order that the instruction session be effective. Unfortunately, during the peak demand for library instruction, this time pressure usually worsens, thus creating a potentially stressful situation. As the instruction librarian realizes how little released time, if any, is available to prepare classes, the frustration level increases.

Providing as many as four or five instruction sessions per day demands a great deal of energy and stamina. Keeping up one's enthusiasm after presenting the same information over and over again is very difficult. One young instruction librarian remarked that at times she felt like a tape recorder programmed with a fifty-minute message. For her, one frustrating aspect of bibliographic instruction was what she called "fading out." After presenting the same lecture several times, she could not recall if she had mentioned certain concepts. When she "faded out," she felt depressed to think she might have failed to communicate an important concept. Furthermore, she had a fear of "blacking out"—totally forgetting everything and consequently not saying anything.

Besides the problem of boredom which might lead to "fading out" or "blacking out," another frustrating aspect of bibliographic instruction is presenting information to a group of total strangers, most of whom the librarian will never see again. There is no time to develop a personal relationship with students being instructed and no feedback on the success or failure of that instruction. Because of this, librarians suffering from burnout have difficulty acknowledging that these classes are composed of individuals who have specific "help me" needs. During the instruction session, such librarians may have very little eye contact with the students and it is difficult for them to convey any enthusiasm about the library.

Related to this problem is the lack of any positive recognition from students and faculty. In a people-oriented job such as librarianship, there are very few instances when people express their appreciation for a job well done. Although this may sound trivial, a sincere "thank you" is as important as a regular paycheck. As one librarian indicated, the thanks he received for a job well done produced an extra boost of energy to keep him moving through his crowded and exhausting schedule. Unfortunately, over a period of time, lack of recognition or reward contributes strongly to burnout.

Although burnout may not strike every instruction librarian, it is pervasive enough that librarians must be able to recognize the problem and to develop strategies to cope with it. If they do not, it may negatively affect their productivity and personal health as well as the effectiveness of the bibliographic instruction they provide.

## NOTES

1. L. Lee Knefelkamp, "Developmental Instruction: Fostering Intellectual and Personal Growth of College Students" (Ph.D. diss., University of Minnesota, 1974); Clyde A. Parker, *Encouraging Development in College Students* (Minneapolis, Minn.: University of Minnesota Press, 1978); William G. Perry, Jr.,

"Cognitive and Ethical Growth: The Making of Meaning," in *The Modern American College*, ed. Arthur Chickering (San Francisco: Jossey-Bass, 1981).

2. Constance A. Mellon, "Library Anxiety in College Students: A Grounded Theory and Its Development," *College & Research Libraries* 47 (March 1986):160-65.

3. Christina Maslach, *Burnout: The Cost of Caring* (Englewood Cliffs, N.J.: Prentice-Hall, 1982). p. 3.

# 7 Human Aspects of Library Technology: Implications for Academic Library User Education

*David King and Betsy Baker*

The introduction of newer information technologies into academic libraries has created special challenges for librarians concerned with the education of library clientele. Many of these challenges emanate from the variety of systems users encounter in their information seeking, both within and, increasingly, outside the library. This technological growth, initially seen as a means for managing the explosion of scholarly publication, can also be recognized as contributing to that explosion; the electronic tools which improve ability to manage information have, at the same time, facilitated growth of the literature and often complicated the task of retrieving information. The evolutionary nature of information systems, in terms of hardware, software, and processes, dramatically affects the ability of librarians and library clientele to remain abreast of the technological power available to them and the technological problems that face them.

A major source of difficulty in discussing technology concerns the meaning of the term itself. Common usage typically equates technology with physical tools, particularly electronic devices, and their mechanisms of control: hardware and software. This common usage envisions technology as inanimate, reducing technology to mechanical and technical terms. It focuses attention on devices and the workings of those devices. The consequences of this perspective on information technology are evident in all corners of library practice and thought: it fosters the notion that information, like data bits, is comprised of discrete units with the characteristics of physical commodities; it fosters the notion that information seeking, like electronic processing, is a set of procedures which can be formalized, followed, and taught as step-by-step sequences; it fosters the notion that tools, especially electronic ones, solve information problems and satisfy information needs. Some library users share these notions.

In contrast to common usage stand the formal definitions and considered commentary of experts. John Kenneth Galbraith, in *The New Industrial State*, uses a definition similar to that found in *Webster's Third Unabridged Dictionary*: "the systematic application of scientific or other organized knowledge to practical tasks."[1] Upon further reading, a much broader interpretation of the term is apparent, an interpretation involving complex organizations and value systems.[2] Physicist Arnold Pacey attempts to express this broad meaning when he describes technology as "the application of scientific and other knowledge to practical tasks by ordered systems that involve people and organizations."[3] Peter Drucker states it simply by explaining that technology "is about work ... human action on physical objects characterized by serving human purposes." [4] In comparison with common usage, which reduces technology to physical and technical terms, the broader meaning envisions technology as human endeavor, individually and in concert as organizations, intended to achieve goals and fulfill needs — using inanimate tools to help attain those ends. It emphasizes the cultural and organizational elements necessary for successful development and application of technology. It challenges the prevalent tendency to think of technology as machines isolated from their human purpose.[5]

As more automated systems are introduced into libraries, the importance of this distinction increases. Library technology adds to the mystery and complexity of libraries. The level and variety of knowledge and skills required of users to successfully negotiate the library are multiplied. Unfortunately, the library user, who approaches the technology as a means for meeting personal information goals, often encounters technology designed primarily to streamline library practices and control library collections. Librarians struggling to maintain a balance between the professional and practice-oriented use of technology on the one hand, and the interests and purposes of their clientele on the other, may easily fall prey to the assumption that technology which meets *their* needs also meets the needs of their constituency. If this were the case, then simply introducing library users to the mechanics and content of library systems would be adequate to ensure that users could successfully and knowledgeably integrate the newer tools into their information-seeking processes. There is little evidence to support the viability of this assumption about library clientele and their application of library technology; in fact, there are strong indications that it is erroneous. Nonetheless, many libraries persist in focusing their educational efforts on the procedural aspects of using technology. As a result, users may be left without a context for the technology other than the library itself: the tools become *library* tools rather than *information-seeking* tools. Users may grasp mechanics without understanding process. Even more disturbing, they may be forced to redefine their personal information goals to meet the inadequacies or requirements (actual or perceived) of the technology.

In fact, library clientele approach library technology in ways that often differ dramatically from the ways in which librarians do, and from the ways in which they approach more traditional library tools. The reasons for this are not well understood, and there is more conjecture than research to support existing theories about the human aspects of technology. This paper attempts to establish a human context for user education in light of newer information technologies. It considers some of the psychological, social, and behavioral factors which may influence acceptance, as well as adoption and successful application of library technology in the academic community. It considers some of the many factors which may affect users' ability to learn about the newer tools. It suggests some of the fundamental problems created by the technology in its current state. And it attempts to identify the place of the library and library technology within the information-seeking processes of students, faculty, and researchers. Throughout the discussion, attention is focused on the human, rather than technical, aspects of library technology, and on the implications for educating library clientele.

# HUMAN-MACHINE RELATIONSHIPS

The realm of human factors in systems development and use is generally recognized as being of critical importance. Yet, there has been little research on human relationships with interactive library technologies. Much of the research that has so far been reported concentrates on system performance and the performance of subjects in accomplishing specific tasks. Such research has provided valuable insights, but is largely outside the scope of this paper. More relevant are studies that attempt to describe the psychological aspects of human-machine relationships. Reviews have been provided by Borgman and by Ramsey and Grimes.[6]

Ramsey and Grimes suggest that three types of psychological modeling serve as a framework for current research on human factors in interactive computer dialogue. The first involves *cognitive* models that attempt to describe the mental processes by which tasks are performed. The second involves *conceptual* models that attempt to describe to the user how and why a system functions as it does, as the user is intended to understand it—not necessarily as the system actually behaves. Conceptual models are often built around analogies, graphical display, and other descriptive techniques designed to communicate to the user learning the system an overall context for system behavior as well as specific points about system operation. The third involves *mental* models: the understandings of the user about the system, which may or may not conform to either actual system behavior or any accurate conceptual models of that behavior.[7]

At the current stage of research, any results must be considered preliminary. Even so, the studies tend to confirm the suspicions of many librarians involved in user education. Among the research reviewed by Borgman and by Ramsey and Grimes are studies which suggest that users trained according to conceptual models perform better than those who receive simply procedural or step-by-step instruction in system use. Users who receive only procedural training can perform isolated tasks, but cannot relate them to similar tasks or explain how the systems worked. Users who receive concept-based instruction seem to be better able to perform more complex tasks with the technology. Moreover, users who are not provided a conceptual foundation for manipulating the technology develop mental models which often lead to misunderstanding, or worse, ineffective system use.[8]

Not enough research has accrued in the area of psychological modeling to explain all the factors that affect human-machine relationships, how and why they develop as they do, or their impact on successful utilization of technological capabilities. Yet, since the psychological aspects of human-machine relationships have such strong implications for the way in which technology is used, as well as when, how, why, and by whom, some broad generalized theories have been proffered. Perhaps one of the more useful for librarians is the work of Sherry Turkle.[9]

Turkle suggests that there may be two different types of human-computer relationships. For some persons, the computer is simply a machine, a tool to be mastered and controlled. Computer commands and dialogues are viewed as means of controlling the machine to achieve particular results. The dialogue is inanimate and ultimately under the mastery of the user. Most librarians, and users familiar with library systems, probably perceive their relationship with the technology in this way.

The second type of human-computer relationship suggested by Turkle is anthropomorphic: the user ascribes human characteristics to the machine. The computer, because of its interactiveness, its question-answer dialogue, and its increasing "user friendliness," tends to be perceived as proxy-human. This type of relationship may be more typical of users less familiar with the systems, users to whom the dialogue appears to have a feel of spontaneity. The major effect of anthropomorphizing the computer, according to Turkle, is the tendency for the user to relinquish control of the dialogue to the computer.

If Turkle's theory of human-computer relationships is accurate, new and infrequent users of library technology may be tempted to anthropomorphize the systems. But even if they do not, it is probably a mistake to assume that users, especially students and inexperienced users, hold the same mental models of library technology and relate to the systems in the same way that librarians do. They encounter it infrequently; they use it for intensive periods; they have little understanding of the bibliographic and organizational principles upon which its design is founded; and perhaps most important, they use the technology for their own purposes — purposes which may differ substantially from those of librarians.

The psychological relationship between human and machine influences how choices about technology are made and how effectively the technology is used. Some of those who anthropomorphize the system, or who feel the interaction involves loss of control over the search process, may have a negative response or may find their interaction unproductive. Some of those who envision the system as simply a tool to be controlled, who find the pseudohuman dialogue and repetitious menus of the system cumbersome or annoying, may respond with impatience or exaggerate the limitations of the technology. For many, the result may be a rejection of the new technology out of hand or perhaps in preference for more familiar tools like the card catalog and printed indexes.

Conversely, some users who anthropomorphize the technology or who enjoy the proxy-human relationship and apparent spontaneity of the system, may experience use as a process of friendly discussion and discovery. Unfortunately, since they may also tend to turn control of the dialogue and search process over to the system, their relationship may result in blind noncritical belief in the outcomes of their interaction, however unproductive. And some of those who maintain a master/tool relationship may enjoy the sense of power and control over sophisticated and complex systems, relishing the contest of overcoming limitations or ignoring them altogether. For many, the result might be a preference for the new technology in spite of its inappropriateness for solving any given information problem or need.

Although little consensus has been reached as a result of research and expert conjecture in the area of psychological human-machine relationships, librarians concerned with the education of their clientele can draw some tentative conclusions to help shape their efforts. It is evident, for example, that factors other than cognitive knowledge about a system can greatly influence attitudes about library technology and affect the ability of users to employ the technology effectively in the information-seeking process. Preformed opinions and attitudes, both positive and negative, about library technology could present significant obstacles to librarians who wish to impart to their clientele, not only the procedural elements of system operation, but also selection and application of the proper tools as and when needed. There is reason to believe that step-by-step procedural instruction, or even worse, rudimentary directions, demonstrations, and printed materials which emphasize the mechanics of searching, are inadequate as a foundation for effective technology use. Library users need sound mental models in order to successfully negotiate complex interactive systems. If librarians do not provide conceptual models within which users can develop their mental understanding of the technology, users will construct their own mental models—models which may prove erroneous and incomplete, leading to misconceptions, poor interaction, and ineffective searching.

The importance of providing users a conceptual foundation for library information seeking has been extolled within bibliographic instruction in recent years.[10] The need for strong conceptual models may be even greater in programs introducing newer technologies.

## HUMAN-MACHINE DIALOGUE

The technical aspects of systems design greatly influence the amount of knowledge users of any technological product must attain in order to apply it well. Many of these aspects are widely discussed in the literature and are beyond the scope of this paper. Yet, the tradeoffs prevalent in the design of library technology intended for public use have important implications that should not be overlooked. Most of these tradeoffs occur in the attempt to develop "user friendly" systems.

In general, the term "user friendly" refers to "information retrieval systems which require no special or prior knowledge to use, so that the full spectrum of end users can be accommodated."[11] Unfortunately, user friendliness is all too often a catchphrase employed in conflicting and confusing ways. As Danny Wallace points out: "There are those who seem to believe, for instance, that a computerized system is inherently more user friendly than a manual system ... or that a menu-driven retrieval system is inherently more user friendly than a command-driven system."[12]

Hidden in the design philosophy of much user friendly software is the belief that it is necessary to sacrifice search and retrieval power, which might require a greater level of knowledge by users, for simplicity of use. Many current user friendly approaches, particularly as implemented in online catalogs, involve intentional technical limitations based upon the assumption that the technology thereby becomes more accessible. Instead of designing software that helps users develop appropriate search strategies or maps from textwords to subject headings, features like full Boolean search capabilities are often eliminated or buried beneath layers of simplified user friendly programs. Not only must one question whether such design decisions have engendered a library technology more primitive than its predecessors, but also whether such decisions are in the best interest of users and are truly "user friendly."

Most user friendly systems are deceptively simple, with their question-answer dialogue, menus, and quick responses listing retrieved items. The process by which the system derives its responses is totally opaque. Users have no way of knowing what the system did, what sort of designed-in limitations are at work, or what other factors, such as terminology and sorting, might have shaped the responses. This opacity creates a "black box" into which users insert words and out of which, magically, references flow.

The lack of transparency of such systems interacts with, and reinforces, the tendency to believe blindly in the results obtained.[13] It may encourage initial tendencies to relinquish control of the search process to a set of preprogrammed prompts and step-by-step procedures. Bernard Dixon, writing in *The Sciences*, describes how such systems distance the user from comprehending process.[14] His assessment is similar to that of Linda Arret, who suggests that simplistic systems that shield the user from the structure and processes employed thwart learning.[15] Others have also begun to question the wisdom of too-simple technology.[16] But, perhaps more important, the user friendly black box creates a situation in which the completeness and accuracy of search results cannot be analyzed or challenged by the user. The system protocols and responses are either accepted on blind faith, or the system is abandoned by the user for meaningful information seeking. For those users who select the former course, Leigh Estabrook concludes that they may obtain less than they would have through the use of other tools and may believe in the completeness of their searches even more.[17]

Early research on the use of interactive retrieval systems attempted to assess the ability of users to successfully manipulate command-driven systems. One of the first and most comprehensive was F. W. Lancaster's evaluation of end-user search performance in MEDLARS.[18] Lancaster discovered that most users had little difficulty with commands, which have been the primary focus in the development of user friendly systems. Instead, he found that users encountered the greatest difficulty in conceptualization and formalization of information needs, selection of appropriate terminology (particularly in regard to controlled vocabulary), and development of search strategies that could exploit the interactive power of an online system. More recent research tends to confirm those early findings.[19] These are problem areas in which user friendly design has had little positive impact. In fact, due to the deceptive simplicity and opacity of most user friendly systems, users may be even less aware of search failures that originate as a result of these problems or unaware that retrieval failures have occurred at all.

In the use of any interactive system, but particularly in the use of the most basic user friendly systems, users may lose contact with the overall search process. With manual tools, systematic and diverse approaches to problem solving and decision making are required of the user; the information-seeking process is more visible and the need for planning more obvious; and the effectiveness of the tools and strategies employed are more easily assessed by the user. Definite choices must be made about tools and access points, and about which items to pursue or reject. With interactive technology, the need for such choices may be less apparent and the fact that many of the choices are made within the confines of the black box may not be recognized. Analysis of the process is less feasible due to system opacity.

Perhaps more insidious is the fact that user friendly retrieval systems force users to approach searching according to a relatively inflexible, linear pattern. Many experienced search intermediaries using the most powerful command-driven information retrieval systems often rely almost exclusively on the most basic techniques and strategies, employing predetermined step-by-step search patterns from which they are loath to deviate.[20] But user friendly dialogues afford the user little choice: they are fixed in progressions which cannot be supplemented or circumvented by the user. The rigid search processes embedded in user friendly systems may encourage users to envision the information-seeking process as equally rigid, equally mechanical, and equally one-dimensional. They may be led to think of the world of knowledge in a similar fashion, tempted to isolate information from its much broader knowledge base, and lose sight of the inter-relatedness of all knowledge.[21]

Unfortunately, the deceptive simplicity of user friendly systems militates against efforts that might address these serious concerns. Users, unaware of the subsurface complexities of retrieving information from such systems, often perceive little need for instruction. The opportunities that do arise often consist of brief one-on-one reference or catalog-assistance encounters, and perhaps printed materials available in the areas designated for searching. The majority of instruction provided through these means focuses almost entirely upon explanation of procedures, ways of selecting or using terminology, or answers to specific questions posed by the user. Even were the printed materials religiously studied and assistance sought by the user every time a question arose, these techniques are probably not sufficient to provide the user a conceptual foundation for effective searching. Neither approach affords the depth required for building satisfactory mental models. Neither can convey methods for integrating library technology into effective information-seeking strategies in most circumstances. The personal encounters are usually too brief; the printed materials are usually too mechanical. Too often, as a result, these approaches may actually reinforce belief that library technology does not require (or merit) much time and effort to master.

## PERSONAL GOALS AND PRIORITIES

The amount of time and effort users are willing to invest in learning about newer library technology deserves special consideration. The time and effort individuals invest in any activity have a direct impact on knowledge and behavior. Some persons learn much more quickly and easily than others, and it is difficult to predict how much time and effort will be required for an individual to master particular tasks or concepts. It might seem reasonable, for example, to expect that users with knowledge and skills related to those necessary for mastering new technology would learn more quickly and/or perform more effectively than those without prior experience. Although this is often the case, research suggests that just the opposite may occur. In one study, prior knowledge of typewriting interfered with users' ability to learn text editing; the users assumed too many similarities between the two activities and were consistently error-prone as a result.[22]

There is too little research as yet to determine whether certain types of knowledge and skill are conducive to learning library systems, and whether other types might be obstructive. And certainly, too little is understood about the learning of information retrieval processes and concepts to enable prediction of the time and effort that will be necessary for a specific group or individual to master them. There does, however, seem to be some indication that students differ in their ability to master online systems; Borgman has found that students in the humanities have more difficulty than those in the sciences, and research suggests that knowledge of other computer systems may be beneficial in learning to search unfamiliar bibliographic databases.[23] Although there is little evidence for guidance, it would seem that different educational approaches and concepts for users with different types of knowledge and skills would be optimal. This is an area in which research would be of concrete, practical value to user education librarians.

The expectations held by librarians concerning the amount of time and effort users will require or willingly commit to library activities are sometimes exaggerated. Conversely, the expectations of library users concerning the amount of time and effort necessary to master library tools and develop facility in information-seeking processes may be similarly unrealistic. Online catalog users, for example, tend to spend a great deal of time searching when they first discover the system. But use drops precipitously after a short time and only recovers over a long period of time. There are a number of plausible explanations for this pattern. One involves knowledge: intensive initial use is tied to learning the system, but once mastered, use falls off. The second involves users' needs: users may search intensively at first to satisfy heavy information needs, which are soon satisfied. The third explanation concerns expectations: high expectations about the power and utility of the system, expressed by high initial use, are diminished through frustration or unproductive searching. A fourth explanation involves the "novelty" effect: a new electronic device generates a certain amount of fascination and curiosity, which is soon satisfied.[24] None of these explanations goes far in accounting for the eventual slow rise in use over a longer period of time in isolation. More likely, a variety of these explanations and perhaps others as well, in some complex combination, would be necessary in attempting to understand the pattern for individual users. But it is doubtful that knowledge of the system is sufficient as the sole explanation.

Time is a fundamental human resource, to be conserved and expended on the basis of personal need and judgments of value, so it is impossible to consider time and its allocation independently of personal goals and priorities. For a few individuals, use of the library is an enjoyable way to spend time, particularly if it is viewed as an investigatory adventure. Learning and serendipitous discovery are interesting and valuable activities for such users. For most, however, use of the library and its tools is an intermediate activity, a means to more important ends. The activity, and the expense in time and effort needed to perform that activity at the optimal level, is not high on the priorities list of most in the academic community. The introduction of an online catalog generates a great deal of initial interest. But low attendance at online catalog workshops attests to the fact that most of a library's clientele are simply not willing to invest much time in learning about tools they consider of intermediate value and which they believe should be easy to master.[25]

A disconcerting tendency among some librarians, however, is manifested in expectations about how much time and effort users *ought* to spend on library tools and activities. Such judgmental attitudes frequently surface as discussion of the so-called "law of least effort," which questions the motivations, priorities, and values of those users who limit their searching to certain tools, who settle for items which are easily accessible, or who terminate their searching at a stage librarians consider premature.[26]

In fact, many library users, perhaps most of them, hold different values than librarians and have their own purposes for using the library. Their priorities often conflict with the ideals of comprehensive searching, and personal values may shape quite different judgments about the quality of any given source of information. What is to librarians a law of least effort may be to the efficiency-minded user an expression of personal priorities and values. To those who desire, for whatever reason, to allocate most of their time to other activities, it may express a "law of effective time management." To others, it may reflect one of several mechanisms for coping with information overload.[27] All are probably pursuing the best available information they can obtain and applying the knowledge they have concerning library tools and resources within the context and constraints of their personal goals and priorities. It would be difficult to assume otherwise, that any individual is intentionally performing at a level below optimal. But limitations on time and effort, even those that are self-imposed, may lead to outcomes that are, in the opinion of all concerned, less than ideal.

All of the foregoing is useful in considering how, why, and under what circumstances newer library technology is used. What appears to librarians to be a much easier, quicker, or more effective tool for approaching the literature (whether manual or electronic) may be perceived by some library users as too expensive in terms of time and effort. Some might find it expedient to limit searching to a single tool with full knowledge that comprehensiveness will not be attained. Some might limit the amount of time spent on the tool selected and achieve satisfaction from the first few references retrieved. Such decisions might not be the correct choices according to the standards and values of librarians, but the choices could very well be the best ones possible according to the time and effort priorities of the efficiency-minded user.

The introduction of electronic information retrieval technologies in libraries can be both beneficial and detrimental within this context. Much of the lure of online and other interactive systems is rooted in their speed, efficiency, and capabilities for saving time and effort. Users may, consequently, be attracted to such devices because of the value they place on their time. Modern technology, from hand calculators to supercomputers, encourages belief in the infallibility of such devices.[28] Without a solid mental model of a library system, users are likely to exaggerate the power and utility of the system for meeting their own needs. Technology perceived in this way may be more highly esteemed by those whose emphasis on time and efficiency is great, and whose knowledge of tools, manual or electronic, is limited. Library users who have little experience with manual tools, who do not have a strong grasp of information-seeking methods, who have little confidence in their ability to use the library effectively, or who have little desire or time to become more expert, run a greater risk of erroneous decision making as they attempt to allocate time and effort to library activities.

Librarians, due to the nature of their profession, necessarily function with a certain amount of ambivalence or conflict of values. Comprehensiveness in searching in order to assure that quality sources are examined serves as the foundation of much library practice. It is appropriate, then, that librarians maintain high standards and attempt to educate those users with similar values in effective methods of comprehensive information seeking and critical analysis of the quality of information sources. Such values have been expressed by library user education efforts which emphasize search strategies and the secondary literature. Within this context, as should be apparent, it is equally important that librarians be able to educate their clientele in the most *efficient* methods of acquiring, assessing, and managing information.

Library technology can be a powerful ally to the efficiency-minded user and to the librarian. Electronic information storage and retrieval technologies are not simply different versions of manual tools. They are substantially different in their capabilities and effectiveness when applied to the personal goals and priorities of users. Education efforts which concentrate on comprehensiveness and exhaustiveness in searching, and which present the technology as just another library tool, fail to communicate the power of the technology to positively affect the intellectual life-styles and goals of library clientele. However successfully it is presented, the technology will remain for the user a library tool rather than an information-seeking tool, unless users are educated within the context of their goals and priorities — goals and prorities which transcend that corner of the information environment and academic community occupied by the library. Thus, the goal of academic library user education is not simply to teach library users about the procedures and techniques for searching in library tools, but rather to assist users in their efforts to integrate and exploit the power of those tools in their preferred information-seeking styles.

## INFORMATION SEEKING AND LIBRARIES

The processes by which individuals are socialized into the communication networks and patterns of the various disciplines, and the ways in which the library is integrated into information seeking, are among the most poorly understood of all educational experiences. Much of what is known or suspected about these socialization processes is based on isolated encounters and anecdotal evidence rather than research. But it is relatively certain that, among the factors affecting the development of information-seeking behaviors, the influence of peers, teachers, and significant others is very strong.[29] Except in those rare academic environments with strong, comprehensive, curriculum-based bibliographic instruction programs, librarians probably play a relatively minor role in the development of information-seeking skills.

Faculty in their formal classroom roles often provide the impetus for students to first begin learning about the library and information-seeking processes. It is often through faculty that librarians are able to provide instruction, and it is usually by means of assigned coursework that students are encouraged to use the library. It is not uncommon for faculty to specify the use of particular tools or information sources, either with or without consulting librarians. Conversely, negative attitudes of faculty about the library or the value of library use are often readily apparent to students, even if they are not overtly expressed.

Faculty also have a less visible and more substantial impact in their roles outside the classroom. Advising, counseling, and assisting students outside the classroom becomes more common as students declare majors and progress academically. Advanced undergraduate and graduate students look to faculty as their role models, especially with regard to research and writing, and over time tend to adopt the information-seeking and information-use patterns of those they emulate. In her research on the psychological motivations for information seeking and the sources used to satisfy information needs, Kathleen Dunn found that teachers were the single most important source about information-seeking, and that peers also play an important role.[30]

Library use patterns reflect the information-seeking progressions characteristic of an academic, research-oriented environment. Those who have the least knowledge of the structure of the literature and communicated knowledge of a discipline are also likely to be those who use secondary and tertiary tools most intensively in the library. It has been suggested that the users who most commonly approach information through such sources include: (1) the undergraduate student who requires enough information to learn about a topic, but not the depth or breadth of information required by researchers; (2) the graduate student or junior faculty member who has not yet established strong relationships with the informal "invisible college" networks of a discipline; and (3) the researcher who is changing research emphasis, has not yet learned enough about the subject, and has not yet established contact with others of similar interest.[31]

As individuals become more familiar with the communicated knowledge of a discipline, much different mechanisms of accessing the relevant literature take hold. As Stephen Stoan points out:

> The subject literature, after all, forms a vast bibliographic apparatus indexed by subject, according to the book or article in which footnotes appear, and analyzed in considerable detail.... [T]o an extraordinary degree *the primary literature indexes itself*, and does so with greater comprehensiveness, better analytics, and greater precision than does the secondary literature. [32]

Research on the communication and dispersion of information among faculty, researchers, and practicing professionals, both in academic and nonacademic settings, consistently reveals the irrelevance of secondary and tertiary library tools for most information seeking.[33] By the time most faculty, researchers, professionals, and even graduate and advanced undergraduate students reach the library, unless they are embarking on unexplored subject matter, they are seeking previously identified items. Even in subject searching, few (if any) follow a formally structured, step-by-step, mechanical search process similar to those often promulgated in bibliographic instruction.

One of the principal elements governing information seeking is accessibility, particularly among library clientele who place great value on their time. Librarians have long been aware that users may be satisfied with a readily accessible source, even of dubious quality, rather than invest more time or effort to obtain a source that might be superior.[34] Librarians have long been aware that some faculty would rather rely upon personal and departmental collections that duplicate library holdings than trek continually across campus, and that students sometimes do without rather than use the library. Librarians have long been aware of invisible college networks and the reliance on colleagues and "information gatekeepers" as sources for information. New technological products can have a significant impact on information seeking; during recent decades, the telephone has made a colleague across the country more easily attainable than the journal article written by that colleague, which is shelved in the library stacks.

Users and librarians do not always share the same notions about accessibility and availability. To some librarians, if an item is on the shelf or can be borrowed from another library, it is accessible. If there are terminals for the online catalog in the card catalog area for public use, the database is accessible. But accessibility for the user may not always be the same as physical availability. The availability of a bibliographic record, whether in electronic or paper form, for an item which is properly shelved and available for use, does not ensure that the item is accessible to the user. Although newer information technology may sometimes ease access to library materials, it may also exacerbate some of the problems associated with bibliographic accessibility. Unless an online catalog contains records for all items in the collection, it increases difficulty of access: users must know more tools, when and how to use them, and plan to spend more time and effort than if only one tool were used. Newer information retrieval devices, either in spite of or because of their user friendly design, are perhaps less forgiving of users' lack of knowledge about controlled vocabulary, and are less "browsable" than paper tools. Conversely, they often overwhelm users with results, with relevant items buried in large printouts or multiscreen retrievals. Bibliographic accessibility thus becomes more complicated rather than more simple.[35]

The power of well-conceived and well-applied electronic retrieval technology lies, not in the fact that manual tools are automated, but in the fact that the limitations of those tools may be overcome. Through textword searching and sophisticated logics, investigation of conceptual subtleties and nuances, lost in manual tools, are possible. The complex relational nature of information seeking, appropriate to the needs, priorities, and knowledge of the user, can be pursued through interactive, flexible strategies. Most important, because of the distributability of the technology, library tools finally can be conveniently integrated into the information-seeking patterns of clientele whose goals and priorities do not include extended visits to the library. The technology has the power to positively affect the intellectual life-style of the academic community, rather than simply reincarnate tools that embody the interests and needs of libraries.

Knowledge of this power has grown rapidly. Many faculty, researchers, and others who rely heavily upon the literature have incorporated mediated online searching into their information-seeking patterns. Many more look forward to the introduction of the online catalog with great anticipation, envisioning improved access to the literature. Many have been subsequently disappointed or frustrated. Libraries have not, on the whole, developed or applied technology as tools for information seeking, but rather as tools for bibliographic control and the management of library processes and collections.[36] Remote access, which would enable users to integrate electronic technology into preferred information-seeking patterns, has not been pursued on most campuses. Mediated searching, an opportunity for librarians to become partners in information seeking, has been confined to library offices, behind a barricade of obstructions which include appointment times, fee-for-service, and occasionally even active discouragement. However user friendly, the technology becomes analogous to the friendly librarian—accessible so long as library walls and the traditional office hours are honored.

This proprietary stance toward newer information technology, reflecting a circumscribed vision of information seeking as an activity which does (or should) take place only within the library and positing a limited role for librarians in the overall intellectual life of the academic community, has compromised the power of new technology already diluted by poorly conceived user friendly design. If technology is understood as, not only the technical and physical devices employed, but the organizational and cultural implementation of those devices as well, this proprietary stance has engendered technology which only partially addresses the needs and interests of its users. It has become "halfway technology" which may, in some cases, obstruct rather than facilitate effective information seeking.[37]

Enterprising companies in the for-profit sector, eager to fill the gaps, are promoting products within the academic community that are more easily integrated into personal information-seeking patterns. Although the user friendly software found in these products often shares some of the limitations of user friendly online catalogs, they tend to be more flexible and more powerful. For the moment, database content does not overlap—a situation that will probably change during the next decade as full-text and other bibliographic services match technical progress and economic opportunity. The slow (at present) encroachment of the for-profit sector into a market once virtually monopolized by the library is but another indication of the gulf that exists between library technology and the information-seeking patterns and preferences of those in the academic community.

## BIBLIOGRAPHIC INSTRUCTION IN TRANSITION

Although prognostications about the new electronic library abound, the current state of library technology suggests that it may be some time in arriving. Only in rare instances might it be argued that newer electronic retrieval tools have succeeded in supplanting their manual predecessors. The proliferation of these devices has multiplied the number of tools available, each with advantages and disadvantages, and even though the newer electronic products are intended to simplify processes and improve access, users are more likely to discover that libraries and information seeking become increasingly complex with each new tool or enhancement.

Librarians concerned about the ability of their clientele to negotiate library tools and resources have reached no consensus on which methods are most appropriate for informing users about newer electronic tools. The debate between reference services and more formal educational efforts continues unabated in some quarters, and a few libraries, insisting that one-on-one assistance is not only the most efficient means of instructing users but also the most effective means of teaching, offer little or no opportunity for users to obtain structured classroom introduction to library use techniques and tools.[38] Many libraries discover that stand-alone workshops on the online catalog fail to attract library users in sufficient numbers to justify the expenditure of time, space, and professional expertise, with the result that the workshops are discontinued. Most libraries limit their efforts to brief demonstrations, frequently as part of a tour, printed materials that outline commands and procedures, and assume that users will consult built-in help screens or request assistance when problems arise.

Unfortunately, research on online catalog use bears testimony to the inadequacy of such approaches. Many users never master the tool, most do not consult help screens, and few seek out assistance.[39] The assumption by users that the systems are easily mastered, often implanted by librarians who extoll the simplicity of online searching, may actually deter users from seeking assistance and contribute to the belief that the responses received are actually indicative of library holdings. The value of one-on-one encounters, as has been noted, is significantly depreciated by brevity and specificity, and even when tours, help screens, printed materials, and other approaches of an introductory nature are combined with personalized assistance, an organized conceptual foundation upon which mental models can be built is not conveyed. As a consequence, users tend to learn the newer electronic tools as they have learned manual tools in the past: superficially, inadequately, from peers and by trial-and-error. Considering the many problems that have been discussed so far, particularly since so many of them emanate from the approaches taken in design and implementation of the technology by the library itself, formal educational opportunities for the user should not be viewed as simply a nice gesture by the library, but as an obligation.

Many libraries have experienced some success in recent years with the familiar combination of bibliographic instruction, designed to convey a conceptual framework and strategies for library use, coupled with the individualized methods of one-on-one assistance and/or term paper counseling clinics intended to assist with specific problems users encounter. Evaluations of bibliographic instruction programs suggest that they can lead to better understanding and use of library tools and resources, and may contribute to improved student products, such as term papers.[40]

Integrating library technology into standard bibliographic instruction sessions presents difficulties, however. Due to the additive effects of newer electronic tools, incorporating discussions of the online catalog, for example, into typical one-hour stands can be highly disruptive. Simply adding more tools to the instructional content may result in a disintegration of the session into discussions of the characteristics and use of many different tools. Overall conceptual frameworks may be lost. Moreover, mental models take time to develop, and the conceptual models that might be most valuable for technology use are very different from the strategies-oriented bibliographic instruction approaches commonly employed. Electronic searching is in fundamental ways very dissimilar to manual searching; some of the basics like controlled vocabulary are common to both manual and electronic tools, but the complexity of using interactive tools effectively requires skills and knowledge unlike those needed for manual tools. If the overall strategies orientation of bibliographic instruction is retained, the addition of electronic tools to the content may not allow for proper resolution of these problems. Attempts to cover too much, a common source of difficulty in tool-based library instruction and appearing again with the introduction of technology-related topics, may cause students to be overloaded, unable to absorb or apply the information provided.

In response, some libraries have redesigned their instruction to focus almost entirely on use of electronic tools. Such decisions capitalize on the interest generated by library technology among both faculty and students, and permit more time to convey conceptual foundations for use of interactive systems. Unfortunately, since electronic tools do not supplant manual sources but multiply the decisions that must be made about tools in the library use process, students are still left with an inadequate foundation for their library information seeking. As is true of one-on-one assistance, printed materials, stand-alone workshops, and other approaches which emphasize specific tools or simply address isolated problems, the relationships between tools and frameworks for library use in general, are lost — and often, so are the students encountered at the reference desk.

A few libraries have enjoyed great success with alternatives to the standard one-hour stand approach to bibliographic instruction. Credit courses offer sufficient time to thoroughly address library tools, resources and searching fundamentals, and because of the increasing complexity of library use and the interest generated by unfamiliar library technology, there may be enough impetus on many campuses to successfully establish courses. Other innovative libraries have developed more comprehensive instructional programs, integrated into the undergraduate curriculum at all levels.

Even under these preferred conditions, which permit more time for exploration of techniques and concepts, newer library technology has introduced a set of distinct problems. Among the most difficult is how to teach the fundamental process of searching interactive tools. The mechanics of manipulating the system and the procedural aspects of searching are relatively easy to teach, but the mental decision-making processes required for search strategy development, selection of terminology, and system interaction are not well understood. Even experienced search intermediaries often cannot explain how decisions in the process are made, and though a number of models have been constructed to describe basic strategic approaches, good searches (and good searchers) rarely adhere to a set model. The problem of formulating conceptual models appropriate to the knowledge and skill levels of students, models which will enable students to build useful mental models for successful system use, is an important one.[41]

Equally important is the problem of how to accommodate the varying knowledge, skills, experience, and attitudes of students. Just as factors other than procedural knowledge about a system can affect users' choices about when, how, and why to select tools and can also determine the effectiveness with which a tool is used, a variety of factors other than content can influence users' response to instruction and determine how well they learn. Librarians have little experience shaping instruction to account for such factors, since they are often placed in situations with limited time and no control over class composition. As a result, their instructional aims are often cognitive rather than affective and behavioral; the content is often reduced to a low level of basic information; and concepts and strategies often degenerate into inflexible generic patterns. The pervasiveness and importance of these diverse factors suggest that new approaches to instruction, allowing flexibility and alternative learning experiences for individuals according to their learning styles and a mix of approaches to content presentation, will be necessary to educate users about newer interactive library technology.

The complexity of problems associated with user education in a technological environment reinforces the need for systematic instructional planning and assessment: goals and objectives and evaluation. These are endeavors that have been supported more in word than in deed in the past, and become even more difficult with the introduction of electronic systems. There are major questions concerning how to write good goals and objectives for programs that teach the use of interactive systems, probably a reflection of the more fundamental questions about what to teach and how to teach it.[42]

The number and complexity of problems associated with teaching clientele to use interactive library systems has led to cautionary comments in recent years. Limiting instructional efforts to the use of library technology, particularly the mechanical and procedural aspects of its use, may result in defeat at two levels. First, by focusing on the procedures and mechanics of electronic searching, rather than the conceptual foundations for system use, libraries may fail in their attempt to adequately educate their clientele. Second, by focusing on the technical aspects of technology as a library tool rather than its broader purposes as an information-seeking tool to be integrated into the intellectual life-styles of library clientele, libraries fail in their attempt to provide their clientele the power to apply the technology within the context and patterns of information seeking they prefer or require. The long-range goals of educational effort, to provide users with the optimal skills and knowledge for accessing information, are defeated. A larger perspective on the educational role and instructional activities of libraries will be necessary to overcome the challenges imposed by newer information technologies, roles and activities which build upon the experience of bibliographic instruction, but which transcend its limitations.[43]

## NEW EDUCATIONAL ROLES FOR LIBRARIES

Most predictions concerning the future of the academic library postulate new roles for librarians and increased relevance of libraries in the academic community, but at the same time warn that the possibilities will not be realized automatically or easily. Most recognize the close relationship between technological progress and library progress. Most recognize the need for librarians to demonstrate the qualities of creativity and leadership. But there is some question as to the source of these qualities and the goals toward which they should be applied.

To date, much of the direction for library technology development has been determined by default. The guiding philosophy has been: Do what has always been done, only electronically. The principal question has been: Here is a new tool, what can be done with it? By default, leadership in technology development has flowed from the curatorial tradition of librarianship, with its focus on the physical document: its acquisition, description, storage, and control. It is understandable that, given the circumstances, the emphasis of library technology reflects the practices associated with curatorship: bibliographic control, networking, collection management, records management, and automation of routine processes. The basic assumption has been: If it is good for the library, it is good for the academic community.

Critics have not hesitated to refer to traditional library practices as warehousing, and however electronic its implementation, the current path leads only to high-tech warehousing. Contrary to the images of the future library as prominent in the intellectual pursuits of the academic community, and the librarian as an esteemed information professional, more realistic is the image of the library as repository and service center (much like computing services), and the librarian as technical clerk and caretaker (much like computing center personnel). If the library is to become more than a repository and a service center, librarians must visualize the future they wish to attain, and exercise the creativity and leadership required to transform vision into reality.

There are many within the profession who share the vision of a future academic library that is not only an electronic repository, but also a center for expertise. If this vision is to be realized, it will not occur by default or by doing what has always been done, however electronically. Proponents of the vision, from the early "paperless information systems" writings of F. W. Lancaster to the information management scenarios of Matheson and Cooper, posit a central importance, and critical responsibility, on the educational efforts of libraries.[44]

The dramatic growth and success of bibliographic instruction in recent years is an indication of the potential impact of proactive library services. But there is also a concern that bibliographic instruction has not yet matured, and is not yet ready to assume a position of leadership in the transition. However successful, its emphasis on simplistic search strategies and comprehensive searching of secondary tools, its inability to accommodate the varied learning styles and attitudinal differences of library clientele, and its focus on library use and library tools rather than on broader information-seeking problems and practices, has limited its value to the academic community.

In contrast, more advanced students, faculty, and researchers, who in the past relied heavily on information-seeking and information management techniques that exploited the self-indexing nature of the primary literature, are finding it increasingly difficult to maintain those practices. The explosive growth in volume of the literature in many disciplines has disrupted methods that a decade ago were reliable and efficient. Various coping mechanisms employed to manage the information load, and problems associated with the allocation of time and effort to information seeking and management, have had deleterious effects on the scholarly communication process.[45] Many faculty and researchers are becoming less and less confident of their ability to retain adequate awareness of the literature through their traditional practices. Many are seeking a way out, turning to outside sources for advice and turning to the new information technologies for assistance; others are quietly struggling.

The disparity between library services, including user education, on the one hand, and the information-seeking patterns and problems of the academic community on the other, represents the single most important and difficult challenge facing libraries and librarians today. How successfully the challenge is met will determine the future of the profession and the institution. Almost certainly, a satisfying resolution will not result from simply doing what has always been done, however electronically. Librarians will have to adopt new roles, with strong educational components, in order to bridge the gap.

First, the librarian must become an *advocate*, not of the library, not of the library user, but of the information user. Much as the patient advocate defends the needs and rights of the patient in the face of an impersonal health care system, much as the legal advocate states the case of the client to those who would not otherwise attend, the librarian must become the voice of the faculty and students served by the library. The goal of advocacy is not to educate the user about the library, but to educate the library about its constituencies. As an advocate, the librarian will necessarily face the prospect of challenging many of the assumptions and practices entrenched by two thousand years of tradition. In order to succeed, the librarian will necessarily require a solid understanding of the needs, problems, and practices of students and faculty, not just in general terms, but intimately, and must develop the communication and organizational skills necessary to work within the library structure to effect change. The call to political action within university administrations, issued by some within the profession, is misguided: political maneuvering, however successful, will not convey an image of professionalism or effect a more central place in the intellectual life of the academic community for libraries or librarians. The real political task of librarians lies in the educational role of advocacy.

Second, the librarian must become a *consultant*. Much as the role of the business consultant is not to solve the problems of the client, but rather to provide advice and guidance in the problem-solving process, the role of the librarian as consultant is to provide knowledge and expertise to members of the academic community in solving their information problems. Consulting is in large part an educational activity, customized to the specifications of the client. The goal of consulting is not to instruct the user according to a predetermined formula or to promote predetermined products (including library tools and services), but to offer a context for decision making. In order to succeed, the librarian as consultant will necessarily require the ability to tailor professional knowledge to the needs of the client, whether an individual or a group.

Third, the librarian must become an *educator*. Just as the role of a science faculty member is not simply to train students in the use of laboratory equipment, but to employ the equipment as a means of teaching systematic inquiry into the nature of physical phenomena, just as the role of the philosophy faculty member is not simply to train students in the use of symbolic logic, but rather how to use logic as a tool for analytical reasoning, the role of the librarian as educator is not simply to train clientele in the use of library tools, but rather how to employ tools as a means of managing the information process. The goal of the librarian as educator is not library self-sufficiency for students, or even knowledge of specific library tools, but mastery of the information process. In order to succeed, librarians must dispense with the notion that information is a product and that training in the use of tools is education. The goal of the librarian as educator is to facilitate student learning of the principles and concepts that will enable them to manage that portion of the knowledge spectrum relevant to their needs.

Information retrieval and management technology can be an ally to the educational role of the library. The devices generate enough interest that clientele want to investigate their potential for solving information problems or facilitating the information-seeking process. Librarians cognizant of the needs of their clientele, who understand the information-seeking processes used by the individual or group with which they are working, and who successfully subordinate library use and library interests to user needs and interests, can make strides in effectively serving their clientele.

Librarians serving faculty, researchers, and professionals in the sciences have made early advances. They have made it their job to know how information is communicated in various fields, how individuals obtain and use the information, common practices in personal information management, and current problems experienced by their clientele. They have taken the lead in informing their constituencies about end-user search services, often providing equipment within the library for end-user searching. They have taken the lead in developing programs to teach effective searching of databases relevant to user interests. Knowing that some of their clientele rely on large personal collections of articles, technical reports, and other materials, they have taken the lead in teaching users the principles and techniques for collection management within the context of client knowledge bases rather than library vocabularies and processes.

As advocates, they have worked toward library technology that reflects the needs and interests of their clientele, when possible, by loading relevant databases on library computers for user access, by working a little harder for remote access capabilities, and by developing services that take the librarian into the environment of the user. As consultants, they have taken the lead in advising departments and individuals in the selection of hardware and software for end-user searching and bibliographic management, as well as training. As educators, they have developed programs tailored to the practices and needs of specific groups.

As a result, many of these libraries are establishing a new place in the academic community, founded upon expertise rather than collections. Technology is, in these libraries, not simply a matter of hardware and software, but of service enhanced by electronic tools.

## CONCLUSION

This chapter has attempted to provide an overview of a variety of issues and problems associated with library technology from a human, rather than a technical, perspective. These range from specific problems concerned with human-machine relationships to more general problems in teaching users about the use of electronic devices and from general notions about the nature of technology to specific ideas about the educational roles of the academic library. The intent has not been prescriptive, but rather exploratory: to raise issues, generate ideas, and promote creative thought. In the process, some topics have been treated much more superficially than others. The chapter will have succeeded if it has given some insight into the complexity of library technology as a human endeavor: the relationship between the academic library, the aspirations of professional practice, the needs of the academic community, the aims of technology development, and the personal stake *everyone* has in the way that technology is used.

## NOTES

1. John Kenneth Galbraith, *The New Industrial State*, 3d ed. (Boston: Houghton Mifflin, 1978), p. 12.

2. Ibid., chap. 2.

3. Arnold Pacey, *The Culture of Technology* (Cambridge, Mass.: MIT Press, 1984), p. 6.

4. Peter Drucker, *Technology, Management, and Man* (New York: Harper & Row, 1970), pp. 45-46.

5. David N. King, "Library Technology as 'Halfway' Technology," *Proceedings of the ASIS Annual Meeting* 23 (1986):132-37.

6. Christine L. Borgman, "Psychological Research in Human-Computer Interaction," *Annual Review of Information Science and Technology* 19 (1984):33-64; H. Rudy Ramsey and Jack D. Grimes, "Human Factors in Interactive Computer Dialog," *Annual Review of Information Science and Technology* 18 (1983):29-49.

7. Ramsey and Grimes, "Human Factors in Interactive Computer Dialog," pp. 44-48.

8. Christine L. Borgman, "The User's Mental Model of an Information Retrieval System: Effects of Performance" (Ph.D. diss., Stanford University, 1984). Similar findings in teaching the use of non-library technology have been reported. See the review by Ramsey and Grimes, "Human Factors in Interactive Computer Dialog."

9. Sherry Turkle, "Computers as Rorschach," in *Inter/Media: Interpersonal Communication in a Media World*, ed. G. Gumpert and P. Cathcart (New York: Oxford University Press, 1982); and Sherry Turkle, *The Second Self* (New York: Simon and Schuster, 1984).

10. For examples, see Pamela Kobelski and Mary Reichel, "Conceptual Frameworks for Bibliographic Instruction," *Journal of Academic Librarianship* 7, no. 2 (May 1981):73-77; Elizabeth Frick, "Information Structure and Bibliographic Instruction," *Journal of Academic Librarianship* 1, no. 4 (September 1975):12-14; and Thomas G. Kirk, "Problems in Library Instruction in Four Year Colleges," in *Educating the Library User*, ed. John Lubans (New York: R. R. Bowker, 1974).

11. Lisa P. Brenner et al., "User-Computer Interface Designs for Information Systems: A Review," *Library Research* 2 (Spring 1980-81):63.

12. Danny P. Wallace, "The User Friendliness of the Library Catalog," University of Illinois Graduate School of Library and Information Science *Occasional Papers*, no. 163 (Urbana-Champaign, 1984), p.3.

13. Leigh Estabrook, "The Human Dimension of the Catalog: Concepts and Constraints in Information Seeking," *Library Resources and Technical Services* 8 (January/March 1983):68-75.

14. Bernard Dixon, "Black Box Blues," *The Sciences* 24, no. 2 (March/April 1984):11-12.

15. Linda Arret, "Can Online Catalogs Be Too Easy?" *American Libraries* 16, no. 2 (February 1985):118-20.

16. *Users Look at Online Catalogs: Results of a National Survey of Users and Non-Users of OPAC's* (Berkeley, Calif.: University of California, 1982).

17. Estabrook, "The Human Dimension of the Catalog," p. 70.

18. Frederick W. Lancaster, "Evaluation of On-Line Searching in MEDLARS (AIM-TWX) by Biomedical Practitioners," University of Illinois Graduate School of Library Science *Occasional Papers*, no. 101 (Urbane-Champaign, 1972).

19. For example, Carol H. Fenichel, "Online Information Retrieval: Identification of Measures that Discriminate among Users with Different Levels and Types of Experience" (Ph.D. diss., Drexel University, 1979); other research is reviewed by Fenichel in "The Process of Searching Online Bibliographic Databases: A Review of Research," *Library Research* 2 (Summer, 1980-81):107-27.

20. Fenichel, "The Process of Searching Online Bibliographic Databases," 117-19, 123.

21. David N. King and Betsy Baker, "Teaching End-Users to Search: Issues and Problems" (Paper presented at the LOEX Annual Conference, May 1986; proceedings in press).

22. Sarah A. Douglas, "Learning to Text Edit: Semantics in Procedural Skill Acquisition" (Ph.D. diss., Stanford University, 1983).

23. Christine L. Borgman, "Individual Differences in the Use of Technology: Work in Progress," *Proceedings of the ASIS Annual Meeting* 22 (1985):243-49; Jay Elkerton and Robert C. Williges, "An Evaluation of Expertise in a File Search Environment," in *Proceedings of the 27th Annual Meeting of the Human Factors Society*, ed. Alan T. Pope and Linda D. Haugh (Santa Monica, Calif.: Human Factors Society, 1983), pp. 521-25.

24. A wide variety of factors related to online catalog use are considered in Joseph R. Matthews, Gary S. Lawrence, and Douglas K. Ferguson, eds., *Using Online Catalogs: A National Survey* (New York: Neal-Schuman, 1983).

25. Betsy Baker, "A New Direction for Online Catalog Instruction," *Information Technology and Libraries* 5, no. 1 (March 1986):35-41.

26. The original work on the least-effort concept can be found in G. K. Zipf, *Human Behavior and the Principle of Least Effort* (Cambridge, Mass.: Addison-Wesley, 1949).

27. Joel Rudd and Mary Jo Rudd, "Coping with Information Load: User Strategies and Implications for Librarians," *College and Research Libraries* 47, no. 4 (July 1986):315-22.

28.  For example, see Robert E. Reys et al., *Identification and Characterization of Computational Estimation Processes Used by Inschool Pupils and Out-of-School Adults: Final Report* (Washington, D.C.: National Institute of Education, 1980), ERIC ED 197 963.

29.  Kathleen Dunn, "Psychological Needs and Source Linkages in Undergraduate Information-Seeking Behavior," in *Proceedings of the 4th Annual Conference of the Association of College and Research Libraries*, ed. Danuta A. Nitecki (Chicago: ACRL, 1986), pp. 172-78.

30.  Ibid, p. 176.

31.  David N. King. "Bibliographic Instruction for Research and Information Management" (Paper presented at the ACRL Bibliographic Instruction Section Program, ALA Annual Conference, Los Angeles, June 1983).

32.  Stephen K. Stoan, "Research and Library Skills: An Analysis and Interpretation," *College and Research Libraries* 45, no. 2 (March 1984):103.

33.  See, for example, J. M. Brittain, *Information and Its Users: A Review with Special Reference to the Social Sciences* (Bath, England: Bath University Press, 1970); W. D. Garvey, *Communication: The Essence of Science* (Elmsford, N.Y.: Pergamon Press, 1979); and the general review by S. G. Faibisoff and D. P. Ely, "Information and Information Needs," in *Key Papers in the Design and Evaluation of Information Systems*, ed. Donald W. King (White Plains, N.Y.: Knowledge Industry, 1978), pp. 270-84.

34.  Faibisoff and Ely, "Information and Information Needs," pp. 275, 277, 279.

35.  Arret, "Can Online Catalogs Be Too Easy?" p. 118.

36.  Barbara E. Markuson, "Issues in National Library Network Development: An Overview," *Key Issues in the Networking Field Today*, Library of Congress Network Development and MARC Standards Office Network Planning Paper no. 12 (Washington, D.C.: Library of Congress, 1985), pp. 9-32.

37.  King, "Library Technology as 'Halfway' Technology."

38.  Constance Miller and James Rettig, "Reference Obsolescence," *RQ* 25, no. 1 (Fall 1985):52-58.

39.  See Matthews, Lawrence, and Ferguson, eds., *Using Online Catalogs*, pp. 110, 175; Borgman, "Psychological Research in Human-Computer Interaction," p. 48; Brian Nielsen, Betsy Baker, and Beth Sandore, *Educating the Online Catalog User: A Model for Instructional Development and Evaluation, Final Report* (Bethesda, Md.: ERIC Document Reproduction Service, 1986), ED 261 679, pp. 67-102.

40. Some of the better evaluations are noted by Richard Hume Werking, "Significant Works," in *Evaluating Bibliographic Instruction: A Handbook* (Chicago: ACRL, 1983). Evaluation of efforts to teach the use of information retrieval is particularly difficult and little has been attempted. Description of assessment techniques used with programs that teach end-users to search were presented at the 1986 LOEX Annual Conference (proceedings in press).

41. King and Baker, "Teaching End-Users to Search: Issues and Problems."

42. Betsy Baker, "A Conceptual Framework for Teaching Online Catalog Use," *Journal of Academic Librarianship* 12, no. 2 (May 1986):90-96.

43. Ibid., p. 94.

44. Frederick W. Lancaster, "User Education: The Next Major Thrust in Information Science?" *Journal of Education for Librarianship* 11, no. 1 (1970):55-63; and *Toward Paperless Information Systems* (New York: Academic Press, 1978), p. 158. Nina W. Matheson and John A. D. Cooper, "Academic Information in the Academic Health Sciences Center: Roles for the Library in Information Management," *Journal of Medical Education* 57, no. 10, pt. 2 (October 1982):1-93.

45. Rudd and Rudd, "Coping with Information Load," p. 319.

# SECTION C

## Bibliographic Instruction
## Librarianship

As bibliographic instruction changes from the status of a grassroots movement to that of an established area of librarianship, more attention must be directed toward the theoretical constructs which underlie this area. A recurring theme of the original Think Tank deliberations, reported by Stoffle and Bernero in chapter 1, was the "development of an underlying pedagogy of bibliographic instruction" and an entire section of the Think Tank report focused on the integration of training for bibliographic instruction into education for librarianship. To accomplish the latter, the former must be clearly articulated.

Eclecticism has been the watchword in the bibliographic instruction movement as librarians explored any and all areas that might help them to accomplish their goals. In some instances librarians, struggling to organize the nebulous process of early library instruction, reinvented the wheel—creating theory out of their own experiences, then finding it already existed in another field. The editor is reminded of her first meeting with Keith Cottam, a pioneer in the study of planning for bibliographic instruction. With a doctorate in instructional design, development, and evaluation, she had just delivered a paper at the 1981 ACRL meeting in Minneapolis, describing the implications of this field for design of bibliographic instruction. Keith introduced himself, expressing fascination at the existence of a theoretical area which so closely paralleled his own work. And thus it has been for many of the pioneers in library instruction, as they struggled to order their own learning and to find the terms that would give them access to literature relevant to their needs.

From this vast welter of information (for what is more challenging to librarians than finding every scrap of applicable information?), two major conceptual areas emerged which, at this time, seem to hold great promise as we begin to construct a theoretical base for bibliographic instruction. These areas are the science of knowledge and learning theory. It should be noted, however, that the highlighting of these conceptual areas is a beginning stage in identifying and clarifying what constitutes bibliographic instruction theory; it is not an engraved dictum that THIS, alone and forever, constitutes our theoretical base. Theory-building is an active, not a static, process and as such, requires constant exploration, experimentation, evaluation, and change to challenge the area it is intended to illuminate.

Section C is focused upon the two elements of bibliographic instruction librarianship: education and theory. In chapter 8, the current relationship between bibliographic instruction and education for librarianship is discussed. The authors, both faculty members in the Division of Library and Information Management, Emory University, explain why library schools are not providing separate courses in bibliographic instruction. They provide an overview of the knowledge and skills important to bibliographic instruction librarians and describe how this learning might be attained without major revisions in the typical library school curriculum. The chapter includes suggestions for making library school faculty aware of the needs of bibliographic instruction librarians.

Chapter 9 begins its discussion of the science of knowledge by suggesting that librarians and researchers operate on different levels of knowing: librarians search for information while researchers search for knowledge. It explores this difference, discussing research as process rather than product, and examines how this view of research affects the role of the librarian in general and of the bibliographic instruction librarian in particular.

In chapter 10, the four elements of the instructional situation are described: the student, the teacher, the content, and the setting. It is pointed out that the element which can be least controlled is the student. Theories of learning, which explore how students behave in various instructional situations and why they behave as they do, can help instruction librarians to understand, and thus begin to control, the process of student learning. Several theories are presented which have been found useful to the design of bibliographic instruction.

# 8 Bibliographic Instruction and Library Education

*Rao Aluri and June Lester Engle*

For a long time, bibliographic instruction (BI) librarians, on both sides of the Atlantic, have been interested in seeing library schools offer courses in BI.[1] They view "the design and implementation of a distinct course" as an "indicator of the value placed on bibliographic instruction by library schools." [2] This interest is evidenced by various projects undertaken by the Education for Bibliographic Instruction Committee of the Bibliographic Instruction Section of the Association of College and Research Libraries. For instance, Pastine and Seibert, under the auspices of this committee, surveyed library schools to collect data on their BI course offerings.[3] In addition, the committee has sponsored panel discussions on bibliographic instruction in library school curriculum at annual meetings of both the American Library Association and the Association for Library and Information Science Education.[4] Behind all this interest lie two basic beliefs:

1. BI is important enough in terms of its published literature and practice to merit a separate course in the library school curriculum.

2. New graduates of library schools should be knowledgeable in the theory of BI and should have acquired practical skills in conducting and managing BI programs.

In the main, these beliefs are valid. The practice of bibliographic instruction has matured from the one-size-fits-all orientation program to the sophisticated, carefully targeted, and multilevel delivery that characterizes BI programs today. There is already a large and significant literature on BI, a literature that is itself maturing as it moves away from descriptions of specific programs, whose successes and failures are largely controlled by local institutional and personnel variables, toward theoretical discussions seeking to establish general principles.[5] Assuredly, a new library school graduate interested in reference and BI positions needs to be conversant with the theoretical principles underlying bibliographic instruction.

A cursory review of job advertisements in professional journals shows that there are a number of openings for bibliographic instruction librarians in entry-level positions. Given today's employment climate, the existence of a job market for BI librarians is good enough reason in itself for library school faculties to be thinking in terms of preparing their students for these positions. It is not unreasonable on the part of employers of new graduates to expect them to possess some practical skills, such as lecture preparation and competent use of audiovisual materials. Furthermore, it is to the distinct advantage of both the candidate and the potential employing library if the new graduate is already versed in the design and implementation of BI programs, including the capability to develop such learning support structures as computer-assisted instruction that increasingly characterize BI. One logical way of preparing students for BI positions, of course, is by introducing separate courses that concentrate on the theory and practice of BI.

Given the importance placed by BI librarians on separate BI courses, what is the library schools' response to the demand for these courses? Deans of library schools are, at best, lukewarm to the idea of separate BI courses.[6] In 1980 Pastine and Seibert reported that 11 out of 67 ALA-accredited library schools offered separate courses. When the ACRL-BIS Education Committee repeated this survey in 1984, the number of schools offering BI courses remained the same.[7] Pastine and Seibert's lament that "... the status of bibliographic instruction has not improved substantially ..." continued to remain valid.[8]

The question, then, is why the status of BI has not improved substantially in library schools. Brundin has summarized and responded to the more prevalent reasons for the seeming inattention given to BI in preparing entrants to the field.[9] Alternately, however, the question must be put: Is the perception that the status of BI has not improved in library schools correct?

The first and foremost reason for the so-called lack of substantial progress of BI in library schools is the general insistence of measuring progress by counting the number of schools that offer separate BI courses. If this method of assessing the progress of BI in library schools is dropped in favor of assessing the assimilation of BI-related information in the library school curricula, the progress may not be insubstantial after all.

The purpose of this chapter is twofold: (1) to show that there are significant pragmatic difficulties involved in initiating separate courses on BI, and (2) to show that a number of library school courses can, with some planning, accommodate BI principles and practice.

## FACTORS MILITATING AGAINST SEPARATE BI COURSES

### Length of the Library School Program

The most critical factor affecting many curricular decisions in library schools is the fact that a typical library school program is only one year long. Although there are a handful of two-year programs, the two semesters (or three quarters)-plus-a-summer configuration remains the norm in U. S. schools. Library school faculties are acutely aware of developing new areas that need to be incorporated into existing curricula. BI is one such area that should find a place in the library school curriculum. However, incorporating all the new areas and, at the same time, maintaining the focus of the curriculum on the library and information field is, to say the least, becoming difficult.

One obvious alternative is to increase the length of the library school program to two years. The two-year program can accommodate more courses as well as provide greater potential for specialization on the part of the student. Such programs, however, are generally resisted by both faculty and students. Extension of the program makes library education much more expensive and may result in lower enrollments.[10] Concommitantly, there is no guarantee that the salaries of librarians would rise sufficiently to compensate for the increased cost of the education. When White and Paris surveyed directors of academic, public, and special libraries to elicit their views on the preparation needed for junior professionals, 64 percent of the 382 respondents indicated that they would not give greater consideration to hiring the graduates of enlarged programs over the graduates of one-year programs; and only 15 percent indicated that they would be willing to pay higher salaries to the graduates of extended programs.[11] Once the two-year program is ruled out, BI has to compete with a number of other new and highly relevant courses for a place in the curriculum. And even if that place is won, courses dealing directly with new technology, such as microcomputer applications for libraries and database structure and design, provide stiff competition for the student's attention.

## Qualified Faculty

Bibliographic instruction has its roots in reference and outreach librarianship. For quite some time, it was an activity with no great theory behind it. Witness the criticism that BI lectures tended to be shortened versions of library school reference courses.[12] It is only recently that BI started developing a theoretical base that can compel the attention of library schools.[13]

The major problem with BI, however, from the library school faculty standpoint, is that its theoretical base lies not only in librarianship but also in theories of learning and instructional design. These latter areas are not central to the mission of the library school; hence it is often difficult to find qualified personnel who are knowledgeable in both librarianship and instructional theories. Since it is individual faculty members who develop and propose new courses in periods between overall curriculum revisions, lack of appropriate expertise may be a major factor in the failure of library schools to initiate separate BI courses. This, combined with size and specialization of the faculty and the constraint of existing teaching load, can result in the lack of such courses, even where faculty as a whole are sympathetic to the idea.

In their campaign for separate courses, BI librarians need to be aware of these real world restraints under which library schools operate. In fact, the study by White and Paris demonstrates that, when presented with constraints similar to those faced by library schools, practitioners tend to make curricular decisions similar to those made by library educators.[14]

## Students' Dilemma: Strength versus Breadth

Library school students face a number of dilemmas in planning their curricula, many of which are caused by the students' eagerness to prepare themselves for entry-level jobs and to improve their job opportunities immediately following graduation. One of these dilemmas is whether to plan their program so as to strengthen their general knowledge of librarianship or to specialize in one area, such as reference. A major advantage of the more broadly based program is that the student achieves greater understanding of how various areas of librarianship fit together to form a cohesive whole. The immediate practical advantage of specialization, that is, taking a large number of courses in one area, is that the student will feel more confident during job interviews in asserting (and believing) that she or he actually can do the job at hand.

Faculty, on the other hand, often cringe in fear of overspecialization because the job the student lands may not be the one for which she or he prepared. Specialization is a gamble; and many, sooner or later, end up in jobs for which they were not prepared in library school. Hence many library educators prefer that students use their time at the library school to obtain understanding of the broader principles of the profession and then develop their specializations on the job. Bibliographic instruction, in fact, is a classic example of this approach. Many librarians who are now active in bibliographic instruction started out as reference librarians and entered BI because of the recognized need for such specialization.[15] On the other hand, a student who prepared himself or herself for bibliographic instruction may end up in a library that does not have a BI program, or worse still, in a job that has nothing to do with BI. This mismatch of preparation with the position acquired is one reason why library schools regularly hear complaints from their alumni who wish that they had taken courses in management, in research methods, and in any number of different areas not foreseen as relevant or necessary.

Another dilemma faculty and students face is whether to emphasize theoretical principles of librarianship or the acquisition of certain practical skills. Again, the complaints of many library school graduates that their schools did not prepare them for this job or that job arise from this fundamental conflict. In fact, the debate between the importance of principle and application is common to all professional training.[16] It has ruffled many a feather in the library profession, variously being fought as theory versus practice, knowledge versus skills, and principle versus applications. Whatever the terminology, the basic issue is whether or not new graduates must leave library school with a level of practical skills sufficient to enable them to be immediately productive in their first professional positions. One side of this debate favors acquisition of a large number of appropriate skills,[17] while the other side argues for teaching the sound theoretical principles that undergird the library and information profession.[18]

One reason given to support the position of teaching theory is that practical skills are likely to become obsolete, as new methods, procedures, and technologies are introduced into the workplace. In contrast, the basic principles that underlie professional activities are more stable. Therefore, the argument goes, if one is well-versed in basic principles, one is likely to adapt to the changing world more easily and quickly. Since the library school faculties view their role as that of preparing students for long-term professional growth rather than just for their first professional jobs, faculties emphasize principles over skills. From this perspective, much of BI activity may be seen as acquisition of skills. Although some BI-related skills, such as the ability to organize a class presentation or the ability to stand in front of an audience and present information logically and coherently, are less likely to be time delimited, these skills may be seen by many schools as beyond their mission.

Many practitioners may agree with this view. For instance, DeVinney and Tegler report that practicing librarians believe that "on-the-job training" should be "the primary method of preparing beginning librarians for ... teaching library instruction courses." [19] One respondent to a survey of practitioners conducted by the ACRL Bibliographic Instruction Section Committee in 1984 commented:

> The single most important qualification for bibliographic instruction would seem to be teaching skills, generally gained from experience and perhaps educational training, but unlikely to have come from any course-work in library school. Thus, institutions looking for BI librarians often ask for teaching experience in their job descriptions even though the position may be a beginning one for the librarian. While this does not mean that there needs to be no particular library school preparation for BI, it does suggest that the [ACRL-BIS] committee should be leery of implying that a course or courses in library school may be sufficient to prepare one for teaching in a college or university. [20]

Another respondent questioned the need for a separate BI course by saying:

> A class in BI or integrating the same into other library school courses is all I would see as desirable. The BI movement was the work of librarians with no formal training. Requiring said courses might, in effect, close off opportunity to participate for eager young people with fresh ideas. [21]

Obviously, some BI librarians themselves are not sure if the BI-related skills can be acquired from a formal library school course.

As educators, we notice that our library school students, too, are ambivalent about the knowledge versus skills dilemma. A given course may be criticized as too theoretical by some students and as too practical by others. Some students are bored if they perceive that the course emphasizes the practical and is not theoretical enough. Other students lose interest if they perceive that the course is too theoretical and divorced from the "real world." [22] Striking a balance between these two extremes is not an easy matter for educators. Interestingly, this dilemma is not diminished in the practicum or graduate assistantship situation. In some cases, students are disheartened when the experience emphasizes practical details; and in other cases, they complain that they have not acquired a practical, marketable skill.

A course on BI is open to the same tug-of-war; obviously, many educators themselves are unsure of its appropriate orientation. This dilemma may well exacerbate the reluctance of library schools to initiate a separate course on BI.

## Required Courses versus Electives

A typical library school curriculum includes a number of courses that every student is required to take and a number of others that may be chosen by the students based on their interests and anticipated future development. As an elective course, BI is perceived by many educators as a course related to preparation for reference service. The problem in this instance is that most schools, at least traditionally, have had an abundance of electives in the reference area: courses in humanities literature, government publications, and science information systems, to name only a few. Adding one more course in the reference and public services area may not be helpful to the student already faced with a multitude of choices. In all likelihood, because of various constraints, the student will not be able to take advantage of all the relevant courses available.

### Emerging Areas of Specialization

The flowering of the BI movement during the 1970s, interestingly, coincided with the emergence of computer-based information technologies. These information technologies are having far-reaching impact on both the workplace and the library school curriculum. The enormous growth in the number of automated systems available in the marketplace and the ubiquitous microcomputer are changing the way librarians conduct their business. In view of their impact, complexity, and novelty, the information technologies are demanding an ever-larger share of library school curricula. The computer and information technologies are expensive and demanding; a working familiarity with them is essential for graduating students. One may postulate that it is probably easier for many to pick up BI skills on the job than to pick up computer skills. Further, computers can be used effectively to teach the fundamental concepts of library and information science. What these developments mean is that the library school curriculum is a shrinking place for non-technology-oriented courses, including reference courses, and some may be dropped from the curriculum. A separate course on BI may very well be one of these casualties.

## INTEGRATION OF BI CONCEPTS IN LIBRARY SCHOOL CURRICULUM

The previous section dealt with the difficulties faced by library school faculties in initiating new courses on BI. In contrast to those difficulties, incorporating BI concepts into appropriate courses within the library school curriculum faces no such hurdles. In a sense, this integrative approach may not be a bad strategy at all; library school students will hear about BI from many sources and from different angles. Moreover, BI concepts will reach those students who are not planning a bibliographic instruction career. For the integrated approach to be successful, however, students must be able to transfer the knowledge and skills acquired from their courses to the bibliographic instruction arena.

In 1984, the ACRL Bibliographic Instruction Section's Education for Bibliographic Instruction Committee surveyed its member libraries regarding the proficiencies required for bibliographic instruction activities. The survey instrument asked for responses in two major areas:

1. Proficiencies required for instructional activities, or for entry-level librarians:

    A. Select appropriate educational objectives for a specific instructional activity

    B. Select an appropriate instructional method ...

    C. Evaluate the effectiveness of a specific instructional activity

    D. Conduct various instructional activities

    E. Effective utilize [sic] instructional media

2. Proficiencies needed for administrative, or advanced level, activities:

    A. Conduct a needs assessment

    B. Conceptualize and write a policy and plan for the library's bibliographic instruction program

    C. Obtain the necessary staff and funds to implement a bibliographic instruction program

    D. Train and evaluate the bibliographic instruction staff

    E. Promote the idea of bibliographic instruction to the classroom faculty

    F. Evaluate the overall progress and effectiveness of the library's bibliographic instruction efforts.[23]

Respondents to this questionnaire listed a large number of proficiencies under each of the above categories. Admittedly, many of these proficiencies are best acquired in a course that is completely devoted to bibliographic instruction. As Lutzker points out, "ways to design a class, and effectively present information are subjects which need to be debated and practiced." [24] A full course on bibliographic instruction is the best forum for gaining these competencies. Nevertheless, many library school courses do impart information that will be of use for a beginning BI librarian, as can be demonstrated by the following brief comparison of the BI activities categories identified in the questionnaire with knowledge and skills components of courses commonly found in library school curricula.

1. **Proficiencies needed for instructional activities:**
   *A. Selection of appropriate educational objectives*
   *E. Effective utilization of instructional media*

    The concept of educational objectives and the process of formulating them are covered in audiovisual and information technologies courses offered in the library school curriculum. Because the literature of audiovisual and educational information technology itself emanates primarily from the field of education, both textbooks and supplementary readings in these areas are grounded in instructional theory and practice.[25] Generally, such courses require students to establish educational objectives for specific audiovisual programming and to learn how to use audiovisual materials effectively to achieve specific objectives. They may also require term projects where the students actually prepare an audiovisual program, present it to a general audience, and evaluate its effectiveness in achieving the stated objectives. It is unfortunate, from the standpoint of preparation for BI, that audiovisual courses are more frequently taken by those students planning to go into school libraries and are less likely to be elected by students planning to seek a reference position in academic libraries. Both these groups of students are apt to be generators of BI programs.

B. *Selection of an appropriate instructional method*

Just as above, audiovisual and information technologies courses are the best places to acquire comparative knowledge of various instructional methods. Again, these courses offer hands-on experiences. Interested students can take advanced production classes where they may be able to produce multimedia programs, thereby acquiring better knowledge of the advantages and disadvantages of each of the methods and the most appropriate medium for achieving various learning objectives. Of course, audiovisual courses probably will not be too much concerned with the lecture method, but other techniques fall into their purview.

C. *Evaluating the effectiveness of instructional activity*

The obvious place for acquiring evaluative skills is the course on research methods. A typical research methods course will cover different types of research and then will proceed to introduce the student to the variety of research methodologies available, including various techniques of statistical analysis used to organize and describe the data collected. In addition, this course is likely to provide hands-on experience with statistical packages such as SPSS. Interestingly, despite widespread belief that graduating librarians should possess skills in designing and conducting a research project, research methods courses are not always well-subscribed. Even those students who take these courses often do so for externally imposed reason—for example, to fulfill state requirements for certification as school media specialists. Many who should be taking the course, such as students planning their careers in academic libraries, pass up this opportunity. Once these students graduate and go out to the real world, they will bitterly complain that library schools did not teach them how to conduct research!

D. *Conducting various instructional activities*

Some of the skills required, such as the ability to stand in front of a group of students and give a lecture or conduct a seminar, are usually not acquired in library school. In some courses, students may participate in seminar presentations, but this is usually done under a faculty member's direction and the experience may not be common enough for the student to develop lasting skills. However, other kinds of activities may not be completely unfamiliar to the student. For instance, reference courses may require the student to prepare pathfinders on topics of their choice. Other courses may incorporate preparation of an annotated bibliography for a target group. Such activities require that the student know how to use major indexing and abstracting tools, bibliographies, and other reference tools and how to collect, evaluate, and organize information for a certain audience. A typical instruction session in an academic library makes use of just such competencies. Further, specialized reference courses attempt to develop subject reference expertise, which again, is important for the entry-level BI librarian.

2. **Proficiencies needed for administrative activities:**
   A. *Conducting a needs assessment*
   F. *Evaluating the overall progress and effectiveness of the BI program*
   Conducting needs assessment and designing evaluation mechanisms will involve integrating the knowledge gained from a number of courses. Courses such as collection development and management are concerned with the librarians' understanding of their institutions and their clientele. The research methods course teaches design of survey instruments and use of statistical techniques. Some schools offer specific courses in information needs analysis. Courses on specific types of libraries may also incorporate needs assessment techniques and evaluation processes appropriate to the specific library environment.

   B. *Conceptualizing and writing a policy and plan for the BI program*
   This activity may not be an easy one for a beginning librarian, as some practical experience may be needed for developing policies and for effectively conducting planning activities. Courses on management and administration should, at least cursorily, deal with the planning process, while other courses may provide experience in policy development. Even courses seemingly far removed from the BI function, such as systems analysis, may provide techniques and concepts that can be applied to the process of policy development and planning for the BI program.

   C. *Obtaining necessary staff and funds*
   D. *Training and evaluating BI staff*
   Budgeting processes and personnel management are typically included in courses in library and information center management, with some schools offering advanced level courses devoted entirely to personnel administration. Ideally, the student would have an opportunity in course projects to apply principles from the courses to the BI setting; for example, the preparation of a budget and supporting documents for implementing a new BI program in a general management course or the development of a training manual for BI staff in a personnel administration course.

   E. *Promoting BI to classroom faculty*
   Knowledge and skills needed to promote BI can be acquired in two types of courses: (1) those that deal with the techniques and

processes of public relations, either in a general management course or in a separate course on public relations for libraries (not a frequent curriculum offering), and (2) those that provide an understanding of the institutional setting of the library, typically both the foundations, "library in society," course and the course on types of libraries. Political skill, identified by several of the ACRL-BIS survey respondents as a basic requirement for success in this category, may not be a proficiency the library school curriculum can provide; however, recognition of the necessity for political acuity and for identification and analysis of the political factors in any environment can be developed throughout the curriculum, depending on the attitude and political astuteness of the library school faculty.

In addition to formal courses, students have other opportunities that can contribute to preparation for BI positions: independent study, graduate assistantships, and internships are among the more promising possibilities. Further, a number of courses taken will require term papers and projects. Such courses are perfect avenues for exploring BI at greater depth. These alternatives can enable the student to immerse himself or herself in bibliographic instruction activity and to obtain necessary orientation and training.

## PROMOTION OF BI CONCEPTS WITH LIBRARY SCHOOL FACULTY

The foregoing discussion suggests that it is possible for the knowledge and skills required for effective performance by BI librarians, at both entry and managerial levels, to be provided within the existing library school curriculum without the addition of a separate BI course. That such learning will take place and will be transferred to the BI setting, however, is by no means assured. For BI concepts to be integrated across the spectrum of library school courses, it is necessary for library school faculty to be aware of the competencies needed by BI librarians, for BI concepts to be included in course content where feasible, and for faculty to be alert to the potential for students to use the various course options to develop BI proficiencies. For example, the instructor in research methods can—and (from the BI librarian's perspective) should—include projects evaluating BI programs among the research studies analyzed in the research methods class, and the professor teaching a course in microcomputer applications can suggest a project applying CAI to bibliographic instruction as a possible course assignment. Whether, in fact, such integration takes place can be affected strongly by interested BI librarians, who can assist the library school faculty to identify ways of including BI in existing courses and who can provide opportunities within their own departments for students to participate in BI experiences. For example, BI librarians might provide a practicum for students interested in BI, work with library school faculty in designing appropriate projects related to BI, send copies of BI research studies to faculty for whom such research is relevant, or offer to lecture on BI in classes or talk informally with students in colloquia series or other extracurricular offerings. In their work in promoting BI with other faculty, bibliographic instruction librarians should have become experts in finding ways to integrate the BI concept into the instructor's approach to course organization and delivery. Although they may be accused of trying to propagandize the library school faculty, application of these same techniques by BI librarians in assisting their library school colleagues has potential for improving the status of BI in the overall library school curriculum, without necessarily requiring a separate course.[26]

## CONCLUSION

There are strong factors that act against instituting separate courses on bibliographic instruction within the library education curriculum. In contrast, a number of existing courses already provide basic information that the entry-level bibliographic instruction librarians need and can rely upon. The ACRL/BIS Committee should explore and publicize these options along with their attempt to promote separate BI courses in library schools.

One could argue that the separate course is necessary as an evolutionary step to gain recognition for the importance of BI education before the integrated approach can be effective, much as we had separate courses dealing with online searching and use of the bibliographic utilities before these functions became an integral part of more broadly based courses. The pragmatic realities of today's library school curriculum, however, make such a developmental stage unlikely to occur. And in the long run, it is just possible that the integrated approach will do more to foster support for BI and to prepare effective BI librarians than the separate course so strongly supported by those who became our BI experts without it.

## NOTES

1. Sheila Apted, "Teaching the Use of Information Resources (TUIR) and the Schools of Librarianship," *Aslib Proceedings* 33 (September 1981):357-62; Esther Dyer, "Formal Library Science Courses on Library Instruction," *Journal of Education for Librarianship* 18 (Spring 1978):359-61; Peter Fox, "Teaching the Librarian to Teach: The Situation in Britain," in *Improving Library Instruction: How to Teach and How to Evaluate*, ed. Carolyn A. Kirkendall (Ann Arbor, Mich.: Pierian Press, 1979), pp. 37-59; Sue Galloway, "Nobody Is Teaching the Teachers," *Bootlegger* 3 (January-February 1976):29-31; Nancy Hammond, "Teaching and Learning Methods for British Librarians," in *Putting Library Instruction in Its Place: In the Library and in the Library School*, ed. Carolyn A. Kirkendall (Ann Arbor, Mich.: Pierian Press, 1978), pp. 53-64; Sharon Ann Hogan, "Training and Education of Library Instruction Librarians," *Library Trends* 26 (Summer 1980):105-26; Lisa Howorth and Donald Kenney, "Education for Bibliographic Instruction: A Syllabi Project," *C&RL News* 44 (November 1983):379-80; Carolyn A. Kirkendall, "Library Instruction: A Column of Opinion: Should Library Schools Teach Library Instruction?" *Journal of Academic Librarianship* 8 (March 1982):34-35; John Lubans, Jr., *Progress in Educating the Library User* (New York: R. R. Bowker, 1978), pp. 1-11; Marilyn

Lutzker, "On-the-Job Training for Instruction Librarians," *Reference Services Review* 10 (Summer 1982):63-64; Carla Stoffle et al., "A Modest Proposal for a Library School Course Dealing with Library Instruction," *Journal of Education for Librarianship* 18 (Winter 1978):241-44.

2. Maureen Pastine and Karen Seibert, "Update on the Status of Bibliographic Instruction in Library School Programs," *Journal of Education for Librarianship* 21 (Fall 1980):169.

3. Ibid, pp. 169-71.

4. "Hearing on Bibliographic Instruction in Library Schools" (Panel discussion at the ALA Annual Meeting, San Francisco, June 29, 1981); "Education for Bibliographic Instruction" (Panel discussion at the ALISE Annual Meeting, Washington, D.C., January 5, 1984). Reported in *C&RL News* 45 (April 1984): 188.

5. Anne Beaubien, Sharon A. Hogan, and Mary W. George, *Learning the Library: Concepts and Methods for Effective Bibliographic Instruction* (New York: R. R. Bowker, 1982); Pamela Kobelski and Mary Reichel, "Conceptual Frameworks for Bibliographic Instruction," *Journal of Academic Librarianship* 7 (May 1981):73-77; Cerise Oberman and Katina Strauch, eds., *Theories of Bibliographic Education: Designs for Teaching* (New York: R. R. Bowker, 1982).

6. Charles A. Bunge, "Library Education for Library Instruction: How the Practitioners and the Educators Can Cooperate," in *Putting Library Instruction in Its Place: In the Library and in the Library School*, ed. Carolyn A. Kirkendall (Ann Arbor, Mich.: Pierian Press, 1978), pp. 65-70; Carolyn A. Kirkendall, "Library Instruction: A Column of Opinion: Do the Deans of Library Schools Agree on the Need for Library Instruction in the Library School Curriculum?" *Journal of Academic Librarianship* 2 (1976):240-41.

7. Ellen Meltzer, "Status of Education for Bibliographic Instruction" (Oral report presented at the Bibliographic Instruction Committee Meeting of the Association of College and Research Libraries, Washington, D.C., January 5, 1985).

8. Pastine and Seibert, "Update on the Status of Bibliographic Instruction," p. 169.

9. Robert E. Brundin, "Education for Instructional Librarians: Development and Overview," *Journal of Education for Librarianship* 25 (Winter 1985):177-89. Brundin suggests that seven reasons have been advanced to explain the library schools' reluctance to include bibliographic instruction in their curricula. The reasons are: (1) teaching function is central to BI activity and library schools are not equipped to deal with teaching methods; (2) it is an impossible task to teach BI to students who lack the necessary educational background; (3) little time is available in beginning reference courses to devote to BI; (4) students are either not interested in BI careers or are not aware of the importance of BI; (5) the

faculty, having never practiced BI, consider BI a part of reference service rather than reference service being part of BI; (6) in the conflict between theory and research on the one hand and skills and practice on the other, faculty favor the former; and (7) faculty do not have prior experience with BI or prior teacher training and they are less inclined toward BI than those who have prior experience with BI and prior teacher training. In this paper, we cover some of the same ground and, of course, we do not always agree with Brundin.

10.    Richard L. Darling and Terry Belanger, eds., *Extended Library Education Programs: Proceedings of a Conference Held at the School of Library Service, Columbia University, 13-14 March 1980* (New York: Columbia University, School of Library Service, 1980); Robert M. Hayes and F. William Summers, "Two-Year Library School Programs: Useful Extension or Waste of Time?" *American Libraries* 14 (October 1983):619-20; F. William Summers, "Library School Deans Consider Two-Year Programs but Ignore Alternatives at Columbia Conference," *American Libraries* 11 (May 1980):250-52.

11.    Herbert S. White and Marion Paris, "Employer Preferences and the Library Education Curriculum," *Library Quarterly* 55 (January 1985):1-33.

12.    Anne Beaubien, Mary George, and Sharon Hogan, "Things We Weren't Taught in Library School: Some Thoughts to Take Home," in *Putting Library Instruction in Its Place: In the Library and in the Library School*, ed. Carolyn A. Kirkendall (Ann Arbor, Mich.: Pierian Press, 1978), pp. 71-84.

13.    Beaubien, Hogan, and George, *Learning the Library*; Kobelski and Reichel, "Conceptual Frameworks for Bibliographic Instruction"; Oberman and Strauch, *Theories of Bibliographic Education*.

14.    White and Paris, "Employer Preference and the Library Education Curriculum."

15.    Galloway, "Nobody Is Teaching the Teachers"; Barbara J. Smith, "Background Characteristics and Education Needs of a Group of Instruction Librarians in Pennsylvania," *College & Research Libraries* 43 (May 1982):199-207.

16.    Joe Morehead, *Theory and Practice in Library Education: The Teaching-Learning Process* (Littleton, Colo.: Libraries Unlimited, 1980).

17.    Mark Plaiss, "Countering 'the Guru of I.U.': New Librarians Need Skills, Not Philosophy," *American Libraries* 14 (October 1983):618. For correspondence on Herbert S. White, "Defining Basis Competencies," *American Libraries* 14 (September 1983):519-25, and Plaiss, see *American Libraries* 14 (December 1983):704 and *American Libraries* 15 (January 1984):17-18.

18.    White, "Defining Basic Competencies."

19. Gemma DeVinney and Patricia Tegler, "Preparation for Academic Librarianship: A Survey," *College & Research Libraries* 44 (May 1983):223-27.

20. Education for Bibliographic Instruction Committee, "Questionnaire on Proficiencies Required for Bibliographic Instruction Activities," compiled responses (Bibliographic Instruction Section of the Association of College and Research Libraries, Chicago, 1984).

21. Ibid.

22. Compare Ralph W. Conant, *The Conant Report: A Study of the Education of Librarians* (Cambridge, Mass.: MIT Press, 1980) and Samuel Rothstein, "The 97-Year-Old Mystery Solved at Last: Why People Really Hate Library Schools," *Library Journal* 110 (April 1, 1985):41-48.

23. Education for Bibliographic Instruction Committee, "Questionnaire on Proficiencies Required for Bibliographic Instruction Activities" (Bibliographic Instruction Section of the Association of College and Research Libraries, Chicago, 1984).

24. Lutzker, "On-the-Job Training for Instruction Librarians," p. 64.

25. James W. Brown, Richard B. Lewis, and Fred Harcleroad, *AV Instruction: Technology, Media and Methods*, 6th ed. (New York: McGraw-Hill, 1983); Walter A. Wittich and Charles F. Schuller, *Instructional Technology: Its Nature and Use*, 6th ed. (New York: Harper & Row, 1979).

26. Association of College and Research Libraries, Bibliographic Instruction Section, "Think Tank Recommendations for Bibliographic Instruction," *College & Research Libraries News* 42 (December 1981):394-98; Bunge, "Library Education for Library Instruction"; Vida Stanton, "The Library School: Its Role in Teaching the Use of the Library," in *Progress in Educating the Library User* by John Lubans, Jr. (New York: R. R. Bowker, 1978), pp. 139-46.

# 9 Science of Knowledge

*Sharon J. Rogers*

> There are many ways of knowing, there are many sorts of knowledge. But the true ways of knowing, for man, are knowing in terms of apartness, which is mental, rational, scientific, and knowing in terms of togetherness, which is religious and poetic.
>
> — D. H. Lawrence, *Apropos of Lady Chatterly's Lover*

The world of bibliographic instruction has long lamented discrepancies between the ways in which librarians teach research skills and the apparent ability of the faculty members to conduct perfectly adequate research without using "our" techniques. Indeed, as several studies reveal, the general disinclination among faculty to employ such bibliographic resources as abstracting journals and indexes may appear as an institutionalized aspect of the various disciplines.[1] Yet, it is clear that faculty can and do engage in successful research. It is this seeming paradox that has led Steven Stoan to conclude "that research skills and library skills are neither the same thing nor [do they] bear any organic relationship to each other." He adds, "Research skills center on the quest for knowledge; library skills center on the search for information."[2]

This chapter seeks to explore the apparent rift between the domains of the librarian and the faculty researcher. Do librarians and researchers operate on essentially different epistemological levels? Are they literally trained to talk past one another?

The picture for bibliographic instruction will be grim if such differences are not explored and their implications examined. Students will be condemned to acquire inferior library skills by means of the all-too-familiar "one-hour stand" and the research process will remain enshrouded in the mists that only graduate studies seem to dispel.[3]

## LIBRARIAN AS "TOOL SPECIALIST"

One solution to the dilemma may be to posit a strong, independent role for the professional librarian as a "tool specialist" or as a "research mediator," a librarian who is attuned to the research methodologies of the various disciplines.[4] The librarian must modify his or her *product*-centered (or information source) frame of reference and adopt instead a *process* orientation rooted in the working knowledge of a given discipline or subdiscipline. The librarian, in short, must take it upon himself or herself to learn to "think" like a researcher.

"Tool specialists" have emerged in the various disciplines. The typical researcher, being unable to master the intricacies of, say, an electron microscope, a particle accelerator, or the technique of computer analysis may be forced to "farm out" his or her findings to the tool specialist. The tool specialist then must refashion the data into a form that the researcher can use and interpret. Since each research problem presents the tool specialist with a relatively unique set of parameters, it follows that successful research is dependent upon the tool specialist's creative ability to calibrate the apparatus or adapt a technique to the peculiarities of the data in question. In a real sense, the availability of tools and the abilities of the tool specialist serve to define the range of problems that can be studied.

The librarian is another species of tool specialist. Arguably, the modern research library is just as complex and intricate as any other piece of research apparatus. Its mastery requires a certain kind of skill that only time and experience can hone adequately. The library can no more be learned by the "one-hour stand" than can the skills needed to manipulate an electron microscope.

At first sight, such a program would seem to have much to recommend it; who could deny that library science would gain from a deeper appreciation of the research process? This, however, is one of those cases where the elegance of a proposal may outshine its flaws. What if the notion of a "research process" is not something that can be tapped into easily?

## RESEARCH AS CRAFT

In an attempt to clarify the basic issues, the author will argue that academic research is, in essence, an intensely personal and subjective undertaking. Such a view is based on a conceptualization of "research as craft" which stands in fundamental—while not diametric—opposition to the prevailing articulation of scientific rationality, which holds that research proceeds by means of incremental steps through a mechanistic and rationalized process. The author hopes to illustrate that the notion of "research as craft" locates the academic researcher and the librarian in a single dimension. Both activities entail the acquisition of a set of vague but complex skills that are intuitive and practical in character. Given this, Stoan's assertion that librarians and researchers are engaged in a distinct set of operations may be accepted, but—and the "but" is of crucial importance—both occupations lie along a single continuum[5]. They have convergent aims; however, the skill structures essential to each are largely subjective and, therefore, may be mutually inaccessible. Such a state of affairs, having been made explicit, will actually serve to enhance the work of developing adequate bibliographic instruction. It will at least serve to clear the air of some of the ambiguities that now envelop academic research.

Research, as conventionally received, is a systematic process of expanding knowledge in a cumulative way within a discipline. As Stoan puts it, "The researcher formulates a hypothesis, constructs a research design, gathers empirical data, and tests the hypothesis against the data gathered, offering some kind of conclusion, however tentative." [6] It is assumed that each discipline has its own peculiar type of primary data and its own techniques for the gathering and analysis of that data. It is this set of "techniques" that we refer to when we speak of methodology. Research, from this perspective, consists essentially of two things: the facts, or data, and the tools, or methodology, employed to gather, analyze, and evaluate that data. At this point, it is already clear that the facts are taken often as givens existing independently of the research process. Locating "facts" is one of the contributions librarians are presumed to make to the research process. This, however, is a subtle yet potentially inimical distortion. For it is simply not the case that the "facts" are benign givens. A fact should not be understood as a passive fixture of the universe; it is not merely "out there" awaiting collection and it does not color itself. A fact is instead an intellectual construct. As Ravetz writes, "... a fact is preserved from oblivion only when it is useful as existing information, performing a function in new work analogous to that of a tool." [7] Fact*ness* is therefore a defined status; a fact *is* a fact, or a piece of information becomes a fact only when it fits with and furthers a given research framework.

From the preceding, we can sense the interdependency of facts and methods. They are both aspects of research, and their character is such that a clean demarcation is neither feasible nor desirable. This, however, poses a troubling question: If facts are not the independent and authoritative entities that conventional wisdom would have us believe, then where is the grounding for objective research? How, in other words, can the researcher pronounce upon the truth—tentative though it may be—and be certain of it? This is indeed a difficult question and, as the ongoing controversies surrounding such socio-scientific dilemmas as acid rain, environmental irradiation, and Agent Orange indicate, the answer is far from pat. Much of the difficulty, however, lies with our familiar but overly structured conception of research, with the mechanistic conception that posits the research process as a sort of "black box" that need only be fed raw information in order to produce significant and unambiguous results.[8] This formalistic model does not, according to Collins, "have the potential to resolve differences of opinion over what is a proper addition to scientific knowledge and cannot 'close-down' scientific controversies." [9] While the question of the closure of scientific debate is not our primary concern, it does serve to reveal what has been aptly termed the "soft underbelly" of scientific research.[10] It illustrates how a researcher's judgment must be informed by criteria that are not a necessary concomitant of the data at hand. The decision to find an end point for a piece of research may be defined by a particular research community as a convention that is a social product.[11]

By appreciating the social character of the research process, we may find it easier to accept the idea of "research as craft" and to find a role for the librarian as a "tool specialist." As previously indicated, the formalistic model of research fails to give adequate account for both the facts that go into research and the conclusions that flow out. Thus, it fails at both ends. But, perhaps more important, the mechanistic view fails in the middle as well; which is to say, it fails to illuminate how it is that researchers actually "work through" a given problem.

Table 1 shows the points at which flexibility exists within the formal model of the research process. At each of these points of flexibility, the librarian's role as a "tool specialist" may be utilized by the discipline-based researcher.

Table 1. Flexibility Points within the Formal Model of the Research Process

| Formalistic Research Process | Creative or Intuitive Elements |
| --- | --- |
| 1. Hypothesis formulation | Problem definition and problem setting<br>Ability to relate a puzzling situation to something already known or suspected |
| 2. Construction of research design | Ability to transform problematic situation into terms that can be employed as tools for investigation<br>Ability to abstract raw data into terms that allow for the utilization of research tools |
| 3. Data gathering | Ability to re-form a problematic situation<br>Creative determination of what is to count as data |
| 4. Test hypothesis against data | Ability to manipulate tools for unique purposes<br>Creative determination that tools do in fact measure that data as it has been conceptualized |
| 5. Conclusion | Ability to draw steps 1-4 into a coherent structure<br>Gain acceptance from relevant research community |

In real world situations, the problems which inspire research do not present themselves as givens. As Schon puts it,

> They must be constructed from materials which are puzzling, troubling, and uncertain. In order to *convert* [emphasis mine] a problematic situation to a problem, a [researcher] must do a certain kind of work. He must make sense of an uncertain situation that initially makes no sense.[12]

It is this "conversion" process, perhaps more than anything else, that illuminates the craft-like character of research. For it is at this point that the researcher may be said to intellectually sculpt the amorphous contours of a problematic situation, converting it into a concrete, concise program for research. Again, as Schon says,

> When we set the problem, we select what we will treat as the "things" of the situation, we set the boundaries of our attention to it, and we *impose upon it* [emphasis mine] a coherence which allows us to say what is wrong and in what directions the situation needs to be changed.[13]

Schon is here referring to applied research, but the message remains virtually the same: when the researcher seeks to set or define a problem for research, he or she is engaged in a highly creative interaction with the material of the problem. Research is thus not simply a straightforward matter of applying a prefabricated methodology to the raw and unanalyzed "things" that somehow make up the subject. It is an intuitive and creative process wherein the researcher actually changes the nature of a problematical state-of-affairs. This is perhaps best illustrated by the incidence of so-called "accidental discoveries." Indeed, it is hard even to imagine the magnificent creativity that it must have taken for Becquerel to turn the mere observation of a few spots of an unexposed photographic plate into the basics for a phenomenon that we now understand as gamma radiation. How could such a revelation have occurred if he had actually been limited to a formalistic research methodology?

The creative and craft-like character of research can also be seen in the processes of measurement and experimentation. We are all aware of the enormous complexity of modern experimental apparatuses. In fact, much of what we term "methodology" is associated with the procedures employed to operate these tools of research. But these "procedures" are far from straightforward. There is a lot of guesswork that goes into measurement and experimental procedure for the simple reason that we have no way of knowing the "correct" outcome in advance. In other words, we have no surefire or algorithmic way to determine whether or not an apparatus is actually doing what it is that we would like it to do. This problem is especially acute at the frontiers of a research area, but the basic argument is valid for even the most mundane of experimental exercises. As Ravetz writes of this dilemma:

> In [his or her] work with pieces of physical equipment, the scientist is a very special sort of craftsman, for the objects he [or she] is dealing with are highly artificial. The relation of the readings taken off the apparatus to the objects of ... inquiry is not at all immediate: the establishment of their relevance requires another set of operations.[14]

This other "set of operations" involves the creative act of interpretation. Experimental competence is therefore, in the final analysis, subject to such nonrational factors as the researcher's background, personal style, and value structure. It also entails the approval of the relevant research community. The role of the "tool specialist," as it may be played by librarians and others, creates a certain division of labor in the research process that tends to further weaken the formalistic model. Again turning to Ravetz, we find that:

> There is thus a natural division of labour between tool-experts and their clients; and the tool-experts are not merely individuals serving as auxiliaries to the clients in the work, but themselves can form a

self-contained specialty, a tool-providing field. When two craftsmen with different skills are involved in the same project, they will inevitably see the work from different points of view. The different approaches will be complementary, and can correct and enrich each other; but they can also be the occasion of conflict. For each of the partners may be wanting to get something slightly but significantly different from the project.[15]

What Ravetz is getting at here can be expressed by the notion of a "research dimension" that was introduced above. Earlier, the suggestion was made that librarians and researchers are engaged in distinct yet convergent occupations. The librarian as "tool specialist" cannot teach the library in one hour. Yet by the same token, neither can the librarian realistically hope to grasp the essence of academic research by means of "imported methodologies." As we have seen, the lifeblood of research is composed of the subjective elements of intuition and tacit creativity. From this, it follows that an "explicit analysis of [the various disciplinary methodologies] must be incomplete ... a schematic anatomy representing a complex physiology." [16]

## IMPLICATIONS FOR BIBLIOGRAPHIC INSTRUCTION: LIBRARIAN AS TOOL SPECIALIST

As table 1 made apparent, the notion of research as craft bears significant implications for bibliographic instruction. The librarian, like any other tool specialist, is molded into the research activity in a manner which varies from project to project and, moreover, which may well vary during the different phases of a single project. As research unfolds, it is informed largely by its own peculiarities. Research, in other words, is an interactive process composed not only of the raw materials (what we sometimes refer to as primary data[17] ) that make up the initial problematic situation, but of the character of the research as well. Given this, the librarian, like any other tool specialist, must use his or her creative skills to maintain a certain malleability. For example, it would be only partly facetious to suggest that Becquerel would never have linked anomalies on a photographic plate with the existence of gamma radiation had a librarian failed to imagine along with the researcher and had guided his search only to those abstracts or indexes that deal with photography. Any active reference librarian can provide similar examples from the social sciences and humanities where the event of thinking along with a researcher has given the librarian a share in the excitement of research discovery. The librarian above all knows that the library is an *adaptable tool*. The librarian must come to see himself or herself as a tool specialist or, if you prefer, as a research mediator.

The following points illustrate the basic understanding that librarians have shared as they have functioned in the "tool specialist" role even while not defining it as such. This role for the librarian has implications for both the organization and delivery of instruction.

• If research is indeed a craft, then its perfection entails practice. As Louis Smith writes, "Craft knowledge is practical knowledge; it is of the order of 'knowing how' rather than 'knowing what.' " [18] This understanding obligates the librarian to an instructional role at the reference desk; the librarian will not automatically rush to the rescue of a student who seems especially maladroit in his or her search for information. By the same token, faculty members must be urged from the reserve room to the reference department.

• Perfection entails practice, but practice at what? Many user education activities provide practice at manipulation of reference tools. However, the budding researcher, practicing a craft, may need training in transferring the knowledge gained about organization or materials in one area of study to the organization of materials in another. Librarians by emphasizing a conceptual approach to teaching will emphasize linkages among sources.

• The notion of research as craft allows us to emphasize the social character of research in work with faculty colleagues and in user education. The researcher is, in a very real sense, a member of a research community. He or she therefore has a paramount need to remain "tied in" with the rest of the community. Moreover, this tie should be as direct and as unconvoluted as possible. For instance, the footnote or endnote is the medium through which researchers communicate. Given this, the librarian may restructure bibliographic instruction to concede the secondary or even tertiary importance that researchers often attach to subject-organized abstracts and indexes and emphasize citation techniques for access to various literatures.

• Librarians may become more sensitive to the understanding that different disciplines and indeed different individuals within the same discipline will place a varying amount of emphasis on the different stages that research passes through. Questions to elicit this information may be part of the reference interview. While it may seem clear at first that the historian and the chemist will have broadly divergent needs for information, this equation is muddied by the possibility that a particular chemist may be in need of information that is largely historical or that the historian may need precise technical information in a scientific area. It is the librarian who must maintain the "adaptable attitude" previously discussed.

• Librarians place special emphasis on bibliographic instruction *in conjunction with* basic courses in disciplinary methodology, realizing that the further bibliographic instruction gets from the arena in which students acquire their elemental research skills, the less effective it will be. Librarians argue for the effectiveness of the bibliography as an instructional assignment; but, in this context, with the understanding that it must be used to provide the practice that develops into exercise of a craft. Such a strategy serves to minimize the distance that the student might otherwise place between his or her developing research skills and the tools and professional assistance that will enhance that skill.

• The craft-view of research points to the need for libraries to employ subject-specialists. This may at first seem odd or even contradictory given the earlier emphasis on the subjective nature of research. However, the author also has stressed the notion of the research community. The subject-specialist, then, is not valuable so much as a "bearer of methodology," but rather as an individual who can share a certain "feeling" for research. Granted, the notion of "shared feelings" seems ambiguous to the extreme, but remember — research itself is a highly ambiguous proposition. Schon illustrates this nicely when he discusses the difficulty that baseball pitchers have in articulating just what it means to "find the groove." [19] It is something that they all can do (or at least the good ones), but it is not something they can explain. The situation is similar for research practitioners. A subject-specialist, then, may be more able to appreciate the "grooves" that research as craft seems to imply, and to recognize the necessity of the researcher to find the "groove." In this role, the librarian also may appear as a more appropriate classroom partner.

## NOTES*

1. Maurice B. Line, *Information Requirements of Researchers in Social Science* 2 vols. (Bath, England: Bath University of Technology, 1971), vol. 1, p. 84; Patricia Strenstrom and Ruth B. McBride, "Serial Use of Social Science Faculty: A Survey," *College & Research Libraries* 40 (September, 1979):429; D. N. Wood and C. A. Bower, "The Use of Social Science Periodical Literature," *Journal of Documentation* 25 (June 1969):115-17.

2. Stephen K. Stoan, "Research and Library Skills: An Analysis and Interpretation," *College & Research Libraries* 45 (March 1984):100.

3. Ibid., p. 104.

4. For more on this, see Sharon J. Rogers, "Research Strategies: Bibliographic Instruction for Undergraduates," *Library Trends* 29 (Summer 1980):69-74 and Thomas J. Michalak, "Library Services to the Graduate Community: The Role of the Subject Specialist Librarian," *College & Research Libraries* 37 (1976):257-65.

5. The notion of a "continuum" belongs to McInnis. See Raymond G. McInnis, *New Perspectives for Reference Service in Academic Libraries* (Westport, Conn.: Greenwood Press, 1978), p. 127.

6. Stoan, "Research and Library Skills," p. 100.

*Thanks are due to Charles Herrick and Deborah Masters for extensive searching in the databases for the literature of research on research, which they have finally convinced me is very limited — at least as reported in databases.

7.   Jerome R. Ravetz, *Scientific Knowledge and Its Social Problems* (Oxford, England: Clarendon Press, 1971), p. 88.

8.   H. M. Collins, "The Sociology of Scientific Knowledge: Studies of Contemporary Science," *Annual Review of Sociology* 9 (1983):273.

9.   Ibid., p. 277.

10.   Ibid.

11.   The notion of a research community is elaborated by Kuhn. See Thomas S. Kuhn, *The Structure of Scientific Revolutions* (Chicago: University of Chicago Press, 1978).

12.   Donald A. Schon, *The Reflective Practitioner* (New York: Basic Books, 1983), p. 40.

13.   Ibid.

14.   Ravetz, *Scientific Knowledge*, p. 77.

15.   Ibid., p. 90.

16.   Ibid., p. 148.

17.   Stoan, "Research and Library Skills," p. 100.

18.   Louis Smith, "An Alternative Model," *Anthropology and Education Quarterly* 14 (Fall 1983):178.

19.   Schon, *The Reflective Practitioner*, p. 55.

# 10 Bibliographic Instruction and Learning Theory

*Constance A. Mellon and Kathryn E. Pagles*

Librarians charged with the responsibility of developing user education programs are rarely at a loss for enough material to present to prospective students. In fact, choosing among all the things students should know as effective library users is a task accepted with relish. Getting students to pay attention to, and to understand these things, on the other hand, is a challenge of great proportion. To meet this challenge, bibliographic instruction librarians need all the help they can get! An awareness of learning theory in general and of the work of specific learning theorists can be most helpful in planning and delivering effective library instruction.

Librarians in academic settings are usually no more trained in the design and delivery of instruction than are their academic colleagues, the teaching faculty. Indeed, if instruction librarians look to the typical college professor as a teaching role model, they emulate a mode of instruction used since the Middle Ages — the expository lecture. The popularity of the "fifty-minute lecture" in bibliographic instruction demonstrates that this is just what is happening. In point of fact, it is reasonable that it should happen. Academic librarians are reminded daily by the attitudes of their teaching colleagues that they are not *real* faculty. *Real* faculty are "researchers" and "teachers." Indeed, many librarians have carved out areas of research for themselves; here knowledge of library search often helps to overcome the "inferior faculty" complex which has been thrust upon them. But as to teaching, librarians are told they cannot "generate credit hours" from the library even if they choose to do so. Thus they do not own and control their "classes" in the same way that their teaching colleagues do. All too often they come to believe what they are repeatedly told: teaching faculty are the experts on teaching, not library faculty. So if teaching faculty lecture, should not instruction librarians lecture also?

A sensitivity to the students being taught will dictate the answer: an emphatic "no!" As instruction librarians, we have all looked out upon a sea of uncomprehending or disinterested faces as we held up books, showed slides, described the organization of information, and tried to whip up interest with our knowledge and our enthusiasm. But we know it doesn't work! How then can we find out what will be most effective in our classes?

While learning theory is not a panacea, it is a very useful tool. First, it is helpful just to know that there exists a body of knowledge which addresses why and how people learn or do not learn and that theorists are adding daily to this body of knowledge. It provides a place to turn for help in the design and redesign of courses to better serve our students. Second, through the work of specific theorists who speak to the needs and beliefs of instruction librarians, we become aware of the ways in which students learn, their differing needs, and what we, with our personal strengths and limitations, can do to improve our delivery of instruction.

# THE ELEMENTS OF INSTRUCTION

Before discussing some specific theorists and how their theories might contribute to the design and delivery of better bibliographic instruction, it is important to emphasize one point: instruction is an interaction involving at least four elements: the student, the teacher, the content, and the setting. A problem with any one of these single elements can defeat even the most well-designed instruction. While the learning theories presented in this chapter focus primarily on the student, learning theory alone is not enough. It is fine to suggest, as we do, small group work in the reference area, but if the director of your library frowns on noise and activity and sees it as an indication that you are not doing your job—forget it! You will be so nervous looking over your shoulder that your interaction with the students will suffer. If you are uncomfortable in front of a group or by nature somewhat formal, then developing rapport by telling anecdotes from your own library experience is not for you. If a professor insists that twelve reference sources be presented, ten of which are neither current nor readily understandable, clarity and simplicity may not be possible. Remember, you are the teacher and, as such, are a vital element in the teaching-learning situation. It is important to understand your own personal strengths and limitations when developing an instructional program.

In the opening paragraph, we suggest the major problem with content—there is just too much of it! Instruction librarians are faced with the problem of presenting, often in fifty minutes, everything they think students might need to know to successfully retrieve needed information. No wonder they try to pack so much content into so little time! But since the average attention span is only twenty minutes and the degree of retention of new material minimal, we must concentrate on essentials. If there are only one to two things students will be able to remember, what should those things be?

Finally, the setting in which instruction takes place must be considered. Sometimes a simple thing like a room can conquer the best of us. Our experience includes teaching in a long, narrow room originally designed as a conference room. Located on the perimeter of the building, it was an oven in the summer and an icebox in the winter. The desperately unhappy students were doing well to simply sit there a stone's throw away from comfort, let alone learn anything.

Of the four elements present in the learning situation, the one over which the least control can be exercised is the student. For this reason, a basic understanding of how students operate in the learning situation can be very useful. As we are fond of reminding our students, knowledge is power. With a knowledge of learning theory, instructors can acquire power to affect the outcome of teaching. Without it, too much is left to chance.

There is a vast literature on learning theory and its application, dating from the pioneer work of Thorndike, Pavlov, Tolman, and Hull in the first part of the twentieth century. It is beyond the scope of this chapter to present a comprehensive view of learning theory; instead, it provides a discussion of several theories found to be particularly helpful in the design of library instruction.

# LEARNING AS STUDENT BEHAVIOR

Mention behavior modification to a BI librarian and the response might be that she or he would like nothing better than for some students to have library behavior to modify! Theorists, such as Albert Bandura, have recognized the clumsiness of traditional behavior theory which suggests that learning takes place (1) by trial and error (which Bandura feels can be time-consuming and even dangerous in some instances), or (2) by operant conditioning (which presumes the existence of a prior behavior which then can be modified).[1] In addition to these means, Bandura suggests that many people exhibit an ability to learn using modeling, an extraordinarily efficient "no-trial" process. He describes modeling as essentially a performance (either unwitting or intentional), a pattern of behavior which can be imitated. Bandura further suggests that since performance (the modeling behavior) can provide more relevant cues with greater clarity than can be provided with a verbal presentation, the most effective way to introduce a new pattern of behavior is a combination of verbal and demonstrational procedures.

To design bibliographic instruction which presents appropriate models of behavior, librarians must think in terms of the student behavior they wish to elicit. This will encourage them to incorporate into instruction sessions methods of teaching that call for more than rote responses from students. The design of instruction should begin with developing objectives to define just what it is we want our students to do. While the literature on behavioral objectives is both extensive and contradictory, it is important to mention one value objectives bring to instructional planning. They force the instructor to state clearly and simply just what it is the student should be able to do when they have completed the instruction.

To develop objectives for effective student behavior, imagine dividing your students into two groups, one for those who are successful and the other for those who are not. How can you tell them apart? Teachers who become concerned with what their students should be able to do will, predictably, become less concerned with all the things they want them to know. This will help the teachers to sort out the essential behaviors from the interesting facts.

Once objectives have been stated in terms of things students should be able to do (rather than things which instructors will do for them), library situations can be devised to provide opportunities to model the desired behavior. For example, instructors might demonstrate how to search for information in an online catalog, followed by an exercise where students perform the search under the guidance of the instructor. As instruction librarians begin to think in terms of stating and modeling desired behavior, they will become change agents rather than purveyors of content, allowing their students to see and experience how a person functions effectively in the library.

# LEARNERS AS INDIVIDUALS

Several learning theorists share a belief that each individual possesses a unique way of making meaning from her or his environment and experiences. Some theorists, while acknowledging the presence of the unique environment and experience of each individual, use cognitive styles mapping to help identify and address the special way each person learns.

Cognitive styles mapping involves the use of various types of paper and pencil tests to determine the learning styles of individuals. These tests were devised by theorists who claim that, while each student has a relatively unique way of seeking meaning or knowing, his or her learning style shares certain identifiable characteristics with the learning style of others. These theorists have been able to categorize cognitive strengths and weaknesses, a useful tool for teachers who seek to provide a positive and effective learning experience.[2] While cognitive style can be said to be influenced by a person's family background, life experiences, and personal goals, cognitive strengths and weaknesses can be examined using three sets of criteria: (1) the ability to use symbols (words, numbers, senses), (2) the cultural determinants which affect the way a person derives meaning (individuality, associations with peers, family), and (3) the way a person thinks (in categories, through recognizing differences, by synthesizing multiple relationships, or a combination of all three).[3]

Learning theorists who focus on cognitive styles mapping claim that clues to the way people learn can be found through close and careful observation of their sense of self (physical being). Some even maintain that the verbs which people select and use in unguarded speech can reveal whether their primary and favored means of knowing is through sight, speech, or touch. Contrast, for example, the following phrases: "I see what you mean," "I hear you," "I feel you are right." It is from such observations that tests, called cognitive styles maps, have been developed to help determine the ways in which individuals learn.

Most BI librarians do not have the time to carefully observe students coming to their classes or to apply and analyze such tests in order to devise individualized learning experiences based on each individual's cognitive map. What we can gain from cognitive styles mapping theory, however, is a recognition that students process information differently and, therefore, learn differently. Adding overheads and simple, printed instruction sheets to short expository lectures helps both visual and auditory learners process information. Providing hands-on practice at the card catalog helps kinetic and visual learners alike. The more senses that are involved, the greater the opportunity for learners with varying processing modes to learn.

## LEARNING AND THE ABILITY TO REASON

Two developmental theories that are currently receiving increased attention in higher education are Jean Piaget's theory of cognitive development and William Perry's theory of intellectual and ethical development. These two theories are complementary in use.

According to Piaget, individuals progress through sequential stages of cognitive development.[4] There are characteristic patterns of thought and reasoning at each stage with later stages allowing for more complex and more effective thinking and reasoning. While Piaget describes four developmental stages, only the last two, concrete operations and formal operations, are of importance for the development of college courses.

Individuals who function at the stage of concrete operations are capable of logical thought, but only concerning actual objects and situations or objects and situations with which they have had a great deal of direct experience. Formal operations, Piaget's final stage, are the abstract reasoning processes most college instructors expect to find in their students.

While it was once thought that virtually all college students reasoned at the formal level, research consistently indicates that this is not the case. In fact, most studies indicate that one-half or more of the students sampled reason at either the stage of concrete operations or at a transition point between the concrete and formal stages.[5]

Much college coursework requires formal reasoning patterns; therefore, an understanding of how individuals progress from concrete to formal reasoning becomes quite important. While there are several factors involved, Piaget states that a key factor in the progression from one stage to another is the process of self-regulation.[6]

Self-regulation is an active process by which a person seeks to understand some problem situation or new information and to clear up any confusion or contradiction with his or her current thinking caused by this new information or problem. According to Piaget, this process of self-regulation is a fundamental factor in development,[7] and is thus crucial in facilitating movement from concrete to formal reasoning.

William Perry, a Harvard psychologist, described the stages of intellectual and ethical development of students during the college years.[8] While Perry identifies four main stages of development, only the first three (Dualism, Multiplicity, and Relativism), are relevant to our concerns. In describing the movement of students from one stage to another, Perry has adopted the Piagetian concept of self-regulation.

Most college students who reason concretely fall into the Dualistic stage. These students have difficulty understanding the abstract concept that information in many areas is largely theoretical and that there may be many possible explanations or solutions to phenomena or problems. The students at this stage feel that college instructors should tell them the "right" answer or the "correct" approach.

Individuals who are in transition from the concrete to the formal stage often perceive and order knowledge and values in a manner that Perry calls Multiplistic. They have come to realize that their concrete, right/wrong perceptions of the world are no longer adequate, but they are not yet to the point of being able to realistically evaluate another person's point of view.

It is not until most individuals are firmly entrenched within the stage of formal operations that they can move beyond Multiplicity to the stage of Relativism, where they recognize that values are contextual and relative. This is the stage that most college instructors desire, but which, we are told by the followers of Perry, many undergraduates never reach.[9]

These two theories can provide a rational framework for the development of more effective instruction. Basically, they tell us three invaluable things. First, we must consider the level of cognitive/intellectual functioning of our potential audience when designing instruction. Second, instruction must be designed to facilitate movement of that audience from their current stage of functioning to the desired stage. Third, instructional design must take into account the fact that *stages are sequential and cannot be skipped.*

When considering the level of cognitive/intellectual functioning of a prospective audience, class level alone is insufficient. We cannot assume that students beyond the freshman year are formal reasoners nor that they necessarily have progressed beyond the Dualistic stage of intellectual development. Recent research, in fact, indicates a lower level of cognitive/intellectual functioning than was originally thought.[10]

The design of college instruction using both of these theories is quite plausible. In fact, together they provide a more complete and helpful guide than either can provide alone. The application of these theories requires an awareness of the fact that many college students use primarily concrete/Dualistic forms of reasoning and that the college classroom affords an excellent environment for facilitating movement to higher stages of reasoning. This can best be accomplished by actively involving students in examining not only the course content but also their beliefs and reasoning patterns as well. An important step in this development is self-regulation, the realization that current reasoning patterns are inappropriate or incomplete. Through consistent exposure to formal reasoning patterns and alternate and opposing beliefs and viewpoints, students come to recognize that concrete/Dualistic modes of thought are not particularly useful ways to view the world. This realization may be a threatening experience for many students and resistance may be encountered. In order to establish a situation in which self-regulation is possible, the classroom environment must be considered an integral part of instructional design. It is necessary to produce a setting in which students feel comfortable in presenting and testing hypotheses and in expressing their opinions. In this way, instruction librarians can help to facilitate the cognitive and intellectual growth which they so often claim to find lacking in their students.

## LESSONS FROM THE ECLECTIC THEORISTS

Eclecticism, choosing what is considered the best from many sources, allows theorists to build new theories and to develop new approaches by combining and synthesizing the work of others. We have chosen two eclectic learning theories which we have found to be particularly applicable to library instruction: the conceptual work of Robert W. White and the applied research of Knefelkamp and Cornfeld.

Robert W. White, like his Harvard colleague William Perry, did much of his work in the late fifties and early sixties, yet is only now beginning to attract attention.[11] Combining the work of many of the major psychological theorists who preceded him, White developed the concept of motivation through competence. He defined the latter term as "an organism's capacity to interact effectively with its environment." [12] Motivation, White explained, was derived from a feeling of efficacy; this he called "effectance motivation." Effectance motivation involves a feeling of satisfaction as the organism slowly explores, and comes to master, its environment. The importance of White's concept to learning theory is that it provides a new definition of motivation. In essence, it states that natural motivation accompanies the mastery of learning tasks, the motivation being provided by the satisfaction that competence brings to the learner.

White's thesis argues for "small step" learning, presenting a single task and then providing for practice and mastery, rather than presenting the entire array of tasks that comprise the objective. This is particularly important in the library instruction situation where motivation is a major problem. Instruction librarians rarely have access to classic "reinforcement" through the power of the grade. They do, however, have the chance to help students learn, practice, and begin to feel competent at a single aspect of search. Thus they might present the concept of "searching for information in journals" through the mastery of such steps as determining subject headings in a particular index, identifying articles through that index, and retrieving identified articles through the use of the serials holding list (in whatever local form it might take). According to White's theory, the satisfaction the student feels at being comfortable with one aspect of search will provide the motivation to practice and extend these skills.

White was an eclectic theorist who used a conceptual approach to combining and building upon the work of other theorists. Knefelkamp and Cornfeld, on the other hand, demonstrate how theories can be combined to provide guidelines for actual instructional practice.[13] Their attempt to weave several clusters of prominent theories together highlights the difficulty inherent in designing learning environments to match students in differing stages of development. After years of study, Knefelkamp and Cornfeld concluded that it was possible to combine theories of personality type with those of cognitive development and to use this combination to construct specific classroom experiences. These experiences are designed to facilitate cognitive development and to expand the student's behavior repertoire. Knefelkamp and Cornfeld combined the concepts of such researchers as J. L. Holland (personality types) and William Perry with the thoughts of theorists like Nevitt Sanford (who identified the need for a delicate balance of challenge and support in order to produce developmental change) to provide valuable insights into the design of learning environments which address both the personality types and cognitive development of students. Their goals have been twofold: first, to offer ways to make learning tasks accessible to all personality types, and second, to present students with opportunities to perform at increasing levels of complexity, expanding their roles and task repertoires, so that eventually they are willing to select, and have the capacity to complete, a task which exists outside their preferred mode of operation.

Surprisingly, Knefelkamp and Cornfeld report that instructors often design course assignments to fit their own personal preferences in cognitive styles rather than the actual learning styles of their students. To counter this tendency, they suggest that instructors devise a "task matrix," plotting the course's targeted task competencies as well as all of the options available for students to demonstrate those competencies. Their research indicates greater satisfaction on the part of the students involved in courses where such choices exist.

Those of us who wish to incorporate the concepts of these eclectic theorists into the design of our courses must first accept the responsibility for matching learning activities to the cognitive levels of our students. This is not an easy task. Like our teaching colleagues, most bibliographic instructors resist teaching to where our students are, preferring instead to teach to where we think our students should be. In addition to dealing with this particular reality, we must offer options from which students with various learning styles can choose. Each option should allow students an opportunity to demonstrate the assigned learning task at various cognitive levels. Thus students might choose to locate needed information using an assigned tool, selecting an appropriate tool from an assigned list, or identifying the tool of preference on their own.

## SUMMARY

The task of an instruction librarian has never been easy; it is unlikely that technological advancements will change that fact. If anything, technology is likely to make the teaching of information location and retrieval skills more critical to the maintenance, and even advancement, of human society. With all of the problems attendant to such a task, it makes sense to spend time and effort considering the best and most effective ways to teach these survival skills.

An understanding of the various learning theories, such as those we have introduced, can help instruction librarians better plan their courses for maximum efficiency and effectiveness. The benefits of incorporating principles of learning theory into bibliographic instruction will be apparent to the librarian and student alike. The librarian most assuredly will be rewarded by the attention and competency of the students, and the student will, in turn, benefit from the increased ability to control, rather than be controlled by, an information society.

## NOTES

1. Albert Bandura, "Behavioral Modification Through Modeling Procedures," in *Research in Behavior Modification: New Developments and Implications*, ed. Leonard Krasner and Leonard P. Ullman (New York: Holt, Rinehart and Winston, 1965), pp. 310-40.

2. Nathan Kogan, "Creativity and Cognitive Style: A Life Span Perspective," in *Life Span Developmental Psychology: Personality and Socialization*, ed. P. Baltes and K. W. Schaie (New York: Academic Press, 1973).

3. Joseph E. Hill and Derek N. Nunney, *Personalizing Programs Utilizing Cognitive Styles Mapping* (Oakland, Mich.: Oakland Community College, 1971); Jeffrey M. Dimsdale and Leo R. LaJeunesse, *Introduction to Cognitive Styles Mapping* (Costa Mesa, Calif.: Orange Coast Community College, 1975).

4. Jean Piaget, *The Origins of Intelligence in Children* (New York: International University Press, 1952).

5. Clyde A. Parker, "Improving Instruction in Higher Education: Meeting Individual Needs of Students" (Proposal submitted to the Fund for Improvement of Postsecondary Education, Department of Education, Washington, D.C., 1978).

6. A. L. Baldwin, *Theories of Human Development* (New York: John Wiley, 1967); Jean Piaget, "Development and Learning," *Journal of Research in Science Teaching* 2 (1964):176-86.

7. Piaget, "Development and Learning."

8. William G. Perry, *Intellectual and Ethical Development in the College Years: A Scheme* (Cambridge, Mass.: Harvard University Press, 1970).

9. Parker, "Improving Instruction in Higher Education"; C. Widick, "An Evaluation of Developmental Instruction in a University Setting" (Ph.D. diss., University of Minnesota, 1975).

10. Ibid.

11. R. W. White, "Motivation Reconsidered: The Concept of Competence," *Psychological Review* 66 (1959):297-333.

12. Ibid., p. 297.

13. L. Lee Knefelkamp and Janet L. Cornfeld, "Combining Student Stage and Style in the Design of Learning Environments: Using Holland Typologies and Perry Stages" (A presentation to the American College Personnel Association, Los Angeles, March 1979).

# SECTION D

## Increasing Specialization in Bibliographic Instruction

Bibliographic instruction, as pointed out in chapter 5, consists of many levels. It has evolved from the simple tours and orientations with which it began. Instruction librarians now study the organization of knowledge and the patterns of research which underlie disciplines in order to better train users who seek information in those disciplines. The evolution of bibliographic instruction is similar to the evolution of understanding in individual instruction librarians as they begin to grasp the complexities of their task.

In the spring of 1980, when I assumed the responsibility for developing and coordinating the bibliographic instruction program at the University of Tennessee at Chattanooga Library, I thought my world was perfect. I had degrees in both library science and instructional design, my project was funded by a generous grant from a local private foundation, and the bibliographic instruction program was my only responsibility. Like many librarians with limited reference experience, I was what might be called "bibliographically naive." At first, I took on any and all requests for instruction, frequently finding myself in such a tool-and-strategy maze that even the guidance and generosity of such experienced librarians as Marilyn Snow and Neal Coulter (both long-time leaders in reference work at the University of Tennessee at Chattoonga) could barely extract me in time. It was soon clear to me what I knew and what I did not know. And I learned a valuable lesson.

For the next several years, I concentrated my own efforts on the design of a basic bibliographic instruction program integrated into freshman composition. Combining my training in instructional design with the expertise of the reference librarians in specific subject disciplines, we developed an orientation sequence for each discipline in which frequent requests for instruction were received. The reasoning behind this pattern was simple: You must lay adequate groundwork if you want to develop effective library skills in specific disciplines.

The same reasoning applies to the organization of this book. Basic bibliographic instruction, with its attendant concern for attitudes, was addressed earlier as it must be addressed in people and in instruction programs. But concentration on basic methods of search is insufficient for survival in this information-rich society. In chapters 7 and 9, attention was directed to the ways in which researchers seek and use information, ways that may not coincide with what librarians perceive as "right." It is vital for bibliographic instruction librarians to be aware of the information-seeking patterns of researchers in the various disciplines so that they may develop instruction programs tailored to the real needs of students in those disciplines. Chapters 11 through 13 provide insight into the information-seeking behavior of practitioners in various disciplines and the types of library tools that meet their needs.

In chapter 11, Tom Kirk discusses the goals of science education programs in colleges and universities and shows how bibliographic instruction can be designed to aid in the achievement of these goals. The focus of chapter 12 is bibliographic instruction in the social sciences. Anne Beaubien presents three models of literature used by social scientists, and the corresponding types of reference tools appropriate to their research, as a means of highlighting the key characteristics underlying communication and library research in the social sciences. Chapter 13 rounds out the discussion of research in the disciplines, as Maureen Pastine describes the information-seeking behavior of researchers in the humanities and its implications for bibliographic instruction.

The final chapter of this section, chapter 14, is a natural outgrowth of the increasing specialization necessary for comprehensive and effective bibliographic instruction programs. In this chapter, Carolyn Kirkendall discusses the need for cooperation and interaction with our non-library colleagues, suggesting ways in which this outreach might be accomplished.

# 11 The Role of Bibliographic Instruction in Science Education

*Thomas G. Kirk*

University and college science education programs are asked by various segments of our society to accomplish three general goals: (1) to prepare students for further work in science, (2) to prepare students to effectively participate in a scientifically and technologically based society, and (3) to contribute to the liberal arts education of undergraduate students. While the relative importance of these goals varies among faculty and from program to program, the three occur to some degree in all programs. Achievement of these goals depends on the development of programs which address three fundamental areas of program content: (1) transmittal of factual material, (2) development of an understanding of the scientific process, and (3) development of general intellectual skills. Bibliographic instruction to support course activities which use library and information resources helps to achieve these three goals of science education.

A basic understanding of library materials and search strategies has come to be recognized by academic librarians as an essential part of the beginning of college education; however, this is only an initial step toward effective library use. Students must also become familiar with the organization of library information within their own disciplines and with effective search strategies for retrieving the information they need.

In those disciplines where the primary object of study is history or the expression of ideas (the humanities), rather than the study of concrete objects and their interactions (the sciences), the library is often viewed as their laboratory. It is in the library, as well as in museums, that the statements of ideas and the artifacts of history are collected and made available to students of the humanities.[1] Because of this relationship between libraries and the humanities, the student's need for advanced library use skills is readily apparent.

But what is the library's relationship to the sciences? More specifically, what role can teaching information retrieval and the use of libraries play in science education?

## SCIENCE EDUCATION

To fully understand the role of library use and bibliographic instruction in postsecondary science education, it is important to understand the goals of science education itself. Unfortunately, there are nearly as many expressions of these goals as there are science educators. From the abundant literature on the goals of science education, however, at least three general areas of concern can be identified: (1) preparation for later work in science (for example, graduate school or a vocation), (2) contribution to the liberal arts,[2] and (3) preparation for effective participation in our scientifically and technologically based society.[3] These

145

goals are not mutually exclusive and, in many institutions, courses and curriculum are used to serve all three simultaneously. Moreover, the goals have three threads which are part of the fabric of science education.

The first of these threads is the transmittal of the basic vocabulary and concepts of an area of study. While there is considerable debate about how this should be taught and how much is essential, every teacher of science expects students to master a basic vocabulary and set of concepts.[4]

A second thread is the capacity to solve problems, often called the scientific method. Science teachers expect as an outcome of science education that students will be able to develop a logical argument and/or research strategy which will answer a question about a natural phenomenon.[5]

The third thread is what Arons calls "the development, cultivation, and enhancement of intellectual capacities." [6] Arons argues that science education, and education in general, should provide opportunities for students to step back from the specific subject matter and assess why they know what they know and how they know it. In other words, students should develop a sense of their intellectual powers and reasoning processes.

Whether the goals of science education are discussed in an introductory science course, a collateral course for professional preparation, or an advanced course in a discipline, these threads are present. The fabric of science education literature is woven with the threads of how to convey basic subject matter, how to teach problem solving, and how to develop intellectual capacities. It is critical that these cognitive and affective threads be viewed, not as discontinuous strands, but as interwoven aspects of a complete understanding of science education—its content and process. Therefore science education programs in colleges and universities generally attempt to address all three aims.

## BIBLIOGRAPHIC INSTRUCTION IN SCIENCE EDUCATION

A program of bibliographic instruction within the context of a science program provides a method for achieving some of the goals of science education. Such a program is a conscious effort to provide learning experiences which involve the use of the library and information retrieval tools. Critical to such a program is the recognition that use of the bibliographic apparatus requires completion of a complex series of manual and cognitive steps which a student cannot be expected to learn on her or his own. Because libraries and information systems are complex tools, explicit instruction coupled with experience and practice is essential. Without instructional support, the literature use experience may be frustrating, time-consuming, and, in the use of online searching, expensive. The academic program should provide basic instruction in literature searching and opportunities to practice using the literature. There are many examples of such programs described in the literature.[7] The remainder of this paper is a discussion of the essential elements of such programs and ways in which they support the general goals of science education.

Literature use assignments should be coupled with instruction in the techniques *and* processes of using the scientific literature. For such instruction to be effective it should be grounded in the concept of search strategy.[8] Search strategy provides an orderly process for reviewing the scientific literature based on (1) the nature and purpose of literature types (for example, encyclopedias, dictionaries, handbooks, reviews, abstracting and indexing services, and research literature), (2) the relationships among types of literature, and (3) the familiarity of the researcher with the subject. In the initial stages of bibliographic instruction in the sciences, first-year students, because of their lack of broad experience with the scientific literature, should be provided with a specific search strategy which they can follow. Kirk provides an example of a search strategy for biology students in an introductory course which requires a literature research assignment (figure 1).[9] While the strategy specifies some titles, the process and the role of each type of reference source is emphasized in the instruction on library and literature use. This basic strategy can then be generalized in later stages of a bibliographic instruction program (figure 2).

More sophisticated students who have had several different library and literature use experiences can be given instruction on how to design a search strategy for their specific information need (figure 3). Pritchard and Scott provide a detailed discussion of how the advanced student can develop an appropriate strategy for a particular problem. This strategy encompasses mechanisms for decision making based on the three elements of a search strategy choice: the type of information needed, the subject background of the searcher, and the searcher's knowledge of reference sources.[10]

The use of a search strategy and individual tools illustrates, in reverse, the process by which scientific information emerges from research reports, is picked up in reviews, and finally appears in general sources such as encyclopedias and textbooks. Garvey's excellent illustrations of this process can be used as teaching examples.[11] Furthermore, such an explanation and subsequent use demonstrate the usefulness and limitations of each type of material. This is particularly true when students have an opportunity to contrast the general presentation of a subject in a textbook with the incomplete and sometimes conflicting information in the research and review literature.

The process of using the library and scientific literature also teaches science's factual content.[12] Use of the search strategy results in a natural progression from an introduction to the subject at the student's level of background through more advanced study of the research literature at the level required by a particular library use assignment. Each step provides a progressively more detailed explanation of the subject using a more technical vocabulary and assuming a greater background knowledge of the reader.

This opportunity to teach subject matter through library instruction and use is exemplified in a pheromones assignment given in a field biology class. While the professor teaches very little about pheromones in the course, he wants students to be involved in an independent learning situation. Therefore, students are asked to prepare an oral presentation and short paper on pheromones in two species of animals. The first part of the assignment is to read background material on pheromones. Using such resources as the *Oxford Companion to Animal Behavior*, edited by James D. Hart (New York: Oxford University Press, 1982), students find a definition and brief cataloging of the types of pheromones and the ways in which they function in animal communication. Follow-up of encyclopedia use with texts, such as *How Animals Communicate*, edited by Thomas A. Sebeok (Bloomington, Ind.: Indiana University Press, 1977),

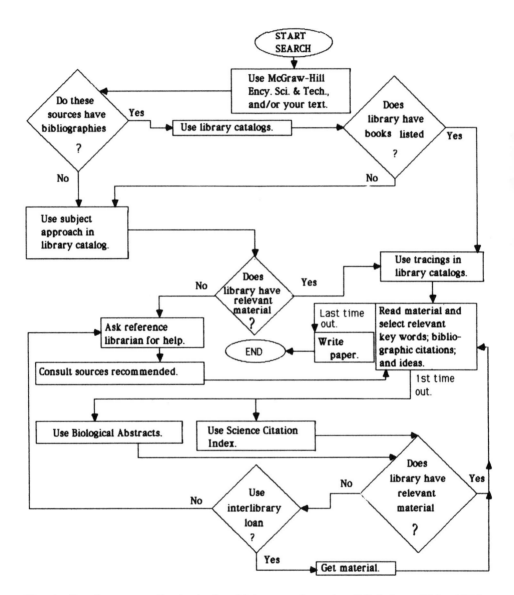

Fig. 1. Search strategy for beginning biology students (modified from Kirk, 1974). Reprinted with permission from *Educating the Library User*, by John Lubans, Jr. Published by R. R. Bowker, Division of Reed Publishing, USA. © 1974 by Reed Publishing USA, a division of Reed Holdings, Inc. All rights reserved.

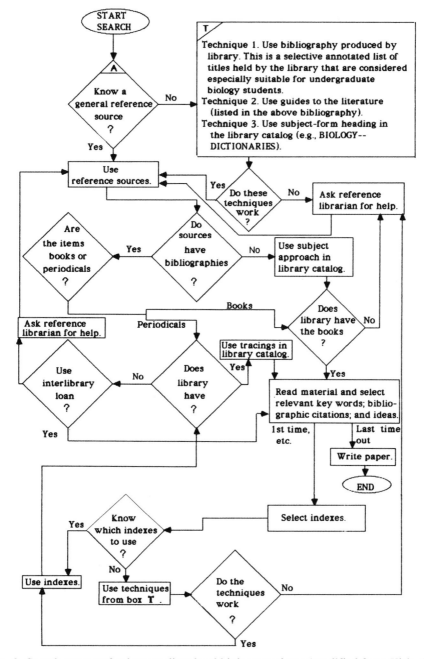

Fig. 2. Search strategy for intermediate level biology students (modified from Kirk, 1974). Reprinted with permission from *Educating the Library User*, by John Lubans, Jr. Published by R. R. Bowker, Division of Reed Publishing, USA. © 1974 by Reed Publishing USA, a division of Reed Holdings, Inc. All rights reserved.

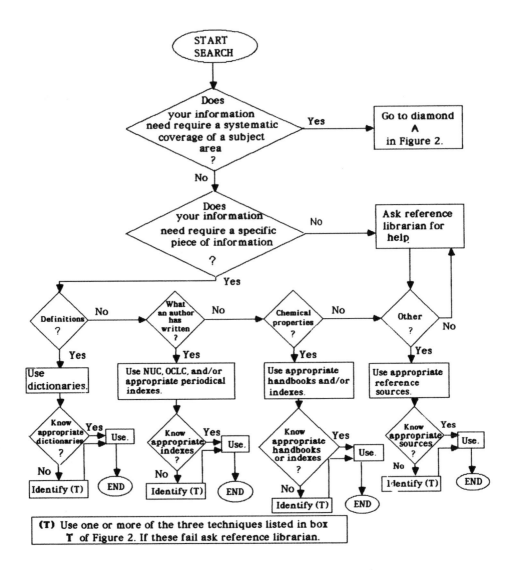

Fig. 3. Search strategy for advanced biology students (modified from Kirk, 1974). Reprinted with permission from *Educating the Library User*, by John Lubans, Jr. Published by R. R. Bowker, Division of Reed Publishing, USA. © 1974 by Reed Publishing USA, a division of Reed Holdings, Inc. All rights reserved.

provides an extensive listing and brief description of research on pheromones in specific species. Such texts serve as a springboard to the research literature. By now the student not only has bibliographic leads to the research literature but has been introduced to the terminology and concepts associated with the study of pheromones. This background prepares the student to find and understand the research literature.

It should be stressed, however, that there are limits to the usefulness of the library and literature use approach to learning a subject. Because such an approach is largely experiential, it requires significant amounts of time for students to complete a project. In addition, subject access to scientific literature may not be organized to meet the students' needs. In fact, it is this characteristic that gave rise to the textbook as a class of scientific literature. Therefore, use of the library and the scientific literature cannot be an effective substitute for the textbook, the lecture, and the demonstration laboratory as primary conveyers of broad subject content. However, for activities that focus on the details of specific subject areas and that are directed at the goal of teaching science as a process, library use based on a search strategy is an effective means to convey subject matter.

In a program of science education, library and literature use assignments should be either problem-solving tasks[13] or background literature searching needed to design a research project.[14] Problem solving creates a situation in which the student must actively engage with the subject matter in order to prepare a synthesis of the conflicting and/or incomplete information found in the scientific literature. The value of problem solving is illustrated by contrasting two types of library assignments. In the first, students are given an assignment requiring them to write on a topic which is an extension of some aspect of the course. The topic may be assigned by the teacher or, more frequently, the students are free to choose their own topic. Usually such an assignment can be done using a minimal set of sources such as texts and encyclopedias. Where use of journal articles occurs as a required part of the assignment, the articles are generally used to provide examples of the phenomena being studied. In the papers or presentations the students prepare, information which has been gathered from these sources is merely assembled and summarized. The teacher is often disappointed with the results of such an assignment because the students do not seem engaged in the subject and have provided no synthesis.

In the second type of assignment, students are asked to solve a problem based on the information they find in the literature. An example of this is provided by the following assignment in an introductory organic chemistry course. Toward the end of the semester, students are asked to propose, on paper, a reaction sequence to get from one compound to another and back to the original compound. The professor specifies the end product which has a carbon-14 marker. The students must design the synthesis starting with a simple carbon-14 marked compound and using their knowledge of type reactions, which they have studied extensively. Having proposed the reaction sequence based on their knowledge, the students must document that each reaction is not just theoretically feasible but actually has been carried out. They do this through searching the chemical literature for a description of each reaction. This assignment effectively combines the application of course material with the use of the library. In the process, students get experience with one of the common information problems of the chemist; namely, finding procedures for producing a specific compound in the laboratory. But most important, the assignment is a problem begging a solution—it requires the students to do more than merely collect and assemble.

Engagement with the subject matter can be particularly effective at illustrating the process of science if the literature contains no resolution of the problem. For example, students in an animal behavior class might be asked to discuss the phenomena of navigation or orientation in an organism group. Such an assignment can be done by assembling information from a series of sources with little integration or synthesis of ideas.

In contrast, the class might be given a series of questions (one for each student), such as "What is the evidence that landmarks assist warbler navigation during fall and spring migration? How does the role of landmarks compare in significance with sunlight as the primary mode of navigation?" Such an assignment requires the student to read the research literature in warbler navigation specifically and bird navigation generally to understand the evidence. Because the literature is filled with several alternative models of the navigation mechanism, often based on the study of different species of birds, a satisfactory response to the questions must be a synthesis. While this type of assignment engages students in the subject matter, it also requires greater engagement in the search process. Students with a specific question to answer can no longer look for information on a topic; they must find material which helps them answer the question. Thus, their research is directed and purposeful.

Using the library and the scientific literature to provide problem-solving tasks for students is an excellent example of how students can experience the process of science.[15] When the student is asked to answer a question, particularly one for which there is no consensus in the scientific community, he or she is placed in the context of scientific investigation. In that context, the student is required to sort out basic assumptions and the basis for the researchers' conclusions. Since that must be done for a body of literature published over some span of time, students can see the evolution of the accepted model of a phenomena. In the case of a phenomena for which there is no consensus, students can see how several models based on different research results exist simultaneously and can see the assumptions upon which they are based. This kind of library use and bibliographic instruction provides an opportunity for students to engage in the basic intellectual activities which Arons has suggested are an important contribution by science education to the general education of students.

Evaluation of a student's work on such assignments should include not only an assessment of the subject content and the effectiveness of the student's writing, but also an evaluation of the reasoning process and the use of the scientific literature. For a program of literature searching and library use instruction to be effective, students must be held accountable for the quality of their search and the bibliography which supports their assignment.[16] This can be accomplished easily, either by requesting that each student turn in a search diary for evaluation,[17] or by incorporating the content of the bibliography and its utilization into the grade for the assignment.[18]

Bibliographic instruction, use of the library and information resources, and problem solving/research form a triumvirate of activities. It is possible, in fact common, to create an assignment using only one or two of the activities. For example, students might be asked to prepare a research design based on selected articles already identified for them; students may be assigned the task of researching a topic with no need to resolve a problem; or students might be given instruction in the use of such library reference tools as *Chemical Abstracts* with no immediate follow-up assignment. However, the synergism of all three activities provides the best example of the scientific process and thus has the greatest potential for achieving the goals of science education: teaching content, teaching the use of scientific methods, and developing an understanding of the basic assumptions of science.

## CONCLUSION

This chapter has developed an argument for bibliographic instruction's supportive role in achieving the goals of postsecondary science education. This argument is based largely on the qualities of the scientific literature, the literature's representation of the scientific process, and the reflection of these qualities and processes in the search strategies taught and practiced in a bibliographic instruction program. Furthermore, library use is an important technique in the repertoire of the practicing scientist. For these reasons, bibliographic instruction should have an important place in undergraduate science education.

## NOTES

1.   Anne K. Beaubien, Sharon A. Hogan, and Mary W. George, "The Research Process in the Humanities," in *Learning the Library: Concepts and Methods for Effective Bibliographic Instruction* (New York: R. R. Bowker, 1982), pp. 109-23; A. R. Rogers, *The Humanities: A Selective Guide to Information Sources*, 2d ed. (Littleton, Colo.: Libraries Unlimited, 1979).

2.   Arnold B. Arons, "Education Through Science," *Journal of College Science Teaching* 13 (February 1984):210-20.

3.   Thomas R. Mertens, "Scientific Literacy and Support for Science Education," *Bioscience* 33 (March 1983):155.

4.   David Butts, "Science Education," in *Encyclopedia of Educational Research*, 5th ed., ed. Harold E. Mitzel (New York: The Free Press, 1982), pp. 1665-75.

5.   National Science Teachers Association, "NSTA Position on Curriculum," *Science Teacher* 29 (December 1962):32.

6.   Arons, "Education Through Science," p. 210.

7.   Scott D. Hawke, "Liberal Arts and the Biology Seminar Experience," *Journal of College Science Teaching* 13 (November 1983):88-90; David Johnson, Susan V. Emerson, and Sharon W. Schwerzel, "Using Bibliographic Instruction to Improve Research Paper Quality," *Fisheries* 7 (October 1982):14-17; Thomas

G. Kirk, *The Development of Course Related Library and Literature Use Instruction in Undergraduate Science Programs* (Richmond, Ind.: Earlham College, Wildman Science Library, 1977); Thomas G. Kirk, *Course-Related Library and Literature-Use Instruction: Working Models for Programs in Undergraduate Science Education* (New York: Jeffrey Norton, 1978); Hannelore B. Rader, "Bibliographic Instruction Programs in Academic Libraries," in *Increasing the Teaching Role of Academic Libraries*, ed. Thomas G. Kirk (San Francisco: Jossey-Bass, 1984), pp. 63-78; Ester Williams, "Introduction to Science Literature: A Library Assignment for General Biology Students," *Research Strategies* 2 (Spring 1984):65-70.

8.   Thomas G. Kirk, "Problems in Library Instruction in Four-Year Colleges," in *Educating the Library User*, ed. John Lubans, Jr. (New York: R. R. Bowker, 1974), pp. 83-103; Kirk, *Course-Related Library and Literature-Use Instruction*, p. 14. Eileen Pritchard and Paula R. Scott, "Formulating a Basic Search Strategy," *Literature Searching in Science, Technology, and Agriculture* (Westport, Conn.: Greenwood Press, 1984); Thomas G. Kirk, "The Role of the Library in an Investigative Laboratory," in *The Laboratory: A Place to Investigate*, ed. John W. Thornton (Washington, D.C.: Commission of Undergraduate Education in the Biological Sciences, 1972), pp. 122-32.

9.   Kirk, "Problems in Library Instruction," pp. 93-95.

10.   Pritchard and Scott, "Formulating a Basic Search Strategy," pp. 6-15.

11.   William D. Garvey, "Scientific Communication: Its Role in the Conduct of Research and Creation of Knowledge," *American Psychologist* 26 (April 1971):349-62; William D. Garvey, *Communication, the Essence of Science: Facilitating Information Exchange Among Librarians, Scientists, Engineers, and Students* (Elmsford, N.Y.: Pergamon Press, 1979).

12.   Constance R. Miller, "Scientific Literature as Hierarchy: Library Instruction and Robert M. Gage," *College & Research Libraries* 43 (September 1982):385-90.

13.   Jerome H. Woolpy, "Information Retrieval for Introductory Science Courses," *American Biology Teacher* 39 (March 1977):162-64, 171.

14.   Kirk, "The Role of the Library in an Investigative Laboratory," pp. 122-32.

15.   Ibid., pp. 122-23.

16.   Assignment, the more general term, is deliberately used instead of "term paper" or "research report" because there are many types of assignments that might be used as the basis for library and literature use instruction. For a discussion of some examples, see Evan I. Farber, "Alternatives to the Term Paper," in *Increasing the Teaching Role of Academic Libraries*, ed. Thomas G. Kirk (San Francisco: Jossey-Bass, 1984), pp. 45-53.

17.    Thomas G. Kirk, "Problems in Library Instruction in Four-Year Colleges," in *Evaluating Library Use Instruction*, ed. Richard J. Beeler (Ann Arbor, Mich.: Pierian Press, 1975), pp. 1-30.

18.    Amy Dykeman and Barbara King, "Term Paper Analysis: A Proposal for Evaluating Bibliographic Instruction," *Research Strategies* 1 (Winter 1983):14-21.

# 12  Bibliographic Instruction in the Social Sciences: Three Models

*Anne K. Beaubien*

Bibliographic instruction librarians have shifted their approach several times since the early 1970s. The shift has been one of emphasis, moving away from drills on how to find and decipher certain types of information toward more generalized logic and problem solving. Where once librarians designed lessons around skills or specific titles, they are now more likely to concentrate on search strategies or the concepts that surround library research and the choice of tools. Clearly this inclination to explain theory and structure is appropriate for bibliographic instruction aimed at specialists in any field, whether undergraduate majors or faculty.

The purpose of this chapter is to help librarians spot the key characteristics underlying communication and library research in the social sciences. Focusing on selected disciplines, this essay will offer three different models of literature use by social scientists and the corresponding types of reference tools which exist to complement and control that literature. From these models readers can extrapolate to other fields as they design specialized bibliographic instruction for their more advanced clientele.

## SOURCES, LITERATURE, AND TOOLS

Every discipline relies on a unique combination of sources, in terms of the relative importance of primary versus secondary materials and the nature of the materials themselves. Insofar as sources are in written form, this unique combination is referred to as the structure of the discipline's literature. Obviously the distinctive structure of any field's literature will have a major impact on appropriate search strategies and consequently on bibliographic instruction.

It is critical for anyone attempting specialized BI to grasp the contours of the literature structure of specific disciplines. Specialists themselves, ironically, are rarely good informants in such matters since they are too close to the creation and flow of new knowledge in their field. Undergraduate majors seldom understand the dynamics of thought and experiment that led to or from the "classics." Doctoral students live in an almost surreal world bounded by their own research with little time to reflect upon the development of their field as a whole.

How, then, can anyone who is not a subject specialist go about exploring the structure of the literature in any of the social sciences? Some answers are: (1) by observation, noting such features as whether eyewitness accounts and original data or documents are prevalent in the field; (2) noting if it is necessary to see all the experimenter's notes or each individual survey response or if summary reports or statistical analyses are sufficient; and (3) observing to what extent new findings are published in journals, which journals, and how quickly. These are examples of an infinite number of possible considerations that bear on the origin and characteristics of the sources, which specialists all too often take for granted. Notice too what sorts of finding tools are available to cumulate and organize this knowledge. Is there a comprehensive periodical index and when did it start? How prevalent are bibliographies? Are there many dictionaries and handbooks and other fact books? If one can describe the structure of the literature to others and how that structure relates to the corresponding reference tool structure, one can tap the resources of the library effectively.

A caution about reference tools—those that exist for one discipline may, for perfectly good reasons, not exist at all, or exist in an outdated form, for another discipline. Similarly, the order in which practitioners consult fact and finding tools varies radically depending on the discipline involved.[1] All veteran reference librarians are at least subliminally aware of these structures, but understanding them becomes crucial when trying to improve them. As someone preparing subject-specific bibliographic instruction to assess the tools for the field, it is the job of the reference librarian to know where the "holes" exist in the printed and online reference works, and to meld this knowledge into coherent presentations to convince the audience that a systematic approach to the library is more thorough and efficient and will help them become better library researchers.

The following disciplines are ordinarily termed social sciences: anthropology, economics, education, geography, political science, psychology, and sociology. In addition, the professional fields of social work, law, and business administration all share some point in common with the social sciences. History exhibits characteristics of both the social sciences and the humanities and is therefore really neither, deserving a separate treatment because of its hybrid nature. Owing to space limitations, it is not possible to discuss all of these disciplines, so four have been chosen to illustrate three distinct models or research approaches.

Psychology exemplifies those social science disciplines, largely dependent on traditional published sources, where current information is of greatest interest. Anthropology represents a field where older literature is often just as valuable as more current sources. The third model, typified by both geography and political science, involves special formats of materials: geography is dominated by maps, while political science relies on a wide variety of "old" materials such as statistics, opinion polls, census tapes, and local ordinances. This chapter will discuss these three models in terms of the characteristics of the literature, most important types of tools, less important types of tools, tools that don't exist, special physical formats, and a typical search strategy sequence. The remaining social sciences generally follow one of these models, so that by comparing them with these models, the reference librarian can readily identify the salient features to highlight in specialized user education.

## ASSUMPTIONS AND TOPICS FOR ANY SOCIAL SCIENCE BI

The suggestions below assume that members of the BI audience are already comfortable with the basic layout of the library, and with its particular services, procedures, and policies. Furthermore, they should have mastered such fundamental concepts as the distinction between primary and secondary sources in general, the nature of each common type of fact and finding tool, the essentials of the library's catalog, and the specifics of a few key titles such as the *Readers' Guide*. In other words, both library orientation and "elementary" — which is not to say easy — BI are taken for granted in what follows. Also taken for granted is a basic familiarity with the nature and content of the discipline, the background one would expect, say, of a junior or senior beginning to concentrate in the field. Without at least that much previous exposure to the principles and landmarks in the discipline, subject-specific library instruction will baffle rather than excite.

Among the most important topics to communicate in any specialized bibliographic instruction are concepts such as:

1. Question analysis: how to break down a social science research question into its component parts; things a person can do before coming to the library in order to make the best use of time in the library.

2. Nature and importance of both primary and secondary sources to the field.

3. Growth of the literature: what sorts of primary and secondary sources appear, at what rate, produced by whom, and what tools exist to control that literature?

4. Bibliographic structure of the discipline: with emphasis on the age of tools, who compiles/publishes them, and the "missing tools."

5. Search strategy: how to exploit the library in a particular field of study. What should be the logical order in which to consult reference materials? When should one go to the card catalog first and when to periodical indexes first, and why.

6. Indexing: concept of an index, difference between controlled vocabulary and key word indexing, prevalence of online databases in the discipline.

7. Other possible topics (depending on what is appropriate in a given discipline) include:
   (a) the role of experts
   (b) importance of outside funding
   (c) group projects
   (d) place of professional meetings
   (e) political incentives or constraints on research and publication
   (f) international interest in the field and foreign language and travel concerns
   (g) crossover between academe and public/private sectors by active scholars
   (h) theoretical versus applied emphasis
   (i) ethics of research and secrecy of findings
   (j) training patterns of new people in the field.

None of these topics will succeed, however, unless each point made can be tied to specific cases in the field in question. The discussions which follow are intended to assist the bibliographic instruction librarian in selecting appropriate ideas to concentrate on in any social science instruction.

## MODEL 1: PSYCHOLOGY

Psychology, the study of behavior and experience, is very much like the physical sciences in that currency of information is very important. Therefore, recent journal articles and conference proceedings are critical, while material appearing in books, because it is older, is less so. When teaching a group of psychology students, a discussion of periodical indexes is essential so that they can have access to the most important literature in their field.

If the library is small and/or the students are not very knowledgeable about the library, the *Social Sciences Index* may meet their needs; however, in many cases introduction to *Psychological Abstracts* (including its *Thesaurus*) will be a natural choice. The librarian could demonstrate how controlled vocabulary puts similar things together, in contrast to key word indexing. While the key word approach to subject searching cannot replace the controlled vocabulary of *Psychological Abstracts*, citation indexes are invaluable, especially in new areas of psychology where jargon first appears in the titles of recent journal articles. Furthermore, when students need to know if current journal articles include a specific reference, citation indexes are the only way to solve the research problem. Almost an hour can be spent fully explaining the *Social Sciences Citation Index*; if the group is advanced, doing so may be appropriate.

It is interesting to note that the primary indexing tool in psychology is compiled and published by the American Psychological Association. Recognizing that it is important to be able to identify quickly current psychology articles, they devote some of their own resources to this goal. The time lag between publication of journal articles and their listing in *Psychological Abstracts* is relatively short, averaging six months to a year. *Psychological Abstracts* is fairly comprehensive because it includes all subdisciplines of psychology as well as some foreign literature and U.S. dissertations. It covers the field so well that there is almost total overlap between its citations on a topic and those listed in indexes covering one subdiscipline, such as *Child Development Abstracts*. The hit rate for additional citations beyond *Psychological Abstracts* is low using *Child Development Abstracts*. However, students should realize that for some topics the indexes for related disciplines, such as sociology and education, should be considered. In psychiatry, one must check both *Psychological Abstracts* and *Index Medicus* for complete coverage.

There is a good annual review for psychology extending back into the 1950s (*Annual Review of Psychology*). This is an excellent place to start a search of literature in order to discover the significant chain of research in a particular area. Chapters in the *Annual Review* identify journal articles reporting new developments in an area. Other than review articles, psychologists usually do not create bibliographies because they take a long time to compile and of necessity, include older materials that may no longer be relevant. Therefore, there is little point in looking for subject bibliographies in the library unless the development of a concept over time is important, or if the researcher wants a historical viewpoint. Unlike other social sciences, psychology can boast several encyclopedias which are relatively comprehensive and current plus a few basic dictionaries.[2]

Biographical sources are not very important in psychology; ideas are of more interest than tracking down extensive information about an author. Because monographs tend to be older, they are seen as less useful sources. It follows, too, that book reviews are not something students of psychology often need to find. Special physical formats that should be covered include psychological tests and survey data.

It takes fewer contact hours to explain research in psychology than in fields such as anthropology for two reasons: (1) there is such good bibliographic control, and (2) fewer formats of source material (for example, journal articles, books, and dissertations) are useful than in other fields. A typical search strategy in psychology works from the general to the specific. Steps include defining the topic (encyclopedia), checking for cumulated research on the topic (annual review), creating a specialized bibliography (indexes and abstracts in all relevant fields), using the citation index to identify more recent work based on relevant citations found to this point, and searching for special formats of materials that may be appropriate (psychological tests, opinion polls, book reviews, and biographical material).[3]

# MODEL 2: ANTHROPOLOGY

Anthropology is the study of human cultures, as they reflect universal "truths" about man and as they exhibit unique features. Anthropology is akin to the humanities in that emphasis is placed on historical versus current information; older materials are just as likely to be relevant as newer ones. Conclusions drawn 100 years ago about a society are often still valid today. Thus, it is appropriate for a library search strategy to include older as well as current materials. Books and journal articles are of more equal value in anthropology than they are in psychology. Also diaries, interviews, and other first-hand accounts of a culture's customs and mores can yield valuable information.

Bibliographies proliferate in anthropology and are key to effectively approaching the literature written before 1970. Books, of course, can also be found through the card (or online) catalog, so a discussion of subject headings and their application in the library will always be appropriate. Probably the best compilation of bibliographies is the *Annual Review of Anthropology*, which was begun in 1972 (preceded by the *Biennial Review of Anthropology* for the period 1959-71). Because bibliographies are important, it is necessary to discuss with students strategies for locating them in the library, strategies such as using the annual reviews, *Bibliographic Index*, and catalog subject headings. In addition to many separately published bibliographies on specific topics, the catalogs of major anthropology collections have been published: the Peabody Museum of Anthropology at Harvard, the Pan American Union, the National Anthropological Archives, and the Edward Ayer Collection of the Newberry

Library in Chicago. Some of these have analytics for journal articles and chapters in books.

Access to periodical literature was very difficult up until 1970 because there were few anthropology indexes or abstracts. The indexing situation has improved over the past twenty years with the advent of periodical indexes devoted entirely to anthropology. However, the indexing that does exist is splintered, being sponsored by a variety of agencies: the library of the Royal Anthropological Institute, Harvard Peabody Museum of Anthropology, *Bulletin Signaletique*, and Baywood Publishing Company. This situation leads to a lack of consistency among the indexes, which are not completely satisfactory since some do not cumulate, some have no subject approach, and none are comprehensive. Furthermore, *Anthropological Literature* has been available only on microfiche since 1983. Explaining these points to students will help them understand why several indexes exist, and will enable them to better choose an index for their needs. Where currency of information is important, indexes such as the *Social Sciences Citation Index* along with the *Social Sciences Index* should be viable alternatives. *Social Sciences and Humanities Index* (and the *International Index*) can be used effectively to locate "mainstream" anthropological journal articles prior to 1970.

Like many of the other social sciences, anthropology lacks a comprehensive encyclopedia in English. The way in which scholars do research in anthropology does not demand one. Students must go instead to the more general *International Encyclopedia of the Social Sciences*. Handbooks (such as the *Handbook of North American Indians*) and dictionaries are important for the study of culture and language. Anthropological research is more likely to be focused on a culture or a geographical area than on an individual so that other fact books, such as biographical directories, are relatively unimportant.

Cross-cultural research is critical in anthropology and the specialized "tool-and-source-in-one," to satisfy that need is the Human Relations Area Files (HRAF). The HRAF files enable students to do cross-cultural research in a way that is not possible with any other method. Being able to take a specific custom, find the code for it, and go directly to source materials describing that custom in several cultures saves the many hours of work required to do the same thing using traditional library approaches. HRAF can also provide a good introduction to microforms if that is how the file is available in a particular library. Depending on the nature of the group and their research projects, the BI librarian could spend an entire hour discussing HRAF, what it includes, and how to use it.

A typical search strategy in anthropology for secondary literature can start with the *International Encyclopedia of the Social Sciences* for general topic definition, *Annual Review of Anthropology* for a review article, bibliographies through the catalog and *Bibliographic Index*, anthropological journal indexes and abstracts, various G. K. Hall catalogs, and HRAF. For primary literature, there is no strategy but several things to be done in any order, such as checking the catalog, the library's manuscript collection, guides to manuscript source materials, and so on. Each topic's search strategy is different, depending on the type of literature required.

## MODEL 3: GEOGRAPHY AND POLITICAL SCIENCE

Geography is a social science focusing upon how human societies deal with use of space/land. Interdisciplinary study for geography could include economics, politics, history, or anthropology as well as natural sciences such as geology, ecology or environment. As White states, "three characteristics tend to distinguish it [geography] from other social sciences: its concern for spatial arrangements, regional or areal complexes, and man-nature relationships." [4] Geography and political science are examples of social sciences where the library research is based on special formats of materials (for example, maps, gazetteers, and public opinion polls) and "library search strategy" in geography may consist simply of locating maps or place names. Compared with other disciplines, traditional formats of materials, such as books and journal articles, are of relatively minor interest to researchers in some areas of research. Because of the unique interest in land, special formats of materials such as maps, atlases, gazetteers, and photographs are more important to students of geography.

It may be more appropriate to spend an hour of BI on maps than on how to locate periodical articles in geography. Students should learn that maps vary widely in purpose. Thematic maps show demographic patterns, agriculture of an area, linguistics, or geology. Topographic maps show terrain. Political maps show the ownership of land by various governments. Planometric maps reflect outlines, either political or natural. Historical maps show an area as it once was. Census maps show fascinating demographic information. Some maps show economics and other factual data. Not surprisingly, the chief producers of maps are government agencies.

It is important to point out to students that not all areas of the world have been mapped equally; some have been mapped often and in great detail, while others have never been mapped at all. Also, the frequency with which maps are updated varies widely. Places that are relatively important and urban areas tend to be heavily mapped, with revisions every few years; remote and/or underdeveloped areas may not have been mapped at all unless the area has military significance.

Although maps are vital for geography, historically they have *not* been individually cataloged in libraries. Maps are, in a sense, like journal articles — the library has a lot of them, but they are not individually listed in the catalog. One must rely on other finding tools (for example, an index) to identify specific maps. Just as journal titles only are listed in the card (or online) catalog, only the names of whole sets of maps may be listed in the catalog.

Since atlases have indexes to the maps they contain, their value is increased. There is as great a variety of types of atlases as there are different types of individual sheet maps. Because of the importance of atlases and their continued usefulness over time, bibliographies of sheet maps are prevalent. Many people are unaware of the map holdings of any library or how to identify maps within a map collection, so these points need emphasis.

Geography is a well-indexed field through *Geo Abstracts*, which not only has many subfield divisions (for example, economic geography and regional and community planning), but extends back to the mid-1960s in paper format and to the 1940s online. Thus, access to journal literature is not difficult. In addition, there are many traditional bibliographies as well as some relevant G. K. Hall catalogs of significant geography collections.

Fact tools are important for geography research. Gazetteers are important not only for identifying place names, but also for giving their coordinates. Dictionaries are useful to determine the meanings of geographic terms. Cartographic handbooks help with map interpretation or assist students who need to know how to calculate the curvature of an area, since math tables and calculations are often included. Directories of map collections are useful to identify possible other locations of needed cartographic resources.

Political science is the study of the politics or government of a society. Political science research often requires many formats of information that do not necessarily fall into any logical sequence or strategy to be followed in the library. It is more a matter of identifying the type of information required (for example, maps, census tapes, or government documents), and then determining how to locate that particular format of information in the library.

Political scientists are as likely to need fact tools (directories and handbooks) as they are to need finding tools (indexes and bibliographies). Political scientists in any given academic environment may be literature-oriented, or they may be more inclined toward computer analysis of data about a country or group of people. If political scientists have a "number crunching" approach, they will most likely be interested in locating long runs of statistical works, abstracts and annuals, as well as census figures for various countries. These figures will be entered in a computer and manipulated to help the political scientists identify past trends and make future predictions. If they are literature-oriented (for example, in political philosophy), researchers will need a wider range of materials than do many other social scientists. In addition to the traditional journal articles, conference papers, and books, they must locate primary source materials, such as newspaper articles and government documents (local, state, national, foreign, and international); maps (mostly those showing political boundaries); diaries and letters; transcripts of speeches; and perhaps videotapes or other audiovisual formats. It is important to know the orientation of the political science department before planning a BI session.

Since the needs of political scientists are not uniform, it may explain why there are so few finding tools in political science. For example, there is no encyclopedia nor any general annual review of the literature (just a few specialized reviews, like *International Review of Administrative Science* [1928- ]). Bibliographies have been compiled to compensate for the lack of comprehensive indexes extending back in time. Indexes to periodical literature are focused, but none provide comprehensive control of the literature as do indexes in other fields, such as psychology, chemistry, or medicine. *United States Political Science Documents* (1975- ) focuses on the United States. *International Political Science Abstracts* (1951- ) is not comprehensive for any country and has a significant time lag. *PAIS: Public Affairs Information Service Bulletin*, good for social issues, goes back to 1913; it indexes things quickly and includes government documents (selected U.S., state, local, and United Nations) and reports as well as journal articles. *C.R.I.S.: The Combined Retrospective Index Set to Journals in Political Science, 1866-1974*, was published recently by Carrollton Press and provides a key word approach to articles published in periodicals back to 1866.

Because of the variety of formats of information and reference materials available in political science, it is important to consider the needs of the group for whom the instruction is intended. Biographical directories are useful for gaining information about political leaders, and handbooks provide basic facts about countries, states, or local areas. Government documents are essential: U.S., regional, state, local, UN, transnational (for example, EEC), international agency, or foreign country. For example, students studying lobbying efforts concerning the quality of the environment should have access to testimony in U.S. congressional and state legislative hearings on bills relating to this topic. If students are interested in wars between nations or international treaties, they should access foreign documents, UN, and international agency publications. British Parliamentary Papers or similar documents from other countries could provide valuable insights for some students. Census data are important to track socioeconomic characteristics of a city or metropolitan area; *Current Population Reports* are significant sources of socioeconomic information between the decennial censuses. If tapes of the census data are available on campus, access to those tapes should be described. At the University of Michigan, researchers at the International Consortium for Political Science Research possess a variety of data in machine-readable form for distribution to over 500 institutional members worldwide. As of 1986, they have approximately 1200 data files available; some are government-produced data (for example, census tapes), some are data resulting from social science research or surveys on attitudes, opinion polls, and the like. Those studying the effectiveness of citizen opposition to local ordinances and zoning will need to know how to approach local records.

If political scientists take a historical perspective about changing political boundaries, learning about maps and atlases will be invaluable. People will be interested in the various types of quick information that can be found in a handbook, information such as land area, picture of the flag, copy of the constitution (or equivalent), and government structure. Handbooks also include the political leaders elected or appointed to each country each year. Newspapers are important for current events, to track the names of top officials if they change frequently over a given year, or to locate names before the handbook is updated. News services, such as the *African Recorder*, report major news items in foreign countries and events of international significance in a current, loose-leaf format. These news summaries are helpful for libraries which cannot afford foreign newspapers. Formats such as microfilm or computer databases may be introduced if the only way particular types of information or documents are stored in the library (or on campus) is through some sort of "non-traditional" means.

What should be obvious here is that there is no particular search strategy for political science. The key to approaching the library in this discipline is to determine what kind of data is needed and then look for it. That is, if students need journal articles, show them indexes; if they need census data, show them the census and/or explain how to get its tapes; if they need government documents, show them the government documents room or explain how to find documents in the library. (It is comforting for students to know that, in some cases, there is no strategy or more effective order in which to approach the library!)

## STRATEGIES

When planning for bibliographic instruction in the social sciences, it is useful to look at the sources students are learning about in order to ascertain what they already know about the structure of the discipline. Then consult a guide to the literature; what reference tools exist in that field to control the literature? Why? What is the array of source materials in the library for that discipline and how does it relate to the array of reference books in the field? The explanation provided to researchers about why specific reference tools exist in their field and how to manipulate these tools effectively should be the basis for library instruction. Good places to start are Sheehy's *Guide to Reference Books* and the *International Encyclopedia of Higher Education*. The latter has articles on various disciplines which discuss how scholars communicate in that field, and lists specific guides to the literature in that discipline, as well as major journals and current bibliographies.

Articles about library instruction in a given social science can be located through usual sources such as ERIC and *Library Literature*. A good source for current articles on user education is the bibliography edited by Hannelore Rader in the summer issue of *Reference Services Review*, and which is reprinted in the LOEX Conference volumes published annually by Pierian Press.[5] At the American Library Association conferences, there is much to learn from ACRL Bibliographic Instruction Section committees and in meetings of the Library Instruction Round Table. Both groups provide opportunities to meet others actively involved in user education. Also consider establishing contact with both subject-oriented groups within ALA, such as the "type-of-activity" sections in ACRL (for example, law and political science), and pedagogically oriented groups within national discipline associations. Discussing ideas with those already doing bibliographic instruction in the social sciences is one of the best ways to test ideas, share them, and gain new ones.

## NOTES

1.   Fact tools are reference works which researchers consult (usually briefly) with specific factual questions in mind, and which yield a fairly discrete answer. Examples include dictionaries, directories, and statistical compendia. Finding tools do not give information directly, as do fact tools, but instead lead the researcher to sources of information in other pieces, such as in a book or journal article. Indexes, bibliographies, and catalogs are all finding tools in this sense.

2.   H. J. Eysenck, W. Arnold, and R. Meil, eds., *Encyclopedia of Psychology* (New York: Herder & Herder, 1972- ); *International Encyclopedia of Psychiatry, Psychology, Psychoanalysis, and Neurology* (New York: Produced for Aesculapius Publishers by Van Nostrand Reinhold, 1977).

3.   For a more complete explanation of the steps involved in search strategy for psychology, see Anne K. Beaubien, Sharon A. Hogan, and Mary W. George, "The Research Process in the Social Sciences," in *Learning the Library: Concepts*

*and Methods for Effective Bibliographic Instruction* (New York: R. R. Bowker, 1982), pp. 135-51.

4. Carl M. White, *Sources of Information in the Social Sciences*, 2d ed. (Chicago: American Library Association, 1973), p. 139.

5. Hannelore Rader, "Library Orientation and Instruction," *RSR: Reference Services Review*, Summer issue (Ann Arbor, Mich.: Pierian Press, 1973- ).

## REFERENCE WORKS CITED

*African Recorder.* New Delhi: 1962- .

*Annual Review of Anthropology.* Palo Alto, Calif.: Annual Reviews, 1972- .

*Annual Review of Psychology.* Palo Alto, Calif.: Annual Reviews, 1950- .

*Anthropological Literature.* Pleasantville, N.Y.: Redgrave, 1979-84. Cambridge, Mass.: Tozzer Library, 1984- . Microfilm.

*Bibliographic Index: A Cumulative Bibliography of Bibliographies.* N.Y.: H. W. Wilson, 1937- .

*Biennial Review of Anthropology.* Stanford, Calif.: Stanford University Press, 1959-71.

*Bulletin Signalétique.* Paris: 521. Sociologie, ethnologie, 1969- ; 525. Préhistorie, 1970- ; 526. Art et archéologie, proche-orient, asie, amérique, 1970- .

*Child Development Abstracts and Bibliography.* Washington, D.C.: 1927- .

*C.R.I.S.: The Combined Retrospective Index Set to Journals in Political Science, 1866-1974.* Washington, D.C.: Carrollton Press.

*Current Population Reports.* Washington, D.C.: U.S. Bureau of the Census.

ERIC (Education Resource Information Center) database. Composed of two printed publications: *Current Index to Journals in Education.* New York: CCM Information Services, 1969- ; *Resources in Education.* 1966- .

*Geo Abstracts.* Norwich, England: 1966- .

*Handbook of North American Indians*, ed. William C. Sturtevant. Washington, D.C.: Smithsonian Institution, U.S. Government Printing Office, 1978- .

*Index Medicus* [New Series]. Bethesda, Md.: National Library of Medicine, 1960-.

*International Encyclopedia of Higher Education.* San Francisco: Jossey-Bass, 1977.

*International Encyclopedia of the Social Sciences.* New York: Macmillan, 1968.

*International Index.* New York: H. W. Wilson, 1907-65.

*International Political Science Abstracts.* Paris: Documentation politique internationale, 1951- .

*International Review of Administrative Science.* Brussels: International Institute of Administrative Sciences, 1928- .

*Library Literature.* New York: H. W. Wilson, 1933- .

*LOEX News, Quarterly Newsletter of the National Orientation-Instruction Exchange, the LOEX Library Instruction Clearinghouse.* Ypsilanti, Mich.: Center for Educational Resources, Eastern Michigan University, 1974- .

*PAIS: Public Affairs Information Service Bulletin.* New York: Public Affairs Information Service, 1950- .

*Psychological Abstracts.* Washington, D.C.: American Psychological Association, 1927- .

*Readers' Guide to Periodical Literature.* New York: H. W. Wilson, 1901- .

Sheehy, Eugene. *Guide to Reference Books.* 10th ed. Chicago: American Library Association, 1986.

*Social Sciences and Humanities Index.* New York: H. W. Wilson, 1965-74.

*Social Sciences Citation Index.* Philadelphia: Institute for Scientific Information, 1971- .

*Social Sciences Index.* New York: H. W. Wilson, 1974- .

*Thesaurus of Psychological Index Terms.* 4th ed. Washington, D.C.: American Psychological Association, 1985.

*United States Political Science Documents.* Pittsburgh, Pa.: University Center for International Studies and the American Political Science Association, 1975- .

## PROFESSIONAL BIBLIOGRAPHY

Beaubien, Anne K. "Library Resources for the Community Organizer: Survey and Bibliography." In *Tactics and Techniques of Community Practice,* edited by F. M. Cox et al. Itasca, Ill.: F. E. Peacock, 1977.

Beaubien, Anne K., Sharon A. Hogan, and Mary W. George. *Learning the Library: Concepts and Methods for Effective Bibliographic Instruction.* New York: R. R. Bowker, 1982.

*Encyclopedia of the Social Sciences.* New York: Macmillan, 1937.

Freides, Thelma K. *Literature and Bibliography of the Social Sciences.* Los Angeles: Melville Publishing Company, 1973.

Frick, Elizabeth. "Information Structure and Bibliographic Instruction." *Journal of Academic Librarianship* 1 (September 1975): 12-14.

Hoselitz, Bernard F. *A Reader's Guide to the Social Sciences.* New York: Free Press of Glencoe, 1963.

Krathwohl, David R. *Social and Behavioral Science Research.* San Francisco: Jossey-Bass, 1985.

McDonough, Kristin, and Barbara Katz Rothman. "The Library Research Module in Introductory Sociology: The Case Study of a Collaboration." *Research Strategies* 1 (Summer 1983): 109-17.

McInnis, Raymond. *Research Guide for Psychology.* Westport, Conn.: Greenwood Press, 1982.

Shapiro, Beth, and Richard Hill. "Teaching Sociology Graduate Students Bibliographic Methods for Document Research." *Journal of Academic Librarianship* 5 (May 1979): 75-78.

Smalley, Topsy N. "Bibliographic Instruction in Academic Libraries: Questioning Some Assumptions." *Journal of Academic Librarianship* 3 (November 1977): 280-83.

*Social Science Encyclopedia.* Boston: Routledge & Kegan Paul, 1985.

Thaston, Lyn. "Dissemination and Use of Information by Psychology Faculty and Graduate Students: Implications for Bibliographic Instruction." *Research Strategies* 3 (Summer 1985): 116-24.

Tuckett, Harold, and Judith Pryor. "Research Strategy for Political Science." *Research Strategies* 1 (Summer 1983): 128-30.

Watstein, Sarah Barbara, and Stan Nash. "Researching 'Hot' Topics in the Social Sciences." *Research Strategies* 1 (Spring 1983): 77-82.

# 13 Bibliographic Instruction in the Humanities

*Maureen Pastine*

The disciplines which constitute the humanities have varied over the centuries, with philosophy, religion, the visual and performing arts, fine arts, language and literature, and the historical sciences most often included. Unlike the sciences, collaborative efforts in producing research are infrequent. Humanities scholars tend to work alone, not sharing their ideas with others until publication. Most prefer a personal, more individual approach rather than a group effort. One's own values and subjective interpretations are far more important than the hard facts upon which scientists rely. There is less of the progressive accumulation of facts used by scientists to build upon, improve, or reject previous research. Instead, the nature of humanities scholarship lends itself to creative new perspectives based on a more subjective analysis than the scientist's objective thrust.

This chapter will be devoted to the characteristics of scholarship in the humanities, types of library research resources available, and scholarly communication. Research methodologies in the humanities will be discussed along with bibliographic control of resources and problems in conducting research in the humanities. It should also be noted at the outset that there are fewer use studies in the humanities than in other fields, creating serious problems in understanding the progression of humanities research.

## CHARACTERISTICS OF SCHOLARSHIP IN THE HUMANITIES

It is known that humanities scholars do not require the use of secondary sources — journal articles, technical reports, and contacts with their colleagues — in conducting research as often as do scientists. Instead, the emphasis is on primary source material: books and monographic publications. While scientific research tends to concentrate on a few seminal works and journal titles, humanities researchers use a wider range of titles, and the time span of materials used is greater. Obsolescence of research resources is less of a problem in the humanities than in the sciences where currency and timeliness of resources are vital. The original text or creative work in the humanities is the key to most humanistic study. Critical literature is in the form of "analysis, interpretation, or commentary on a particular creative work, on a group of creative works, or on the output of a given historical period." [1] A number of books and scholarly journal articles have been published on the art of reading, listening to, or interpreting philosophical, artistic, musical, or literary works.

169

There are innumerable guides on the art of research for every subject discipline in the humanities, many of which provide information on the basic pattern of organization of the literature and bibliographical control of the field of study. Most of these research guides offer sources of data relevant to the field (for example, landmark works, encyclopedias, dictionaries, handbooks, sources of statistics, professional organizations, major bibliographies, and descriptions of specialized library collections).

Barbara Currier Bell, discussing research guides in English, states that "the potential usefulness of research guides is obvious. Yet they are little used ... Students typically do not know what they are, and faculty almost never mention them." [2] She ends her article by stressing the need for English professors to join "with those in other disciplines in emphasizing the importance of learning research skills." [3]

In addition to guides to the literature in the humanities, specialized author, title, and subject bibliographies abound and have been available for many years. Barbara M. Hale suggests some problems researchers encounter in using these bibliographies: "Librarians have from time to time drawn attention to their increasing numbers, to the variety of formats used, to their overlapping and duplication of each other, and have suggested integrated, all purpose bibliographies covering wider fields." [4] She also points out that "little is being done to survey their various forms and relative usefulness or indeed their use by the readers for whom they are intended." [5]

Several authors have noted problems encountered in conducting and studying humanities research. Hale discusses studies which reflect a "reluctance of scholars to use subject bibliographies" partially because of "the variety of arrangements and formats used in the bibliographies available, and lack of knowledge on the scholar's part of such tools and their use." [6] David Nicholas, in reviewing a study of information needs and uses of information by doctoral students in the humanities, points out the lack of "hard data as to the nature of humanities information and its users," and he notes that humanities doctoral students are generally "unprepared for the information-seeking tasks ahead." [7] Eileen M. Mackesy, in discussing secondary access services in the humanities, notes additional problems: the humanists' reluctance to make use of secondary access services in their computer-accessible forms; lack of awareness by humanities scholars of files available for online searching; the humanities scholars' focus on retrospective research versus current awareness services; the lack of controlled vocabulary in humanities databases; and inadequate marketing efforts for available databases.[8]

Surveys of how humanities scholars, students, and faculty use libraries and bibliographic aids, and what other methods they use to obtain information, need to be conducted and the results widely disseminated in both the library and the humanities' literature. The few studies that have been done demonstrate that "literature in these fields ages more slowly ... [and there is] greater need for retrospective bibliography and for co-ordinated control of it." [9]

Humanities scholars are moving away from narrow areas of specialization to interdisciplinary research. The impact of computerization in humanities disciplines is creating new areas for study. Unfortunately, too few humanities scholars are involved in extensive research which incorporates the new technologies and databases; few teach their students about these new avenues of scholarship or solicit the aid of librarians in making these resources available.

There are, however, a number of articles that BI librarians will find useful to orient themselves to databases in the humanities. Examples include Danielle Mihram's article on the Third International Conference on Databases in the Humanities and Social Sciences,[10] Eileen M. Mackesy's "Humanities Databases: An Overview," [11] Maureen Pastine and Laura Osegueda's article on computer databases for language and literature research,[12] M. Mahapatra and S. C. Biswas's article on PRECIS role operators for social science and humanities literature,[13] and Willy Martin's "On Uses of the Computer in Literary Research." [14]

## BIBLIOGRAPHIC INSTRUCTION FOR HUMANITIES SCHOLARS

In teaching humanities students and scholars the most effective research methodologies and how to use research resources, it is important to review fundamental issues affecting their ability to locate relevant information. The starting point in the humanities research process is often with the original work. In the humanities, there is first a close study of the primary text or original work. Beginning with a special perspective about this text or work, the scholar may also wish to study variant editions of the original (for example, a second edition), an original handwritten manuscript, or correspondence related to the work. In the humanities, this may require gaining access to resources held by a special collections department in a specific library, museum, or archive. Travel might be required and special privileges requested as a visiting scholar in order to use the resources in the holding institutions. In such cases, the scholar needs to be aware of national union catalogs or tertiary reference tools that will help one locate the item. If the item is not available locally or on interlibrary loan, the scholar often travels to the location of the library holding the item.

Prior to research travel, it is a good idea to review existing secondary and tertiary sources about the original work so that one is as knowledgeable as possible about the original and does not have to make additional trips to check out information that had not been considered initially. Tertiary tools are often more important initially than secondary sources which provide criticism of the work.

At this point in provision of bibliographic instruction, a discussion should take place on the value of specialized handbooks, encyclopedias, dictionaries, atlases, histories, and biographies in the field. Through such sources, the scholar will discover important facts, theories, and other relevant information relating to the author, artist, musician, or dramatist studied.

Certain questions should be considered. For example, were there variations of the original work completed? Did these variant editions change the focus, theme, or value of the work? Did the work fall into a relevant time period or movement which affected the original meaning or value of the work? Was the originator of the work influenced by others, and, if so, how? Is there any correspondence related to the work, and, if so, does it still exist and where is it located? Was the work translated or reformatted (for example, from a novel to a play, as a short story later incorporated into a novel, from a musical score to a recording)? Did the translation or reformatting change the original intent? By sorting through relevant ephemeral data provided in tertiary sources, the scholar may adapt or redefine his/her interpretation prior to further study.

The next step is to scan the secondary or critical literature on the subject. Scholars need to be aware that certain authors, musicians, and artists are considered major to a particular discipline and thus, are more easily researched. At this point, the bibliographic instruction librarian could discuss the major guides and bibliographies to the field, noting that many of these are devoted to a particular time period, genre, theme, nationality, or individual.

These books and serial publications are especially useful when researching an individual considered to be one of the "greats" of the subject field. If the individual studied is of lesser renown, or a recently rediscovered figure, the major reference sources will not be as useful. At this point, one could discuss the specialized bibliographies that were published during the time period in which the individual lived, since popularity rather than time-tested reputation may have meant inclusion in an older reference work and exclusion in a newer one.

This is also a good point at which to discuss the less scholarly reviewing and citation sources for retrospective runs of popular newspapers and magazines of the time of the original work. While annual reviews and *Festschriften* volumes will be valuable sources of information on individuals considered to be of renown, these seldom cover minor figures or important figures with limited output.

For scholars studying the more recent literary, artistic, and musical figures, bibliographic control is difficult due to time lag in appearance of citations in the major indexing, abstracting, and other bibliographical resources. In addition, scholarly journals are slow to accept and publish articles on less well known or less established figures. In such cases, the scholar will have to rely on the more popular indexing tools to newspapers, magazine reviews, and commentaries.

Indexing and abstracting sources and compilation of online databases have been much slower to develop in the humanities than in the social and natural sciences, and coverage of retrospective journals and subjects is not as good as in some other fields. Thus, humanities scholars have a greater need to browse library shelves and contents pages of current journals. Proceedings of conferences where critical papers are presented are less frequently published than in many other disciplines, but humanities scholars may still locate useful material by using the *Index to Social Sciences and Humanities Proceedings* (Philadelphia, Pa.: Institute for Scientific Information, 1979- ). A search of *Dissertation Abstracts International*, Section A: Humanities (Ann Arbor, Mich.: University Microfilms, 1966- ) can be quite fruitful for the humanities scholar, as can the use of *Arts and Humanities Citation Index* (Philadelphia, Pa.: Institute for Scientific Information, 1976- ).

In addition, humanities scholars need to be aware of the many fine arts, small press, and little magazine publications that are often more likely than the scholarly journals to publish the works of, and critical articles on, the "lesser-knowns," as well as the newer types of criticism. Bibliographical control of these publications is a real problem as many tend to cease publication after the first few issues. Libraries are less likely to subscribe to them because of billing problems, lack of reviews, and lack of continued publication of many of them.

There are fewer textbook publications in the humanities than in most disciplines, but there are a great number of anthologies and monographic series. These anthologies and monographic series of primary and secondary source materials are of great importance in the humanities and most are carefully indexed, albeit slowly, in sources devoted to such publications.

Modes of communication and communication sources are somewhat different in the humanities than they are in the sciences, but the research process is teachable. Some excellent sources for use by bibliographic instruction librarians appear after the "References" section in this chapter. However, it is much easier to approach beginning instruction in the humanities through a specialized field of study where one can focus on a course topic or on an individual's specialized subject. This approach is preferred because, with so many research resources available, effective research strategies will vary, depending upon such factors as whether major or minor figures are studied, the nationality of the individuals studied, the genre, the time period, and/or the medium studied.

## CONCLUSIONS

Humanities scholars have been using libraries for centuries. And, although they have been among the libraries' most knowledgeable users, humanities scholars seldom use libraries today. Retrospective materials, literary texts, and bibliographies are often considered by faculty and librarians to be of great importance, yet they are rarely used. Instead poets, philosophers, artists, musicians, novelists, and other humanists have relied on their own files and their colleagues to provide needed literature citations. Few studies have been made of research methodologies and use of library resources by humanities scholars; consequently, little hard data exists on the nature of humanities research. Such neglect has led to serious problems in the field of humanities scholarship. Controlled vocabularies are almost nonexistent. The development of comprehensive and retrospective online databases has been slow.

The individualistic nature of research carried on by humanities scholars (focused in a narrow subject field or area of specialization) is changing. An interdisciplinary research approach is gaining recognition as our society becomes more technologically oriented and as lines between disciplines become blurred.

Students must be better prepared to integrate their liberal arts humanistic education into a technological or mechanistic society. *A Nation at Risk* by the National Commission on Excellence in Education (Washington, D.C.: U.S. Government Printing Office, 1983) documents the problems inherent in today's education. A large percentage of our total world population is functionally illiterate. Moral and ethical values are declining. The loss of humanistic values is related to the declining ability of our educational system and libraries to meet the needs of society. Information management has become far more difficult due to the proliferation of both print and electronic publishing. Libraries have not kept pace with technological change and other less humanistic organizations have begun to assume the library's traditional role.

Major changes in bibliographic instruction activities for humanities education must be considered. For many, the library is the last place one goes to get information. Why has this pattern been set? What are the implications? What can be done to reverse the trend and strengthen lifelong learning through regular library use?

At one time, libraries were developed by scholars who donated their collections to build repositories of recorded knowledge and who used their creative energies and abilities to help develop inquiring minds. Over the centuries, these repositories grew under the direction of the highly intellectual minds of great scholars. But somewhere along the way, the emphasis has been shifted. Libraries are no longer central to the educational process, but rather, they are supplementary, supportive at best. As noted, a problem is the lack of research on user needs and research methodologies and an inability or lack of interest in keeping abreast of and adapting technological development taking place outside of the educational sphere (in business and industry) to higher education and to libraries.

A disturbing trend which has been observed is the individual's inability to cope with the information explosion brought on by technology. Difficulty in keeping pace with this information explosion is seen most clearly in the decline in the ability to read and write at a level appropriate to advancements made in the "high tech" environment. There are, no doubt, many reasons for this phenomena: higher rates of population mobility causing interruptions, inconsistencies, and stress in one's ability to gain a quality education; an increasing stream of minority groups with inadequate educational opportunities; lack of adequate state and federal financing to respond to educational, informational, and cultural needs; and the declining ability of educational systems to attract quality leaders, scholars, and teachers.

To combat these problems, libraries must assume a greater research role in determining information and cultural needs of users and nonusers, in discovering research methodologies currently used by humanities scholars, and in adapting technological and electronic advancements to meet informational needs. In order to do this, educators, information vendors, librarians, and political and business leaders must collaborate far more than is presently the case.

From the little research available, it is readily apparent that doctoral-level students in the humanities are woefully unprepared to conduct research in their own disciplines and that our educational systems lack the appropriate resources and expertise to resolve the problem. Unless educators, automation experts, librarians, information vendors, politicians, and business and industry work together to combat the problem, little progress can be made.

At the academic level, librarians need to develop a strategic plan by which these problems can be addressed. The following suggestions should be considered:

1. Bibliographic instruction librarians and library administrators could identify research methods courses in humanities disciplines and offer to team-teach these courses. This emphasis, however, might prove far more difficult than the current focus of offering nonhour library sessions to freshman English classes.

2. Academic librarians could work with sociologists to develop effective instruments to survey how scholars conduct research in the humanities disciplines and could then revise bibliographic instruction accordingly.

If it appears that scholars' research methods are inadequate, special workshops and seminars might be provided to improve their knowledge of research methodologies and search skills.

3. Humanities faculty and librarians could work together to develop library assignments that build research skills, thus increasing the ability of students to evaluate sources and to complete their research.

4. Librarians could publish their findings on humanities research in journals of the appropriate disciplines to keep humanities scholars informed of services available.

5. Humanities scholars could be encouraged to meet regularly with librarians to discuss mutual problems and ways to improve current research and access tools.

6. Strategic short- and long-range plans, with specific objectives and deadlines, could be devised by both library and humanities professional associations working together to combat these problems.

As we have seen, effective bibliographic instruction in the humanities cannot be considered as a simple task concerned only with an increased understanding of tools and an improvement in methods of presentation. Rather, it requires awareness and exploration of existing problems and a concerted effort at partnership with our humanities colleagues.

## NOTES

1. A. Robert Rogers, *The Humanities: A Selective Guide to Information Sources*, 2d ed. (Littleton, Colo.: Libraries Unlimited, 1979), pp. 2-3.

2. Barbara Currier Bell, "Research Guides in English," *College English* 44 (April 1982):390.

3. Ibid., p. 403.

4. Barbara M. Hale, *The Subject Bibliography of the Social Sciences and Humanities* (Elmsford, N.Y.: Pergamon Press, 1970), p. 24.

5. Ibid., p. 26.

6. Ibid., p. 70.

7. David Nicholas, "Reviews," *Journal of Documentation* 38 (June 1982):139-40.

8. Eileen M. Mackesy, "A Perspective on Secondary Access Services in the Humanities," *Journal of the American Society for Information Science* 33 (May 1982):146-51.

9. Hale, *The Subject Bibliography*, p. 72.

10. Danielle Mihram, "Third International Conference on Databases in the Humanities and Social Sciences," *Reference Services Review* (Spring 1984): 27-30.

11. Eileen M. Mackesy, "Humanities Databases: An Overview," *Literary Research Newsletter* 8 (Summer and Fall 1983):103-6.

12. Maureen Pastine, and Laura Osegueda, "Computer Databases on Academic Libraries: Implications for Language and Literature Research," *Literary Research Newsletter* 8 (Summer and Fall 1983):107-17.

13. M. Mahapatra, and S. C. Biswas, "Concept Specification by PRECIS Role Operators: Some Technical Problems with Social Science and Humanities Literature," *LISR* 7 (January-March 1985):53-74.

14. Willy Martin, "On Uses of the Computer in Literary Research: A Congress Report," *Review of Applied Linguistics* 8 (1970):3-8.

## SELECTED SOURCES FOR PROVISION OF HUMANITIES BIBLIOGRAPHIC INSTRUCTION

### Background Information

Asheim, Lester. *The Humanities and the Library*. Chicago: American Library Association, 1957.

Bry, Ilse, and Lois Afflerbach. "Links Between the Humanities and the Literature of the Human Sciences." *Wilson Library Bulletin* 42 (January 1968):510-24.

Dudley, Fred A. *The Relations of Literature and Science*. Ann Arbor, Mich.: University Microfilms, 1968.

Foskett, D. J. *Science, Humanism, and Libraries*. New York: Hafner Publishing Co., 1964.

"The Future of the Humanities." *Daedalus: Journal of the American Academy of Arts and Sciences* 98 (Summer 1969).

Jones, W. T. *The Sciences and the Humanities*. Berkeley, Calif.: University of California Press, 1965.

The National Commission on Excellence in Education. *A Nation at Risk, the Imperative for Educational Reform.* Washington, D.C.: U.S. Government Printing Office, 1983.

Northrop, F. S. *The Logic of the Sciences and the Humanities.* New York: Meridian Books, 1960.

"Theory in Humanistic Studies." *Daedalus: Journal of the American Academy of Arts and Sciences* 99 (Spring 1970).

Urguhardt, D. J. "The Needs of the Humanities." *Journal of Documentation* 16 (September 1960): 121-31.

## Research Process in the Humanities

Beaubien, Anne K., Sharon A. Hogan, and Mary W. George. "Research Process in the Humanities." In *Learning the Library: Concepts and Methods for Effective Bibliographic Instruction*, pp. 109-23. New York: R. R. Bowker, 1982.

Bowles, Edmund A. "The Humanities and the Computer: Some Current Research Problems." *Computers and Automation* 15 (1966):24-27.

Huston, Mary, and Willie Parson. "A Model of Librarianship for Combining Learning and Teaching." *Research Strategies* 3 (Spring 1985):75-80.

Mellon, Constance A. "Information Problem Solving: A Developmental Approach to Library Instruction." In *Theories of Bibliographic Education: Designs for Teaching*, edited by Cerise Oberman and Katina Strauch, pp. 75-90. New York: R. R. Bowker, 1982.

Mitchell, J. L., ed. *Computers in the Humanities.* Minneapolis, Minn.: University of Minnesota Press, 1974.

Oakman, Robert L. *Computer Methods for Literary Research.* Athens, Ga.: The University of Georgia Press, 1984.

Rogers, Sharon. "Research Strategies: Bibliographic Instruction for Undergraduates." *Library Trends* 31 (Summer 1980): 69-81.

## Methodologies for Humanities Research

Corkill, C., M. Mann, and S. Stone. *Doctoral Studies in Humanities: A Small-Scale Panel Study of Information Needs and Uses 1976-79.* Sheffield, England: Centre for Research on User Studies, University of Sheffield, 1981.

Gibaldi, Joseph, ed. *Introduction to Scholarship in Modern Language and Literature*. New York: Modern Language Association of America, 1981.

Hale, Barbara M. *The Subject Bibliography of the Social Sciences and Humanities*. Elmsford, N.Y.: Pergamon Press, 1970.

Rawski, C. H. "Bibliographic Organization in the Humanities." *Wilson Library Bulletin* 42 (April 1966): 738-50.

Stone, Sue, ed. *Humanities Information Research: Proceedings of a Seminar*. Sheffield, England: Centre for Research on User Studies, University of Sheffield, 1980.

## Relevant Reference Sources

Bell, Barbara Currier. "Research Guides in English." *College English* 44 (April 1982): 390-404.

Kenney, Donald J. "Publishing BI Articles in Discipline Journals." *Research Strategies* 1 (Spring 1983): 64-76.

Rogers, A. Robert. *The Humanities: A Selective Guide to Information Sources*. 2d ed. Littleton, Colo.: Libraries Unlimited, 1979.

Slavens, Thomas. *Information Sources in the Humanities*. Ann Arbor, Mich.: Campus Publishers, 1968.

Stevens, Rolland E., and Donald G. Davis, Jr. *Reference Books in the Social Sciences and Humanities*. 4th ed. Champaign, Ill.: Stipes, 1977.

Winckler, Paul A. *Humanities: Outline and Bibliography*. New York: Graduate Library School, Long Island University, 1971.

## Bibliographic Instruction Methodologies

Ford, James E. "The Natural Alliance Between Librarians and English Teachers in Course-Related Library Use Instruction." *College & Research Libraries* 43 (September 1982): 379-84.

George, Mary W., and Mary Ann O'Donnell. "The Bibliography and Research Methods Course in American Departments of English." *Literary Research Newsletter* 4 (1979): 9-23.

Keresztesi, Michael. "The Science of Bibliography: Theoretical Implications for Bibliographic Instruction." In *Theories of Bibliographic Education: Designs for Teaching*, edited by Cerise Oberman and Katina Strauch. New York: R. R. Bowker, 1982.

Knapp, Patricia. *The Monteith College Library Experiment.* New York: Scarecrow Press, 1966.

Kobelski, Pamela, and Mary Reichel. "Conceptual Frameworks for Bibliographic Instruction." *Journal of Academic Librarianship* 7 (1981): 73-77.

Miller, Constance. "Scientific Literature as Hierarchy: Library Instruction and Robert M. Gagne." *College & Research Libraries* 43 (September 1982): 385-90.

Oberman, Cerise, and Katina Strauch, eds. *Theories of Bibliographic Education: Designs for Teaching.* New York: R. R. Bowker, 1982.

# Bibliographic Instruction and the Higher Education Community: Working with Professional Organizations and Academic Professionals

**14**

*Carolyn Kirkendall*

All academic library programs and services benefit from the support of interested and knowledgeable faculty. It is when "imaginative development and wise utilization" of an institution's library resources are *not* seen as indispensable to instructional and research programs throughout the disciplines that frustration among library administrators and staff results.[1] What does this unfortunate but common state of affairs have to do with bibliographic instruction? Can the field of BI assist in making the library accepted as a more vital campus resource for the intellectual endeavors of the institution? Can communicating with teaching faculty about the teaching role of the library help to develop an awareness of the library as an important means for academic excellence? The answer to these questions is an unequivocal "yes."

Librarians actively involved in bibliographic instruction know that faculty acceptance of the importance of library services can be one result of a successful library instruction program. We recognize that it is no longer necessary to begin from scratch each year to convince faculty that teaching students effective library use is important. Word of mouth and results of programs have their effect and, on any campus where there is BI activity germane to the curriculum, teaching faculty have seen that such instruction helps students prepare for an information-based society, permits their classes to do better work, and can make teaching a more rewarding experience.[2]

Through local campus efforts, teaching faculty can recognize and understand the library's mission in higher education as they see it in action: they can develop a clearer recognition of the librarian as a peer in the educational enterprise; and they can participate in an ongoing flow of communication and consultation.[3] The BI librarian has frequent opportunities to educate his or her colleagues about the library—what it is, how it operates, and what kinds of support it needs—opportunities as frequent as those of the library director.

This one-to-one librarian-to-teaching-faculty method of working locally to improve the library's instructional role and potential has been widely used, tested, refined, and reported upon in the literature; there is no longer a major need to preach its necessity. But, BI librarians *and academic librarians in general* also need to be in the mainstream of change, both in the library profession and in higher education.

We are seeing exhortations for this in much of today's professional literature. It is clearly time for librarians to move from inward, institutional activities to more direct interaction. Our present mandate, to build bridges to our own profession and to all of higher education, can help us become recognized as full partners in the academic enterprise.

In May of 1982, the ACRL Committee on an Activity Model for 1990 issued an appropriate challenge to BI librarians: to look for ways to "affect alliances with and to enhance an awareness of the role of academic and research libraries .. among higher education associations, scholarly organizations, and agencies that share interests with academic and research libraries," and "to represent academic and research library concerns within other professional bodies." [4] This mandate echoes the conclusions reached by the ACRL Bibliographic Instruction Section,[5] and the series of recommendations offered by the BI Think Tank,[6] which included the fuller integration of user instruction into the fabric of the library profession and the mounting of a substantial effort to relate our mission to the "outside world." In addition, it reflects the goals of the ACRL BIS Bibliographic Instruction Liaison Project which predated the Think Tank: to promote cooperative efforts with other higher education associations, to assist librarians to participate in programs and activities of non-library professional associations through funding for registration fees, and to generally help integrate libraries into the mainstream of academia. The current ACRL Professional Association Liaison Committee continues the efforts begun by the Liaison Project.

Librarians have long been concerned with the negative image of the library held by many university faculty and administrators, an image that results in viewing library services with indifference, impatience, lack of understanding, or at best, benign neglect. While much has been written on interacting with faculty, librarians also need to know how and when to communicate with various administrators on campus. As Moffett explains, the integrity of the library is rarely of concern to academic administrators who are otherwise vitally concerned with the quality of the institution's educational programs.[7] The responsibility for communicating the purpose of the library and its potential instructional role to the higher education community rests with the academic librarian, who must speak confidently about its services and offer needed help and information.

This chapter describes the development of mechanisms to ensure that communication within the higher education community is effective. The thoughts expressed herein are based upon the author's experiences and observations as program officer for the ACRL BIS Liaison Project, and upon the work of Carla Stoffle, former vice-chancellor at the University of Wisconsin-Parkside and currently associate director of the University of Michigan Libraries. Her willingness to share her thoughts and notes, particularly on the topic of working with administrators, has contributed greatly to the development of these ideas.

## DEVELOPING AN UNDERSTANDING
## OF HIGHER EDUCATION

First, it is necessary for librarians involved in user instruction to recognize that the field of BI, as vital as it is and will continue to be, is a rather narrow concept from which to view the relationship of the academic library to the local institution, to academic research, and to the goals of higher education in general. BI librarians have been sharing news of successful programs and experiments for the past fifteen years. This concentration on individual programs and the propensity to talk among ourselves were necessary first steps in the development of BI. There is, however, no longer a major need to address these issues. It is time to stop directing our primary efforts toward BI programs with only ourselves as speakers and listeners. A substantial and organized effort must be made to share our accumulated knowledge with those outside the library field.

Academic librarians must take stock of their collective expertise and must honestly address the following questions:

1. What is there for us to know about higher education?

2. How are we to learn what we need to know?

3. What ought to be done once we've learned?

Edward Holley has outlined four areas of knowledge important to academic librarians in addition to professional library skills. These areas include a background in the history and development of higher education, an appreciation for the history of scholarship and learning, an understanding of how knowledge is obtained in various disciplines, and the ability to evaluate research findings.[8]

In addition, librarians must be able to (1) communicate with and speak the working language of faculty and administrators, (2) understand how they operate and think, and (3) recognize what is important to faculty teaching in each particular discipline. Also necessary is a better understanding of the academic setting in general, as well as how the political milieu, both on and off campus, affects librarians and their services. Librarians must begin to appreciate the organizational behavior of those who teach and those who administer in the broader higher education field of which they are a part.

In past years, BI librarians have often expected teaching faculty to adopt their way of working and thinking as well as their programs and services. But faculty are experts in their fields, and librarians must respect the expertise of faculty if they wish to gain their attention and respect. It is the librarian's responsibility to consider how library services can assist and augment the expertise of faculty and support the general mission of the institution.

This is the reason the Think Tank recommended a study of governance and power structure of colleges and universities, the history and nature of higher education, and the priorities and socialization of teaching faculty and administrators. Holley reminds us that we are "living in a dream world if we believe multi-million dollar operations [like the library] can function without involvement in the political process, or an understanding of fairly well-defined structures that reflect basic academic values."[9]

How can librarians learn and understand the things they need to know? Perhaps in a manner different from the traditional, safe, and somewhat ineffective way. It has been assumed that it is necessary to hold an additional master's degree beyond the professional library degree in a subject field that reflects the librarian's interest. This second degree, however, is no guarantee of acceptance by the teaching faculty of a particular discipline.

While an additional degree may help a librarian find a better job, it does not necessarily teach him or her how faculty think about research and teaching, or how to communicate with instructors and administrators. Nor will the subject degree add to a librarian's skill in and knowledge of organizational behavior. The emphasis on additional education in specific disciplines will not directly improve the present position or future of the academic librarian; such education is often narrow or incorrect. Academic librarians interested in working within the fabric of higher education need more.

Library schools who train academic librarians need to sponsor more courses in the structure of higher education and to address the issues raised by research on attitudes of faculty toward research. Seminars on the organizational behavior of institutions, ACRL continuing education courses on how faculty approach research, workshops on the role of the library in the history of higher education and on the history of learning and scholarship can help BI librarians understand the setting in which they operate. In addition, librarians need a regular mechanism to provide current information on higher education research; perhaps a newsletter, similar to *Library Currents* for library administrators, could be designed for this purpose.

Library schools, or ACRL, should consider developing a course on how to effectively involve the academic library in the mainstream of higher education politics. The current studies on the state of secondary and higher education have ignored the library's role. The College Board omitted library skills from its list of recommended subjects and skills to be mastered. Librarians were not included among the panels and committees devising recommendations for improving education in the United States, yet librarians did not protest their exclusion. We missed the opportunity to do this as each study lacking a library component came out. It is the responsibility of the library profession to keep tabs on these working parties and to aggressively inform them of library concerns. Emphasis through library schools and ACRL courses can teach librarians the means by which this can be done. Seminars to accompany apprenticeships or residency programs for library school students interested in working in academic libraries should be more widespread.

Instructional opportunities such as these would help students understand important aspects of the higher education milieu: how faculty operate on their own turf; how librarians can work with administrators to make the library more cost-effective (such as through BI programs); how to discuss, collaborate, and negotiate with campus officials; and how to work with teaching faculty to identify information about libraries and information-seeking behavior for inclusion in textbooks. These experiences can prepare the potential academic librarian for the types of situations she or he will confront in the world of higher education and can assist in developing academic librarians who are a vital part of the structure of higher education and real contributors to its goals.

## INVOLVEMENT IN NON-LIBRARY ASSOCIATIONS

A less formal route by which academic librarians can contribute to the goals of higher education in a significant way is through discipline associations and other agencies in higher education to which faculty and administrators belong. The ACRL/BI Liaison Project investigated ways for librarians to do this effectively and, in the May 1984 issue of *College & Research Libraries News*, published their recommendations.[10] They suggested that academic librarians work with non-library associations, particularly on the state and regional levels, attend meetings as often as possible to become acquainted with non-library colleagues who share their interest in a specific discipline, and compile articles and bibliographies for publication in association newsletters. Working on a local or regional level with these groups is a much more realistic and feasible goal for librarians than to aim for more competitive accomplishments, such as presenting a paper at a national conference or publishing an article in a major higher education or discipline journal.

To assist librarians interested in joining non-library associations, ACRL might consider establishing membership agreements with selected professional organizations. For instance, during a specified trial period, perhaps five years, librarians might be charged reduced rates to attend professional association meetings and conferences. The organization would benefit, as well as the librarians, through higher attendance than could otherwise be expected. Offering such an opportunity, with increased interaction between association members and librarians, might provide participating associations with two further benefits: additional memberships and activities to improve access to information in their discipline. Exhibits and publications might be expanded, using the expertise of librarians, and the teaching emphasis of the discipline could be enhanced and improved through better use of library resources. Such activity would provide visibility and legitimization for library professionals.

By working with faculty on local campuses, librarians will learn how faculty operate, what pressures are involved with their jobs, what control they have over their own curriculum, and how the library might develop alternative activities and services to facilitate classroom teaching. By communicating with faculty on a regular basis, librarians learn about the trends and studies conducted in higher education and in specific disciplines and can design relevant services to meet current needs. Such information can also help librarians to analyze their own institutions, raise their awareness of campus politics, and where feasible, serve as agents for appropriate change.

## WORKING WITH CAMPUS ADMINISTRATORS

In addition to working with local and regional non-library associations, academic librarians need to capture the attention and imagination of their administrators to maintain effective library service. Administrators express interest in improving education and the library holds the potential for doing just that. Administrators' perception of the academic library and the impact that administrators have on these libraries is an important topic for academic librarians, one that should be pursued in the library school curriculum, through continuing education opportunities, and by ACRL. Stoffle has described the areas of academic administration which should be familiar to librarians: the identity of an institution's administrators, its administrative decision-making structures, the values of the institution, and the institutional environment.[11]

As many university administrators are former faculty members who have worked their way up through the ranks as department chairs and deans, the history of this progression, where it exists, has implications for the library. Good administrators still consider themselves educators and, when properly approached, can appreciate new concepts to enhance the quality of service offered by one of the most traditional parts of university life, the library.

The experience of such administrator with the academic library has been primarily through their students, their teaching, and their personal research; few are aware of or interested in current issues of academic librarianship. With a limited view of the role and potential of the library and the professional expertise of the librarian, they rarely make any efforts of their own to change or upgrade their original understanding.

Academic librarians can play an important part in making sure that campus administrators realize the library's potential. Some suggestions for achieving this might include the following: discovering the interests of administrators and identifying ways to access current information in their fields; developing networks which include faculty and campus staff; becoming involved in the daily life of the institution including attendance at student activities; delivering quality service; and finding ways to let the administrators know that the library and its professional staff are aware of campus concerns and, whenever possible, are committed to helping find solutions.

While such activities take much time and effort, academic librarians must be willing to make this effort if they are to be effective. Technological developments and information management are changing the way librarians interact with library users. In this electronic age, it is especially vital for BI librarians to keep current and to use technological changes to advance what they do. Rather than rendering library instruction unnecessary, technology can be incorporated effectively into the BI program when instruction librarians remain flexible and open to change. Administrators will come to view the academic library as a central component in information management if the library and its librarians are aware of their potential role and if library services reflect institutional priorities.

## SUMMARY

To summarize, academic librarians need to learn as much as possible about their campus political situation by working with faculty, by studying how administrators operate, by reading and learning about higher education, and by involvement with professional organizations in a broader and more active way. For those involved in the field of bibliographic instruction, this knowledge and appreciation of the higher education milieu should offer more opportunities to provide instruction in library and information skills. It will help us to create opportunities to debate and communicate among ourselves, thus keeping the BI field alive and flexible, and to criticize each other's work constructively, thus keeping our services current and germane. Moreover, it might help us recognize and synthesize our own philosophical goals and values. This, in turn, could lead to the development of criteria for assessing potentially good BI librarians and of BI performance standards to assess the quality of the programs we have established.

With a thorough understanding of the operational structure of the institutions in which we work, more BI practitioners will be available to help resolve the questions of the role of the library in higher education today. And by appreciating the concerns of other professionals on campus, librarians will be better able to design library services to support the university's curriculum, thus making better and more visible use of the funds and resources allocated to the library.

Many BI librarians already know what quality programs can be offered and how they will support the teaching process. By demonstrating an understanding of our colleagues' concerns, philosophies, and work styles, we can capture their attention as fuller partners in the educational enterprise.

## NOTES

1. William A. Moffett, "What the Academic Librarian Wants from Administrators and Faculty," in *Priorities for Academic Libraries*, ed. Thomas J. Galvin and Beverly P. Lynch (San Francisco: Jossey-Bass, 1982), p. 16.

2. Evan Ira Farber, "The Importance of Teaching Use of the Library," *Library Issues: Briefings for Faculty and Administrators* 2 (November 1981):4.

3. Moffett, "What the Academic Librarian Wants from Administrators and Faculty," p. 14.

4. "ACRL's Committee on an Activity Model for 1990: The Final Report," *College & Research Libraries News* 5 (May 1982):167.

5. Donna Senzig, "Bibliographic Instruction in the Discipline Associations," *College & Research Libraries News* 10 (November 1980):297.

6. "Think Tank Recommendations for Bibliographic Instruction," *College & Research Libraries News* 42 (December 1981):394-98.

7. Moffett, "What the Academic Librarian Wants from Administrators and Faculty," p. 16.

8. Edward G. Holley, "Defining the Academic Librarian," *College & Research Libraries* 46 (November 1985):463.

9. Ibid., p. 464.

10. Association of College and Research Libraries, Bibliographic Instruction Section, "Working with Discipline Associations: A Tip Sheet," *College & Research Libraries News* 45 (May 1984):240-41.

11. Carla Stoffle, "Enhancing the Role of the Academic Library: The Administrator's Perspective" (Notes from an address to the Chicago Area Library Council, September 30, 1983).

# PART III

## THE NEXT GENERATION
### Reflections on the Future

In the preceding sections of this book we have explored the components of what has come to be called the "Second Generation" of bibliographic instruction librarianship and we have described the event which may well prove to have marked the transition between generations, the Bibliographic Instruction Think Tank. From the early, unorganized efforts of the First Generation of bibliographic instruction librarians has grown a recognized area of public service in academic libraries, an area with its own literature, theory, content, and concerns. But bibliographic instruction is not a static area. Existing as it does in a milieu of constant change and development, bibliographic instruction itself will be altered, modified, and perhaps transformed in ways we can only begin to imagine. Moreover, as it changes and develops to meet the needs of different student bodies in different institutions, it will probably continue to be controversial. Proponents of varying methods or particular theories will argue among themselves and with colleagues, both within and outside the profession of librarianship, about the value of the instruction they offer.

Midway through the preparation of this book, the editor assembled a group of authors and other leaders in the bibliographic instruction movement to discuss its future. This discussion was to lay the groundwork for the final part of the book. Polite conversation gave way to hot debate when the issue of the term "bibliographic instruction" was raised. Proponents of a name change to encompass such concepts as "information," "search," and "management" based their recommendations on a whole new approach, not only to bibliographic instruction, but to academic librarianship as well. Responding to technological changes, both current and projected, this group conceived of librarianship as a field in flux, one in which terms like "bibliographic instruction" and perhaps even "librarian" might have no real place.

In direct opposition was a second group who saw technology as merely another form in which to store and retrieve information just as were the clay tablets of Ashurbanipal or the various microprint technologies introduced several decades ago. Search, retrieval, and use of information, this group argued, maintained certain basic and teachable concepts regardless of the form in which the information appeared. So heated was this controversy that it engulfed the time allotted for speculation on the future of bibliographic instruction. None of the participants suggested that such a discussion should be resumed.

Looking to the future is not a simple task in a profession where technological, sociological, and political changes rage about us. Clearly, the two hours we had allotted for this task was insufficient. However, plans are currently being discussed for a second Bibliographic Instruction Think Tank to explore new issues which have risen from our changing environment since Think Tank I was held. Perhaps these deliberations, should they occur, will take us one step beyond the thoughts and ideas set forth in this book into the future of bibliographic instruction.

In the meanwhile, we have asked Donald Kenney to provide a concluding note to this exploration of bibliographic instruction's Second Generation. Don, a participant in the original Think Tank meetings, a faithful member of the editorial board for this publication, and an active part of the library instruction movement from its early days, reflects upon bibliographic instruction, past and current, and raises some important questions to be addressed as the Second Generation moves on toward the twenty-first century.

# 15 Library Instruction in the 1980s: Where Has It Been and Where Is It Going?

*Donald J. Kenney*

> Wherever we are, it is but a stage on the way to somewhere else, and whatever we do, however well we do it, it is only a preparation to do something else that shall be different.
>
> — Robert Louis Stevenson

The hazards of predicting the future are markedly demonstrated by recalling some of the famous forecasts of the past. Indeed, it seems likely that most major jumps to the future have been undertaken accompanied by predictions of failure. In 1490, a panel of Spanish sages examined Columbus's plans for his New World voyage and came up with six reasons why it was impossible.[1] As scientific and technological advances have increased, so has the number of errant predictions. Many experts insisted that a new invention called the railroad would kill its passengers, who would not be able to breathe when traveling at such high speeds.[2] It was reported in a 1940 *Scientific American* article that a rocket bomb was too farfetched to be considered.[3] And most of us recall the public skepticism expressed at the idea of landing a man on the moon.

The height of the art of prediction was reached in the science fiction writings of the late nineteenth and early twentieth centuries. One of the most famous of the literary prognosticators was Jules Verne, whose imagination encompassed such future developments as the submarine and voyages to the moon. Of equal note is the American science fiction author Hugo Gernsback, who predicted television, radar, and communications satellites.

Forecasting and prophesying are not new. Sages, prophets, astrologers, and mystics are part of the common thread of civilization. The twentieth century, however, has added a new dimension to predicting the future: numerous public movements designed to influence government and society are based on predictions of possible future disasters. Environmental groups demonstrate in an attempt to preserve the environment. Antinuclear activists take to the streets to persuade national governments to forsake nuclear weapons. The terms "futurism" and "futurology" have taken their place in our vocabulary and in our dictionaries. While forecasting is not new, contemporary man has attempted to make it less of an art and more of a science.

Both government and industry are relying more and more upon futures forecasting to establish policies and goals. Public policy is now made chiefly on the basis of looking into the future. The founding of the Rand Corporation after World War II established modern futurism.[4] Today numerous institutes and centers are devoted exclusively to predicting the future. Government has also become involved. The Office of Technology Assessment was established in 1972 to aid the United States Congress in evaluating the potential impact of technology for the purpose of legislation. The Congressional Budget Office was set up in 1974 to monitor and assess the long-range impact of budgetary decisions. The Census Bureau, charged with taking a national census every decade, has begun making predictions based on the numerous data which it collects.

With the advent of the 1980s, much was predicted, reported, and written about what this new decade would hold for us. The soothsayers of librarianship were no less busy than the economic, political, and social prognosticators. Much has been, and will be, written about what the future will be like for librarians. Professionalism, AACR2, automation, salaries, collection development, networking, cooperation, governance, funding, and a hundred and one other topics have been included in discussions about the future of libraries in the 1980s.

The author also has had his place among the prognosticators: the Bibliographic Instruction Think Tank, of which he was a part, took on the task of predicting the future of library instruction. During the two days we spent in a closed room in San Francisco discussing this topic we never dreamed that we would still be talking and writing about those deliberations in 1986. While the group explored a host of problems, concerns, and issues, the discussion kept coming back to bibliographic instruction in the future or, in the words of one participant, the "Second Generation." This book represents the continued interest, and perhaps controversy, surrounding the Think Tank recommendations about the future of bibliographic instruction.

While politically and socially, the 1980s did not begin on a particularly hopeful note, the state of bibliographic instruction was more promising. By this time, bibliographic instruction had begun to assume the status of a profession, maturing at least to the point where there was no question as to whether or not it should be done. Concern about evaluation, or at least the lack thereof, had surfaced, giving rise to a whole series of questions about the long-range effect of instruction upon users and whether users' skills and attitudes toward the library change for the better as a result of instruction. Moreover, the impact of automation raised vital questions about bibliographic instruction and how it might meet the challenge of automation in the coming decade.

One issue emerging from the Think Tank discussion, which still hangs over us as we approach the decade of the 1990s, is the role that bibliographic instruction plays in the grander scheme of higher education. By the 1980s, librarians involved in bibliographic instruction no longer saw themselves as teachers of basic library skills or of research methods in a particular discipline. Rather, they realized that they had a great deal to offer to the process of higher education in general and that integrating bibliographic instruction into the university curriculum was important since "in the increasingly specialized and divided groves of academe, the need for an integrative role of BI is even greater." [5]

## THE PROFESSIONALIZATION OF
## LIBRARY INSTRUCTION

In the library profession, the late 1960s and 1970s could be called the decades of library instruction. Numerous job descriptions highlighted its importance; workshops and conferences featured library instruction as focal themes. Varied techniques of instruction, evaluation, and funding were advocated, explored, and debated. The literature was filled with articles devoted to library instruction methods and the merits of providing it.

The Summer 1980 issue of *Library Trends*, which was devoted to library instruction, features an article by John Mark Tucker, "User Education in Academic Libraries: A Century in Retrospect." [6] Tucker pointed out that library instruction had been with us for more than a century. In the 1883 "Annual Report of the President," the president of Columbia University, Frederick A. P. Bernard, stated,

> The average college student ... is ignorant of the greater part of bibliographic apparatus which the skilled librarian has in hourly use, to enable him to answer the thousand queries of the public. A little systematic instruction would so start our students in the right methods, that for the rest of their lives all work in libraries would be more expeditiously accomplished. [7]

In a 1902 article published in the *North American Review*, W. R. Harper observed:

> The equipment of the library will not be finished until it shall have upon its staff men and women whose entire work shall be, not the care of books, not the cataloging of books, but the giving of instruction concerning their use. [8]

Starting in the mid-1960s, library instruction experienced its keenest revival, resulting in the establishment of various programs throughout the country. The revival was characterized by various pedagogies, eclectic methods of evaluation, and a proliferation of workbooks, instructional materials, and audiovisual aids. Librarians worked earnestly to convince faculty, administrators, and even other librarians, of the need for providing bibliographic instruction. Librarians of all types—school, public, and academic—began to establish library instruction programs. Efforts to establish both state and national standards for bibliographic instruction saw results, with several states establishing standards for library instruction. On the national level, there was increased recognition of the legitimacy of the BI movement, demonstrated by the establishment of a Bibliographic Instruction Section (BIS) within the Association of College and Research Libraries (ACRL). In addition, there were other units within ACRL devoted to bibliographic instruction. The Community and Junior College Libraries Section (CJCLS) organized their Committee on Instruction and Use in the mid-1960s and the Education and Behavioral Sciences Section created their Committee on Bibliographic Instruction for Educators in 1977. The Library Instruction Round Table (LIRT) was formed in January 1977.

It was necessary to formalize these groups to bring about the professionalization of bibliographic instruction but more important, it introduced camaraderie and a formal place for librarians to share ideas and issues related to a common concern. This formalizing of what Boisse and Webster in chapter 3 of this volume, have called a "grassroots movement" has been essential to the integration of user education into the operational framework of academic libraries. ACRL's

Bibliographic Instruction Section has just begun to identify and address their major concerns and is attempting to establish a framework for bibliographic instruction at the academic level. While the Second Generation of instruction librarians may be confronted with numerous issues and problems, the organizational structure to support their efforts is firmly established. Consequently, time and effort can now be directed toward the important questions which will take bibliographic instruction into the twenty-first century.

## HAS BIBLIOGRAPHIC INSTRUCTION MADE A DIFFERENCE?

Bibliographic instruction programs are intended to teach library users the skills needed to make effective and efficient use of libraries and information. At academic institutions, bibliographic instruction is also intended to teach students how to use scholarly and highly specialized resources. The typical program includes orientation to basic research tools, use of specialized bibliographies, and practice in locating materials through card catalogs, indexes, and abstracts. The next level of bibliographic instruction programs is designed to teach the library skills necessary in locating research reports, government documents, and journal literature. As a result of the instruction, students should be prepared to do original research papers and to read research findings within a specific subject field.

Most programs attempt to evaluate through practical, related exercises and tests whether students have actually acquired intended research skills. It is difficult to design a test which measures the application of learning: there is no easy method to ascertain whether or not a person who presumably has acquired these skills makes use of them. Checklist evaluations are used and of course, examinations are part of courses taught for credit. Seldom is any effort made to find out if bibliographic instruction does make a difference in students' use of the library, in their ability to succeed in academic course work, or in their subsequent use of sophisticated tools for specialized research or information gathering.

Evaluation of instructional programs is important not only to measure the results of instruction, but also to determine the cost-effectiveness of such efforts. Since librarians devote considerable time to this endeavor, both in designing instructional programs and in teaching, the payoff has to be determined. Today, even more than in the past, libraries are confronted with reductions in both budget and staff. Dollars and staff have to be stretched to meet increasing demands on the library. Day-to-day maintenance of the collection has increased in cost; automation is taking a bigger chunk of the budget. All these factors must be considered in deploying staff for instructional programs. What then is the payoff for conducting a program of bibliographic instruction?

## THE IMPORTANCE OF INSTRUCTION

Effective instruction can result in users who are able to make intelligent, independent decisions about research and information. To be able to use a catalog to retrieve needed information or to recognize that libraries use classification systems to organize materials are two examples of the fundamental knowledge that every student, indeed every citizen, should possess. Euster's observation in chapter 4 that "technology is creating a new public consciousness of information as a consumer good" is already evident in the way people are changing their attitudes toward libraries and information. Librarians are no longer viewed as trustees of knowledge who parcel out bits and pieces of information from a reference desk. The technological revolution has changed the public's view of information and the public in turn expects changes in the methods used by libraries to deliver the information. This is the challenge for the next generation of instruction librarians: to change the traditional method of information delivery. To some extent, that pressure is already upon us as a result of new technologies.

Today's student, despite current criticism of American education, is doing far more research earlier in his or her college career than did the students of twenty years ago. Students are required to read and to prepare papers based on original research very early in their academic pursuits. Core collections no longer satisfy the curriculum for most college students today. Reading and reacting to current research is very much a part of undergraduate courses. This fact, combined with the realities of "library anxiety" in beginning researchers as described in chapter 6, points to the need for early, systematic training in library skills. Without such training, either students do badly in research-oriented courses or the courses become watered down to meet the lack of skills found in the majority of students.

On the other hand, the better students respond to the increased emphasis on research and diversity of materials by demanding more of libraries and librarians. They demand more service, current research sources, and instruction on the use of the library. Academic librarians no longer can be merely givers of information, but must provide instruction on the retrieval and use of information.

Long-range financial commitment for instructional programs is necessary if bibliographic instruction is to remain stable. Reduced funding for libraries has meant fewer books, journals, and staff available to users. It is through the bibliographic instruction programs that users are taught to make the most of those resources still available. Lack of staff and monies should not lead to a reduction in instructional efforts; rather, it should spur on those endeavors. However, making maximum use of the collection and developing informational skills requires that library instruction go beyond the traditional fifty-minute introduction to the card catalog and the *Readers' Guide to Periodical Literature*. Interpretation and evaluation integrated into search-and-retrieval skills, information access through computer databases, and methods of information management must take their place in the bibliographic instruction programs of the Second Generation.

## LIBRARY INSTRUCTION FOR THE 1980s

Automation has been the watchword for the 1980s. As we entered this decade, online systems and computers began to dominate our professional lives. We have moved quickly beyond the mechanization of the card catalog to information retrieval systems. DIALOG, BRS, and InfoTrac information retrieval services are dominating job descriptions, conferences, and the professional literature.

What does this mean for library instruction? Do we supply students with ready-made bibliographies and statistical data retrieved from online information sources rather than teaching them search strategy? Moreover, with the increasing availability and ease of search offered by online retrieval sources, end-user searching has become increasingly popular. Has automation and online retrieval terminated the need for library skills instruction?

These new tools and sources, it is being discovered, are clearly not supplanting the need for bibliographic instruction; instead, increased and more sophisticated instruction is required. While librarians need to reconsider what they are to teach and how they are to teach it, any new method which will help users find the information they need should be accepted gracefully and gratefully. This does not mean an end to teaching many of the fundamental skills and concepts of traditional bibliographic instruction; users need to know traditional search methods as well as new ones. Research strategies are important regardless of where they lead: card catalog, COMcats, book bibliographies, footnotes in journal articles, printed indexes, or Knowledge Index.

With the advent of online retrieval and information systems, instructional responsibilities will increase. These new sources cannot be expected to decrease the questions, problems, and indeed laziness, of library users. Much of the same ineptness that users display as they encounter the traditional card catalog and printed indexes will be duplicated as they approach computer-generated or computer-managed systems. In many ways, these new information technologies will increase user problems and frustrations. The paramount misconception concerning automated catalogs and information sources is that they are a panacea for those with information needs. Some users are under the impression that the problems they encounter with a manual catalog will automatically vanish with the advent of technology. Information, they believe, will be forthcoming for all seekers who push the right button or give the right command. Discounting these misconceptions can be considered one of the main objectives of bibliographic instruction for the next decade. Users need to realize the vast potential of online information systems and automated catalogs but at the same time, they need to have realistic expectations and to understand that systems are only as good as the information they contain. Users are still going to need skills to access and interpret electronic sources of information.

## INTO THE FUTURE

Bibliographic instruction will increase in importance as libraries tie in to national networks and full-document delivery becomes standard procedure for users. User education for the future must be considered as important as the cataloging or checking out of materials. Only educated users will be able to make libraries work for them. Librarians who do not educate their patrons are doomed to do their work for them; a role and an image that instruction librarians are particularly anxious to eradicate. With the growing complexity of libraries, especially in the area of increased automation, and with the rapidly rising cost of traditional library services, education of users will become the only practical approach to public service in an academic library.

In the 1980s, bibliographic instruction in higher education is both "in" and innovative. For the coming decade, instruction librarians will build upon what they have learned as they help patrons adapt to the use and potential of an online environment. The new decade will be one where instruction must extend beyond the accepted activities of retrieval and interpretation to include the complexities of information management. The Second Generation of bibliographic instruction librarians, far from being the final generation, must provide the drive and leadership to move us effectively forward into the twenty-first century.

## NOTES

1. Samuel Eliot Morison, *The Great Explorers: The European Discovery of America* (New York: Oxford University Press, 1978), p. 380.

2. Hoyt Gimlin, *The American Future* (Washington, D.C.: Congressional Quarterly Inc., 1976), p. 4.

3. Roy H. Copperud, "Is Atomic Energy Near?" *Scientific American* 163, no. 1 (July 1940):16.

4. Gimlin, *The American Future*, p. 5.

5. Frances L. Hopkins, "A Century of Bibliographic Instruction: The Historical Claim to Professional and Academic Legitimacy," *College & Research Libraries* 43 (May 1982):197.

6. John Mark Tucker, "User Education in Academic Libraries: A Century in Retrospect," *Library Trends* 29 (Summer 1980):9-27.

7. Frederick A. P. Bernard, "Annual Report of the President of Columbia College, Made to the Board of Trustees, May 7, 1883" (New York: Columbia College, 1883), p. 46.

8. W. R. Harper, "The Trend of University and College Education in the United States," *North American Review* 174, no. 545 (1902):458.

# Index